T0367722

Managerial Lives

Organizations are often complex and unwieldy, and many managers have difficulty in combining ideals and positive identities with the complexities and imperfections of life. They are expected to be strategic and competent, while at the same time human and empathetic. This engaging book takes a fresh look at managerial work as experienced and understood by managers. It examines the central tenets of managerial life, such as the work expectations that managers have, the significance they assign to different activities and the difficulties that they face. It also takes a wider view of working life by looking at subordination in the managerial context. The theoretical material is supported by in-depth interviews with thirteen managers from different organizations. This book will appeal to those with an interest in management, and leadership and identity questions in modern working life.

STEFAN SVENINGSSON is Associate Professor of Business Administration at the School of Economics and Management, Lund University, Sweden. He has been visiting researcher at Cardiff Business School, Cardiff University, and Melbourne University. His research interests include strategic and organizational change, leadership and management of knowledge work. His most recent book is *Changing Organizational Culture, Second Edition* (2015) edited with Mats Alvesson.

MATS ALVESSON is Professor of Business Administration at the University of Lund, Sweden; at University of Queensland Business School, Australia; and at Cass Business School, London. His research interests include critical theory, gender, leadership, identity and organizational image. His most recent books include *The Triumph of Emptiness* (2013) and *Constructing Research Questions* (2013), edited with J. Sandberg.

Managerial Lives

Leadership and Identity in an Imperfect World

STEFAN SVENINGSSON
School of Economics and Management, Lund University Mats Alvesson

MATS ALVESSON
School of Economics and Management, Lund University

CAMBRIDGE
UNIVERSITY PRESS

CAMBRIDGE
UNIVERSITY PRESS

University Printing House, Cambridge CB2 8BS, United Kingdom

Cambridge University Press is part of the University of Cambridge.

It furthers the University's mission by disseminating knowledge in the pursuit of education, learning and research at the highest international levels of excellence.

www.cambridge.org
Information on this title: www.cambridge.org/9781107121706

© Stefan Sveningsson and Mats Alvesson 2016

First published 2016

A catalogue record for this publication is available from the British Library

ISBN 978-1-107-12170-6 Hardback

Contents

Figures

Tables

Preface

This book is the result of a number of studies of managerial work, identity and organization which we have conducted over more than a decade as members of the organization studies group at the Department of Business Administration at Lund University. Our main purpose is to examine essential elements of modern working and organizational life at close quarters. This has been done through in-depth studies of a number of people who work as middle or senior managers. Our aim is to understand the typical relationships between experience, work situation and identity in an organizational context. In doing so, we attempt to describe, interpret and theoretically highlight how organizations and occupational groups work. We highlight the dilemmas and problems which lie beyond the impression given by more formal and official descriptions.

Organizations are often complex and unwieldy, and many occupational groups and managers have difficulty successfully combining ideals and positive identities with the complexities and imperfections of life. Modern-day working life is, in many ways, contradictory and complicated – what seem like good ideals and clear recipes for success can easily cause deadlock and become traps for managers.

The research which has led to this study has taken place in a number of sub-projects, with varying emphases. We are grateful for the research grants received from FAS, Vinnova and Handelsbanken's Research Foundation. We would also like to thank our colleagues Johan Alvehus, Tony Huzzard, Dan Kärreman, Daniel Nyberg, Jens Rennstam, Robyn Thomas and Robert Wenglén, who have contributed with both empirical material, which we have used in the book, and creative discussions on managerial work and identity.

We would also like to thank the managers who have taken part in the studies – in particular the thirteen people we studied in depth, who with immense candour (and perhaps not a little courage) placed themselves at the disposal of research. But the other eighteen interviewees also deserve our thanks, as do Johan Alvehus, Ola Håkansson and Nadja Sörgärde, who have read and commented on the manuscript.

Lund, May 2015
Stefan Sveningsson Mats Alvesson

PART I **Managerial life: managerial work and the managerial identity**

I Introduction

"Manager" is a term which covers a rather disparate collection of job holders. Sometimes it implies that the person who has this position is superior to and should manage other people, who, being non-managers, are co-workers or subordinates. However, the term is often also used for individuals who are responsible for a particular task. Many HR, information, sales and financial managers are mainly responsible for personnel administration, information leaflets, their own sales or accounting systems respectively. In this book, we are only interested in managers in the first sense, that is to say those who have a job where they are expected to lead subordinates in some way. What this actually implies is not always clear.

Managers are a popular topic of interest. Leaders – a common term for managers, and one which managers themselves like to use – are an even more popular topic of interest. However, we are not following fashion here, but are interested in those professionals who are managers in the sense we have just described. Whether they also practise leadership and can be seen as leaders is a question we will try to answer. The widespread interest in managers is partly linked to the general growing interest in how people experience expectations, challenges and demands in modern organizations. Naturally, everyone in an organization acts according to specific expectations and demands, but this is perhaps particularly true of managers (Watson 2008, p. 122). There is a large industry offering ideals and templates for managers and leaders. Managers cannot just "be themselves" as they please but are undoubtedly expected, more than others, to represent organizations, to be leaders, competent decision makers, strategic, knowledgeable and to be seen to be in charge. At the same time, they must make an effort to be human and empathetic – someone you can trust – in order to establish and maintain good, and thereby productive, relations with their co-workers. Against this background, our aim in this book is to portray managerial work as it is experienced and understood by managers, with a particular focus on the importance they attach to different demands and activities in their work. We will therefore describe how a number of managers from different organizations form their managerial work. Why do they want to be managers and what expectations do they have of their work? What do they actually do as a manager? What significance do they assign to different activities, and what do they hope to get out of their positions as managers? How do they see themselves and their personal development? What difficulties and dilemmas do they come up against? These are some of the questions we take up in this book, which thus address questions of managerial identity, experience and efforts to fill their work with meaning.

We approach this with some scepticism – which we believe is healthy – and hope thereby to avoid ideological overtones associated with reverence for "the superior" which can easily lead to confusion when studying typical fields of status such as leadership, professions, competence development, the knowledge society and more (Alvesson 2013a). In this book, we also take co-worker aspects seriously. Subordination is a central aspect of organizations and working life. Disregarding this in a managerial context is as unwise as attempting to understand men without taking into account women, or analysing parenthood without considering the children. Our main focus, however, is on the life of managers – although we do not ignore the relationship dimension or the fact that managers themselves are almost always subordinates, often more so than they are superiors.

Since managers are the object of a great deal of attention, there are, of course, numerous interpretations and images of what their managerial activities consist of. We therefore begin this chapter with a brief account of five common, if somewhat contradictory, images of managers and managerial life. These give us a background to how managerial work is often viewed in various contexts. This is followed by a clarification of our aims and, specifically, a short section on the importance of identity. We end the chapter with an outline of the book's purpose, target group, structure and content.

IMAGES OF MANAGERS AND MANAGERIAL LIFE

There are undoubtedly images in the literature which show nuances of managerial life, but these are more often found at the top or bottom end of the scale. The former includes the idea that managerial work is something special and important, the latter that it is often disorganized and boring.

Managerial life is attractive

Managers are often described as being privileged in terms of status, titles, high salaries, bonuses and other symbolic and physical benefits which come with the role. Sometimes managerial life is even portrayed as a matter of glamour, luxury and abundance. Sometimes it is pointed out that managers have power and influence and opportunities to influence not only their own working situation but also organizations and society as a whole which other, "ordinary", people lack. In addition to the high standard of living, the emphasis is often on the attractive work tasks and, in general, a working life which includes things that anyone with the right qualities has reason to aim for.

The image of the privileged manager is at times complemented by images of managers as forceful and inventive – they stand for change and contribute to the development and welfare of organizations. In particular, the ability of managers to exercise leadership in many situations is held up as being especially necessary and important. School principals, for example, are expected to demonstrate "pedagogical leadership" in order to produce well-run schools and good academic results.

Becoming a manager is clearly an ambition for individuals who are talented and goal-oriented. This is traditionally true for men, at least. For women it has been – and to some extent still is – rather less evident. But as the ideal of gender equality is increasingly embraced, and by a growing number of people, the ideal of becoming and remaining a manager is also becoming typical for the majority of talented women interested in making a career (the number of female managers has also increased, at least up to middle management levels).

When it comes to the view of management as a privilege, we tend to think of managers in slightly higher positions – although most people probably imagine that "normal managers" also have a richer and more interesting working life than the "normal co-worker". It is much more appealing to be seen as a leader than a follower, and without a managerial position, leadership is difficult and you are left to do followership instead. In addition to the benefits, what is seen as making managers special is perhaps that they have interesting tasks, a key role and major opportunities to influence.

Managerial life is influential

It is sometimes easy to have the impression that the manager is responsible for everything that happens in and around organizations. In comparison with many other groups, managers do, of course, often have a somewhat more privileged situation. It is not unusual for them to have greater opportunities to influence the way resources are distributed and utilized in organizations than many other members. Managers are often surrounded by a certain authority which is based on formal requirements, traditions and norms. They are often assumed to have a greater influence than many others on the direction and development of the workplace; we sometimes talk about how managers formulate strategies and control organizational change. They are also expected to do leadership. It is the responsibility of the manager to ensure good working outcomes within the work unit and that the interfaces between units work well. Any disparities must be corrected so that productivity and quality are satisfactory. The manager is also expected to be a key player in many so-called soft questions, including those which are concerned with developing organizational culture and personnel. These are questions which involve, among other things, recruitment, career development, promotion and motivation, as well as general employee care.

In much of the classic management literature, but perhaps even more so in pop-management literature, managers are portrayed as more or less omnipotent. An organization's or department's performance is seen as an effect of how well it is led. Managerial work and/or leadership is seen as the hub around which the co-worker wheel revolves. The manager is seen as important, not to say crucial, for how things work.

Managerial life is (as a rule) complex

Most managers are part of complex contexts in which they are often subordinate to an overall hierarchy. Even more so for senior managers – a company manager can be kept on a tight leash by the executive committee and a CEO can be forced to limit their actions in line with the decisions and principles of the owner and board of directors. Middle managers may be regarded by their superiors as more of a subordinate than a leader and, in a strongly result-focused context, as a disposable commodity. Managers are also part of working processes where there is often considerable dependence on and pressure from other steps in the production chain. A unit manager in a factory must start with a given input of products to be processed according to stipulated demands and then achieve a specified output. A sales manager in a particular region in a larger group of companies is normally given a fixed product range and expected to reach a specified sales volume. A personnel manager is often forced to respond to all kinds of emergency calls and perform administrative tasks and meets little understanding for a request to "delegate" these in order to be free to work with personnel strategies and act as a consultant to senior management (Alvesson & Lundholm 2014). The majority of managers do what they are told to do, rather than developing goals and taking initiatives based on their own ideas. Nonetheless, it is the latter image which is often communicated: leaders lead others – and are not led to any great extent by more senior managers. In most leadership literature, the managerial world appears to consist mainly of colonels and generals – and not of sergeants and lieutenants who are expected to put into effect what their superiors have decided within rather narrow limits (Laurent 1978).

Neither are the employees always particularly receptive to influence. Some strive for independence or may even express counter dependence; that is to say, they are willing to fight against authority. Managers who believe they have good ideas sometimes come up against counterarguments or disinterest, and often have to back down or seek a compromise (Lundholm 2011). There are, of course, times when messages from the manager – suggestions, requests, instructions, talk of values – which are accepted in themselves have little effect because the employees are busy with other things and do not have time. Managers are not the only ones who try to influence: there are colleagues, customers, senior managers, unions, regulations, procedures, practical arrangements, temporary work problems (such as faulty deliveries, computer problems, illness) – all these mean that the manager's efforts to lead rarely go according to plan. Adapting and dealing with disruption are often just as central elements as leading, in line with ideals and individual ideas about goals and ways of working. Doing what you have been instructed to do is central. The time pressure is often huge (Holmberg & Tyrstrup 2010).

Managers' influence is often limited by changes and developments in an organization's environment. Rather than managing by self-governing, goals and objectives, management becomes a question of adapting to the situation and various circumstances.

There are, however, those who say that this development has made the role of the manager even more important. Managers are expected to take responsibility for an organization's adaptation. Capturing trends and changes, along with making internal preparations for and implementing organizational change, is seen as distinguishing successful managers. Leading an organization, or at least a working group, in times of change is more often than not seen as a privilege. It is exciting, dynamic and demands real leaders. In most organizations, describing change and uncertainty and other similar problems as challenges for managers is standard vocabulary. Yet this is often expressed in euphemisms: dancing to your customers' tune, trying to keep up with the latest organizational trends, or, in public services, being forced to follow the decisions of politicians in order to demonstrate ability to take action; these are often portrayed as "change-oriented leadership". There are times when "adaptive followership" might be a more appropriate label. There is no doubt that change can lead to positive development, but the impression is that changes, in practice, contribute to making managerial work more uncertain and fragmented. Not everyone enjoys working with reorganization and new administrative systems; it often results in the breaking down of systems and relationships which have been painstakingly built, and a great deal of time and energy goes into building something new. More often than not, change projects, which are embarked upon, come to nothing (Alvesson & Sveningsson 2015).

Managerial life is (very often) unclear

Even if it is possible to point, as we did earlier, to a number of areas which must be coordinated, it is often unclear and uncertain whether and how this is achieved in actual terms. We can certainly say that managerial work is, in a sense, about strategy and organizational change, but it is rarely clear what this means in real terms. There are, of course, many models and ideas for how to support this work, but managerial work is, nonetheless, often seen as vague and ambiguous by managers and other members of organizations. After interviewing numerous managers about what they do, we are left with a rather confused and contradictory impression of, for example, leadership (see e.g. Alvesson & Sveningsson 2003b). It frequently involves very broad, and imprecise, ambitions and interests ("have an open door", "make people think", "be open and honest"). Although this offers managers scope for action, it also leads to uncertainty and anxiety about what is actually to be done in addition to delivering specific results. As it is often the subordinates who do the actual delivering, it is not obvious what the manager exactly contributes.

Managerial life is (sometimes) boring and tough

Organizations, particularly large ones, contain a great deal of administration. Managers are seldom exempt from spending a lot of time working with this. Sometimes it is impossible to maintain the distinction between being a manager and being an administrator. It is not self-evident for everyone that a promotion from an ordinary job to a managerial job provides a boost in terms of tasks and well-being. One manager of a construction company felt that promotion to a more senior managerial post in reality only meant more administrative hard work which "sucks you dry". Many professional organizations, such as universities, consulting firms, advertising agencies, law firms and hospitals sometimes find it difficult to recruit people to managerial positions. At universities and colleges, for example, there is no doubt that most people find research work and teaching a more attractive proposition than being the head of a department or faculty and working with administration. In most cases, the elected managers (as a rule) hold their posts for a limited period of time (an electoral period) and then return to their ordinary tasks. More often than not, they do so with a sigh of relief.

A number of other personnel issues, which are not about developing co-workers but about taking care of those who are ill, or have problems with some form of addiction, high levels of absence, poor performance, conflicts with other people, and so on, are also important managerial tasks which not everyone appreciates. One-off efforts rarely lead to any noticeable improvement in the work of underperformers or people with other kinds of problems. This also includes not giving people what they want or think makes them feel good. Not even the most co-worker-oriented manager can give everyone the salary they themselves think they deserve or offer expensive in-service training; more interesting tasks; fancier titles or less challenging pupils, patients or customers (in schools, hospitals and companies respectively) as co-workers sometimes request. Managerial work often means saying "no" to people, which is not always seen as an attractive task. But some may not see it as a negative factor. A certain exercising of power can have its attraction. It is sometimes claimed that the willingness to exercise power (in the interest of the business) is the characteristic of good managers (McClelland & Burnham 1976; Zaleznik 1997). But this is seldom emphasized, either in the management literature or by managers.

MANAGERIAL WORK IN PRACTICE

That is all very well, you may now be thinking, but in that case, which of these images is true? Are managers mainly occupied with exercising their power of influence, are they leaders who lead? Or is it rather about administration and parrying? Is it about interesting or boring tasks? How unclear is it really? Perhaps notions of complexity are exaggerated.

It is not easy to give a straightforward answer to these questions, even though there are countless empirical studies (we ourselves have spent years on research). One reason is the enormous variation – the meaning and consequences of managerial work are very different. Different organizations, levels and jobs may have little in common. There is also a large variation from a co-worker perspective. A pharmaceuticals sales representative does not have the same expectations of the sales manager as does a star researcher, striving to develop new ideas and make progress in product development, of the company's R&D manager. Leadership styles are often influenced more by the behaviour and attitude of the subordinate than by the strong personality of the manager. It is easy to be a good manager if you have good co-workers – it is not so easy if your co-workers are less competent. This is a highly complex question with many implications. A strong manager can (unwittingly) produce passive or dependent co-workers. A weak manager can (unwittingly) mean co-workers take more initiative and responsibility and thereby develop.

Managers and management have been the object of a great deal of attention in various contexts. Given the general view that managers are extremely important for both the results and quality of working life, it appears essential to examine their work. Since managers are assumed to have a strong influence on how resources are allocated, not just in organizations but also in society at large, the large volume of management research and the significantly greater volume of pop-management literature, which talks about what managers should do, or presents dressed-up descriptions of what managers work with (decision making, strategies, leadership ...), is understandable. Sometimes it presents celebrity portraits of "super managers" – generally without any great knowledge of the person they are praising. A deeper insight would only complicate and spoil the picture. This is very typical of the mass media, but academics eager to reach a broad audience also provide misleading descriptions (Spector 2014).

"Should do" questions in particular have attracted a great deal of interest, from both managers and organizational scholars (and others with a public interest). Since the work of managers has long been considered diverse, the interest has often been directed towards attempting to explain what managerial work should actually involve. Over the last hundred years, there have been many attempts to formulate principles and guidelines for what managers should occupy themselves with, in particular which areas they should make decisions about. This literature contains a wealth of normative ideas about what a manager should do, more often than not expressed as a number of overall principles. These have often been about clarifying the decision-making process, which is normally seen as a rational process in which you first analyse and plan what you are going to do and then implement these plans using organizational arrangements. This kind of managerial work is about taking a long-term view, working to plan and design the overall orientation and organizational infrastructure. Many of these ideas look good on paper, but few have proved to be of any great help to managers or provide good explanations of what managers actually do in practice (Carlson 1951/1991; Mintzberg 1973; Tengblad 2003).

One problem is that "reality" is framed by different representations of "reality". This is true of all phenomena. "Youth", for example, is shaped partly by our ideas of young people. Young people today – when we see a long drawn-out period of youth and the idea that young people are very special people in need of policies, efforts, psychologies and such – are in some ways different from the young people of a hundred years ago, when the transition from childhood to the adult world was more abrupt and final. In the same way, managers' reality is framed by concepts, theories, models, values, norms, changing fashions, wishful thinking and more. Managerial reality is intimately linked to managerial myths. In working life, we find cultures where the manager as leader–hero or bureaucrat plays an important part in assumptions, expectations and other representations. People act and interpret according to their representations or frames of reference, albeit rarely in an unambiguous way. It should be pointed out that perceptions and representations are often unclear, contradictory and confused – we go into this more deeply later in the book.

Understanding managerial life thus largely means understanding representations, values and ideas and how these frame, but are also occasionally disconnected from or ambiguous in relation to, managerial work and the relationship between managers and others. This is one of the main points made in this book.

Nonetheless, one important way of attempting to understand what managers do is to observe managerial work. The interest is thus in behaviour rather than in representations, experiences, meaning, and so on. The aim in this "managerial work" tradition is to attempt to provide more realistic descriptions of what managers actually work with and, based on these, to formulate principles, areas or roles which describe and can act as guidelines for their managerial work. The starting point is thus not what managers should do – good principles for managerial work – but what they actually do at work. Most people in these traditions would agree that managerial work is fragmentary, pressured and action-driven (Mintzberg 1973; Tengblad 2012a). Sometimes it appears chaotic, at least on the surface. It might, however, be the case that flexible, varied and apparently disorganized managerial behaviour helps to bring order to the business (Lind 2011). But what appears to be fragmented and disorganized can also play a part in, and reinforce, ambiguity and confusion in a business.

Among other things, a number of models of different roles which managers can practise, depending on what kind of work they do, have been developed in an effort to explain managerial work. We discuss these in more detail in the next chapter. In this Introduction, we simply mention that although these roles provide a more diverse and credible picture of managerial work than the traditional roles, they are, nevertheless, limited by a rather strict focus on managers' tasks and behaviour. As a consequence, personal circumstances in particular are toned down, as are what the various activities mean – significance and relevance – for managers. The thinking behind behaviour and more subtle attempts to influence emotions and values are not taken directly taken into account. Questions of identity – how they see themselves and their personal development – have also been left out. In this book, however, we aim to take these conditions seriously. In order to come closer to the people behind managerial work, our effort is broader and relatively more open than many other portrayals of managerial work. We have consequently tried not to structure the discussions with the managers in advance through the use of standardized questions based on existing characterizations of roles or managerial positions. The point of departure for this book has instead been to give the managers the opportunity to talk about the areas which they themselves feel to be most important.

In our attempts to clarify managers' experiences and experience of managerial work, we will often talk about identity, a topic which makes it possible to get closer to people's understanding of themselves and their situation. At the same time, we go far beyond a simple account of people's personal experiences and seek to achieve a deeper, in part more critical, understanding of managerial work and managerial identities. Simply registering, recounting and summing up personal statements about experience and experiences gives a naïve and superficial picture. It is easy to take statements made in interviews at face value, but these sometimes follow a script or manuscript for how to talk about yourself and your leadership. In today's society, with its passion for leadership, there are countless guidelines for how to talk about motives, driving forces and action – and these can be misleading. Managers – like other people – sometimes have a more limited understanding of themselves, their business and their relationships than is apparent. They are not always so reflective (Koot & Sabelis 2002; Schaefer 2014). Our research therefore uses, as far as possible, the statements made by co-workers and others about the managers studied – which can be very different from the assertions made by the managers themselves. Observations of leadership efforts also often give an impression which is different from the managers' own words. Rich and varying data – and not only single interviews with managers – together with interpretation, critical reflection, theoretical understanding and links to previous research, are essential for understanding managerial work (Alvesson 2011a).

MANAGERS' IDENTITY

Managers' identities or self-views are central to managerial life and managerial work. There are many reasons for this. One is that identity speaks to almost everyone, since our self-view is something that most of us reflect on at some time in our lives. We try in different ways to understand ourselves, who we are, what we really want and what we stand for in different contexts. Identity is, in other words, about our attempt to create a coherent and relatively stable idea of who we are. The seemingly increasing importance of these questions can be partly understood against the background of a growing feeling that we are living in changing and complex times. What is perhaps even more important is the promotion of all the ideals being offered for sale and the seductive images of how we should behave and develop (Alvesson 2013a). The emergence of a multitude of changeable and contradictory standards and ideals contribute to making identity an ongoing and fragmented project, rather than something more static and coherent which gives some stability to our existence, at least during certain phases of our lives (Knights & Vurdubakis 1994). It is, however, also possible that variation and incoherence in terms of ideals and discourses can be combined and balanced and thus lead to a form of stability. As Clarke et al. (2009) write, "people tend to employ multiple competing and often inconsistent sensemaking frameworks to explain chronic problems and to rationalize inconsistent policies and beliefs. That is, identities may be stable without being coherent, and consist of core statement but not be unified" (p. 341). This is hardly unproblematic, and tensions are difficult to avoid.

The growth of managerial and leadership ideals in recent decades has also led to uncertainty about managerial identities (Sinclair 2011). As a manager, you are presented with a large number of idealizations of how you should be: from strong to humble, strategic to present (i.e. around and available for others), result-oriented to sociable, demanding to therapist, moral role model to business-like, and so on (Alvesson & Spicer 2011; Koot & Sabelis 2002). Few come close to the cherished ideals of leadership, and if anyone does come close to an ideal it quickly collides with, or is replaced by, something else, in line with rapidly changing trends. There are, of course, many cases where the passion for change and following fashions can be seen to be beneficial for organizations in which people strive to renew and improve themselves, just as with any other project, but it can also cause identity problems among many co-workers and uncertainty about where their organization is heading, what one should do as a good leader and the implications for oneself.

"Identity" is a convenient term, since it can be used to describe many different circumstances on both a collective and an individual level. We can talk about organizational identity; professional, individual and social identity; and, not least, managerial identity. Sometimes these different descriptions are linked in different ways – we may say that social or professional identity, that is to say, how we define ourselves according to an organization or profession, influences how we view who we are, that is to say our individual identity (Dutton et al. 1994; Haslam 2004). A strong corporate identity can rub off strongly on self-view – we might, for example, see ourselves first and foremost as an IKEA employee or Volvo engineer and be reluctant to change employer. In cases like these, identity has also come to be an important element of control in organizations; many types of activities in today's organizations can be seen as attempts to control and regulate ideas and views about who we are and what we can do, such as cultural change programmes, feedback on management and leadership, leadership development, coaching and ideas about authentic leadership. Yet identities can also be based on professional norms and other convictions and thereby be a source of a certain level of independence.

As has been mentioned, identity is usually something which is discussed in times of change and turbulence, since that is when we often feel that demands, expectations and the content of our work change and it can be difficult to maintain a coherent picture of who we are and what we can do. Change is partly about personal development in different life phases, such as when we choose the direction of our studies or occupation, or consider changing jobs, starting a family or applying for promotion. But external changes are also important, as they can require us to reflect on our self-view and priorities. Times of change can mean new challenges, inspiration and personal development. But they also often bring feelings of inadequacy and anxiety and, consequently, a more active search for stability. Given the complexity which accompanies change, it can sometimes be difficult to create continuity and coherence in our existence (Sennett 1998). This is particularly true of managers, since they are expected to be good role models and lead the way for change, increased flexibility and renewal in general. It is not always easy to "make the best of it". There may be times when they feel as though they are prostituting themselves when they, say, put a lot of effort into making co-workers embrace a new management system which they themselves do not think provides good management or accept core values which they consider false or filled with meaningless, empty rhetoric produced by a wishful thinker of a CEO or hired consultants.

In this book, we show that change and turbulence are more than a platform for inspiration and development. Diverse and changeable demands and expectations also make it more difficult to maintain identity and often lead, whether or not with justification, to doubt, uncertainty and anxiety, although the latter is often toned down in management literature or interpreted as resistance to change which must be overcome.

THE BOOK'S PURPOSE AND TARGET GROUP

The purpose of this book is to give a thorough and in-depth portrayal of how managers experience managerial work. Our aim is to understand what influences managers and their work and how managers approach and understand different circumstances – organizational, economic, social, cultural and political – which affect them. It is also important here to understand how to create meaning in the managerial work, in particular when ideals and notions of what is natural and important for oneself conflict with an imperfect organizational reality. In the book, we identify countless forces which demand the manager's attention and commitment. Given that these forces are often contradictory and ambiguous, they cause stress and vulnerability. It is not always easy to make your self-view match the demands and expectations of the people around you, or to live up to alternative and often competing ideals about how you should behave as a manager. It is therefore important to attempt to portray how managers fight and struggle with different circumstances and how this struggle affects their understanding of themselves and their chances of upholding a relatively stable image of themselves in their managerial work.

By highlighting how middle managers ("normal managers", as opposed to top executives in large companies) position themselves in modern organizations, we also aim to give a realistic picture of significant circumstances in modern organizations. What is happening in organizations today? What are the topics which dominate organizations in the question of social relations? What dilemmas do they struggle with? We hope that by following a number of managers and their work, we will gain an insight into the trends and other circumstances in today's organizations. The middle-management category is a key segment for understanding organizations. This is, of course, a vast and highly diverse category and it is impossible to generalize, as there is great variation among nations, industries, occupations, organizations, areas and, perhaps above all, individuals. Most of the managers we studied are Swedish, but as most of the issues we raise are also addressed in international studies, we believe that the book's content is of broad international and cross-organizational value. We anticipate that many of the themes covered in the book will have some general relevance, but the exact range is impossible to establish. We also indicate variations – for example, between more or less successful efforts to deal with identity issues – and here there are likely to be heterogeneities across samples. The ideal of our kind of study is to offer insightful examples and useful concepts and ideas, and not to contribute with quantitative findings.

The book is aimed at a wide readership with an interest in management, managerial work, leadership and identity questions in modern working life. We aim both to give "in-depth" descriptions, that is to say rich and insightful portrayals, and to develop a more theoretical understanding and contribute to a new way of thinking in the field of management/leadership and identity. We take our point of departure in, and give a lot of scope to, the voices of managers themselves, but interpret these critically at times and thus also make theoretical contributions. We hope these will be of value for research, but they also provide an important entry to managers' self-reflection and ability to deal with their often complicated situation. Much of what we have to say is highly relevant in different contexts of management and leadership education. There is every reason to think carefully about what you are doing when you appeal to both aspiring and new managers' expectations of a glittering career.

THE STRUCTURE AND CONTENT OF THE BOOK

After this introductory first chapter, there follows a chapter in which we briefly describe some of the central terms – management, managerial work, identity and leadership – in other words, the school of thought the book belongs to. As we have already mentioned, there is no shortage of literature on what managers should do or studies of what they actually work with – the subject has a long and colourful history – and it is important to point out how our book can make a contribution over and above what has already been said on the subject. In Chapter 2 we also discuss identity and leadership. The concept of identity is central, and we believe it enables an intensifying of managerial work by highlighting how people interpret and understand their management, based also on more personal interests and individual backgrounds. Leadership is another central concept in this context and one which regularly recurs among our managers. The concept exists in many forms, and our aim in this short chapter is simply to draw attention to some central ideas which are relevant for our managers' own descriptions of leadership.

After two introductory chapters, it is unquestionably high time to begin to listen to our managers' experiences of their work. The book's second part, "Managerial life: roles and identities", begins with a gallery of people and organizations. In the book, the reader will become acquainted with and follow a number of managers from different organizations. The main actors are thirteen managers whom we follow in more or less equal measure through all the chapters of the book. We have studied each of them closely, through, among other things, repeated interviews and observations. We are also very familiar with the majority of their organizations, which we have particularly studied. These main actors are flanked by other managers, whom we call our secondary actors. The secondary actors have slightly different, and varying, experience from the leading actors, sometimes from other industries, which helps to both broaden and deepen the discussions and analyses of managerial work and managerial identity. The secondary actors also appear regularly in the book, albeit not to the same extent or in as much depth as the main actors. These secondary actors have generally been interviewed twice. In all, the reader will meet thirty-one managers from different organizations and industries.

In Chapter 3, we discuss the attraction of becoming a manager. How do our managers feel about their work, and what makes them think they have what it takes to be a manager? In this chapter, we meet managers who talk about their expectations of management and what they hope to achieve as managers. We also hear why they think they make good managers, what it is that makes them of the right managerial material. In this chapter, we focus on the aspects of managerial work managers identify with when they begin this phase of their career.

In the following two chapters, Chapters 4 and 5, we report how managers talk about and describe managerial job when they are actually working with it. What do they say they do as managers? How do they talk about what influences and directs their work and how do they see their own opportunities to influence what managerial work should consist of? In Chapter 4, we discuss the fact that managers are keen to stress the importance of the manager as change agent, strategist and networker. This is about the big, all-embracing questions, and many of the managers stress that this aspect of the managerial role is also a question of moral importance – it involves keeping to the big questions and not disturbing your co-workers too much in matters where they are deemed to know best. Many also describe this aspect of management as something which suits them particularly well in their leadership – they frequently talk about authentic leadership as a fundamental principle of managerial work. In Chapter 5, we continue our portrayal of how managers describe their job situation and focus on the manager as humanist and moral authority. The managers stress on the importance of listening, maintaining an open dialogue and being accessible to co-workers. Here, acknowledging co-workers and creating well-being are central. This managerial work, too, is described in terms of morals.

In the book's third part, "Management: ironies, labyrinths and pitfalls", we attempt to illustrate managerial work in practice. We go beyond the managers' descriptions of what kind of persons they are, and their wishes and what they do in general. While we allow the managers themselves to speak in most of the previous chapters, this part contains more analysis and interpretation. An interest in practice implies a more critically interpretive effort, where we do not simply take the managers' words and possibly idealized views for granted but try to elicit their practice. We have learnt that managers describe themselves as strategists and people who understand human nature, but to what extent do these (articulated) identities correspond with their actions? This leads us into the pitfalls, problems and perils associated with the managerial job.

In Chapter 6, we discuss the problems of working with strategies and other overall questions in practice; much of the work seems to involve more administration and other things they do not really want to work or identify with. We also point to the problems of acting as someone who understands human nature; it is not easy to combine the ideal of being an understander of human nature with the ideal of being a determined leader. The organization's need for the machinery to work sometimes clashes with these ideals, and the individual's self-view is not always confirmed by what they actually work with as a manager. Co-workers can also be hard to please and may not adapt to suit the manager's leadership ideal. This is the element of the managerial job which poses a challenge, and can undermine what appears to be a stable managerial identity.

Chapter 7 is taken up with a deeper discussion of the problems which first emerge in Chapter 6. Here, the focus is, above all, on the problem of the lack of confirmation of the managerial identity. Managerial work may appear to be highly prestigious and attractive and in itself contribute to a strong confirmation of identity. The ambiguity and complexity of the managerial job may, however, contribute to a heightened need for confirmation. When confirmation is lacking, or vague, this can lead to serious identity problems and, subsequently, anxiety and uncertainty. Although many managers describe themselves as natural managers and leaders, the need for, and thereby the dependence on, the approval of those around them is surprisingly strong. The question of what knowledge they have as a manager and their ability to assess the core of the business and the activities also leads to uncertainty about their own managerial identity and contributes to the anxiety. We discuss how important these circumstances are in making it possible to maintain the managerial identity which is linked to self-esteem and self-confidence.

Chapter 8 addresses the identity problem in its entirety. We identify a number of difficulties in building a positive picture of who you are as a manager. In the best of worlds, ideals and reality always go together, but what actually happens when this is not the case? What happens when the ideal of reality clashes, or comes into conflict, with what actually happens? What happens to self-esteem and self-view, and what are the consequences for the managers and the organizations in which they operate?

In the final chapter, we discuss the outcome of managerial work in more general terms. We point out the irony that in a job which, on closer inspection, is vague, contradictory and often frustrating, it is still largely described as special and attractive. We also point out some fundamental problems in the strong relations and confirmation orientation which managers express. This is linked to specific difficulties associated with the idea that a manager should maintain some distance from operative matters in the organization and what the co-workers do. Many managers express a reluctance to "interfere" or "get involved". But deciding that you will only work with overall matters and the co-workers' psychology is not without problems. We end with some opinions which we believe can help managers to deal with identity questions more successfully than often seems to be the case today.

2 Management

Work, identity and leadership

What do managers actually do? This is a question which has given rise to countless studies and articles over the last hundred years, yet despite this it is claimed from time to time that we do not know as much about managerial work or management as we think (Mintzberg 1991). This is undoubtedly due to the great complexity of managerial work and an extremely wide diversity in the question of what is hidden behind the apparently straightforward label "managers". It is not particularly easy to see management as a special occupation, in the same way as for a baker, a firefighter or an accountant. We probably have a reasonable picture of what the person does as far as the latter are concerned, but if we think of management, it instantly becomes much more ambiguous and vague. Perhaps we think of managers as the people at the top of the pyramid who make decisions, but the question is whether this is better seen as organizational management rather than management in the more usual sense of managerial work. Organizational management consists of more than managing subordinates – it includes dealing with owner relations, external relations, questions of financing and market analyses, among other things – and typically also covers staff – CFO, CIO, COO, etc. – who work with financial markets and policies, follow up results, and so on. Most managerial work is not organizational management. The CEO of a large organization and the manager of a small sales department or production unit have little in common. On the other hand, managerial work and organizational management are often similar in smaller organizations, but organizational questions are less interesting in smaller organizations with a couple of dozen employees than in situations where it is essential to make a multitude of departments and roles work together to form a complex entirety. In this book we concentrate on managerial work in larger organizations and only touch on organizational management/top executive work activity.

We begin this chapter with an overview of management and address the classic principles of managerial work. Numerous studies of what managers do, however, have shown that managerial work deviates from the classic principles. The results of these studies have often resulted in formulations of different managerial roles, and we will here give an account of some of these which are relevant, given our result. This is followed by a discussion about managerial work and identity where we propose that identity can enable a deeper and wider understanding of management and managerial work. Leadership is a central theme in the identity work of our managers, and we therefore end the chapter with a review of differing perspectives on leadership and also declare our own school of thought.

MANAGEMENT – AN OVERVIEW

Management is a function which consists of, or is held by, people, called managers, who are formally responsible for an organized collection of tasks and individuals. In this book, management is seen as a function and formal role, but also as something that we approach informally. Managerial work is a result of how those who occupy this function interpret, view and work with the role and the often implicit expectations, demands and mandates associated with it.

Since management, unlike some other professions, does not consist of a number of clear and explicit demands and expectations, the question of what constitutes managerial work is actually rather difficult to answer. A fundamental problem is, as has been mentioned, the sheer number of different managerial positions and tasks. Being a manager covers everything from being prime minister or group chief executive to cleaning staff supervisor or sales team manager. The variation is not just about the size and type of business but also about the specific conditions. Imagine a school principal who has a team of qualified teachers with an average of twenty-five years of experience, in a school with well-adjusted pupils, and then imagine a principal in a problem school where fights and vandalism are everyday occurrences, where most of the staff are temporary employees, and those on contract may only be there because they cannot get jobs in other schools. There may be few similarities in the work even though the job descriptions are similar. The former may lead a well-balanced existence, while the latter spend most of their time dealing with emergencies.

Many of the studies which have been conducted in this field have, however, attempted to clarify what managerial jobs consist of, despite the differences, and a number of key principles and roles which managers ought to practise when exercising management correctly have been articulated (Barnard 1938; Fayol 1921/1949). Managerial work in practice looks different from the principles (Tengblad & Vie 2012). Many studies of the work of the manager in practice (Carlson 1951/1991; Jönsson 1995; Mintzberg 1973; Tengblad 2006) present an accurate description of managers' behaviour. They have often focused on the way working time is spent on different activities, but the focus on behaviour comes at the expense of a certain richness and vividness in the description. The people behind the managerial roles are marginalized. It is the behaviour and the doing which is emphasized, while thoughts, motives, emotions and interpretations of events and outcomes disappear from the picture. The external behaviour alone does not always tell us very much. It is clear that a certain percentage of the manager's time is spent talking to people, taking part in meetings or sitting in front of the computer, but the mechanics of this are not particularly interesting unless the aspects of content and experience are taken into account. The "internal side" of managerial work – as of other reasonably qualified and thought-dependent activity – is central.

Who are these individuals who become managers, and what is the force that drives them? How do they experience management? How do they see themselves, their jobs, their achievements and their relationships with others? Positioning yourself as a manager means, as we mentioned above, forming your managerial work and its content based not only on external demands such as role expectations but also on your own background, interests and aspirations. The managerial work is also influenced by how you understand yourself as a human being and person. A central theme of this book is that the way in which management and managerial work are shaped and exercised is linked to the way in which people understand and see themselves in different contexts (Watson 2001). This has a bearing on ambitions, actions and the interaction which can be said to constitute the core of managerial work.

At the same time it is, of course, also important to go behind the notions, intentions and self-view of the managers and include the opinions of co-workers and others, and also to place the managerial experiences in a wider context. There are many circumstances which play a role and take place behind the manager's back – both open and hidden forces and mechanisms influence managers' attempts to combine their self-views with an image of the world. Ideals and norms, new trends, seductive leadership language and the multiplicity of demands lead to many managers floundering about and almost tying themselves into knots to make it all work: to be a coach and be charismatic, to be a moral authority with integrity and to adapt politically to suit the circumstances, to be clear but absolutely not authoritarian, and so on.

Managerial work – the classical theorists

Much of what is written today about the work of managers has its historical roots in writings about managers from the beginning of the twentieth century. The studies of managers' work gathered momentum when people began to pay serious attention to how organizations are led effectively. The classical authors include Henri Fayol (1921/1949), who laid the foundation for what has sometimes been called the administrative school, in which a number of activities for good company administration were formulated. These activities are planning, organizing, commanding, coordinating and controlling. Fayol also formulated a number of fairly abstract principles for good administration; these involve the division of work and responsibility, upholding discipline and putting the right person into the right place. The classical theorists also include other writers who influenced the way in which management came to be viewed in the early twentieth century. One well-known variation of these rationalistic and normative frameworks is the American political scientist Luther Gulick's specification of the manager's activities in the acronym POSDCORB. According to this, the central tasks are

- *planning*
- *organizing*
- *staffing*
- *directing*
- *coordinating*
- *reporting*
- *budgeting*

A uniform style of management with strict line responsibilities is central in this system, in which managers drive through their activities by means of discipline, force and persuasion. The classical theorists share a view of organizations as somewhat closed and stable systems. Organizations are seen more or less as machines, which is why relations with their external environment of the kind which are common today, such as market orientation or being expected to follow trends and fashions, are not so central. Increased production and productivity (*efficiency*) are the most important things. The theorists tried to design universal management principles based on a strong production-oriented management logic. These are characterized by rationalism, and the senior management – with special leadership traits and management styles – is assumed to have a strong influence (*top-down*) on organizational events. Taking their starting point in a fairly autonomous and consequently strong position, albeit one curbed by the market, organizational management is expected to act rationally in crucial and strategic issues, to some extent decoupled from daily activities (Tyrstrup 1993).

Today, when most of what is produced bears the mark of an affluent society, with its overproduction (in relation not only to need and demand, but also to time for consumption), creating and influencing demand is central not only for many companies, but also, to some extent, for public sector organizations such as schools and higher education colleges and universities, where market orientation and efforts to sell the right image of oneself are also seen as essential (Alvesson 2011a). This has complicated the picture somewhat. Modern organizations are often more complex and obscure – which in turn makes managerial work more complex.

Even if many characterizations of managerial work in practice have shown that the classical theorists' depiction of managerial work is an oversimplification – and, above all, that it tends to portray managerial work as well organized, clear and rational – many of these notions of what the manager does still dominate. The idealistic picture communicated by the classical theorists has been upheld in various ways in countless management books and popular writings about management and leadership. The emphasis in the majority of management literature is thus still on planning, strategy, overall orientation and symbolic work with general values. We can take strategy as an example. Even if most people – academics as well as practitioners – believe today that company strategies develop gradually in long-term learning processes, the majority of textbooks in the field still place great emphasis on analysis, planning and implementation. And even if it is common to stress increased dynamics, it is not unusual to view the CEO as the Great, decisive Strategist, who makes his or her impact on the business. Montgomery (2008) claims, for example, that even if strategy today is vastly different from that in the past, the most important implication is that the CEO works with this continuously:

Watching over strategy day in and day out is the CEO's greatest opportunity to shape the firm as well as outwit the competition.

The consequence of this view is that other actors appear as less central figures – even managers appear almost as performers in The Great Strategist's creation and recreation of the company (Carter et al. 2008). In practice, strategies tend to develop gradually, in interplay between different actors and the circumstances of individual organizations and environments. Strategies are usually controlled by efforts to adapt to changes which may at times be rather rapid and are sometimes difficult to assess (Mintzberg 1991).

Managerial work – in practice

Studies of managerial work in practice have, as has been mentioned, shown that the rational ideas launched by the classical theorists present a different picture of what managers actually do. According to these, time for analysis, planning and reflection is marginal. Managers spend most of their time on operational and function-oriented questions, such as purchasing and production issues. Decision-making, commanding and strategy occupy a far less important place in their managerial work. The image of the manager which emerged in Carlson's (1951/1991) classic study was hardly the military general with an overview, but rather "the marionette in a puppet show", with hundreds of people pulling the strings and forcing him to act sometimes in one way, sometimes in another.

Many other studies have confirmed this image (see, for example, Koot & Sabelis 2002; Mintzberg 1973; Tengblad 2006; Watson 2001). One that has attracted particular attention is Mintzberg's (1973) observations of the daily activities of five senior managers. Mintzberg states that managerial work is diverse, fragmentary, action oriented (rather than analytical) and verbal (in meetings and on the telephone) and that it takes place under severe time pressure. To describe this fragmented managerial work, Mintzberg articulated ten managerial roles, organized in three overall role categories (Table 2.1).

The first meaning of management is acting in different interpersonal roles. As *figurehead*, the manager performs social, ceremonial and symbolic duties. The role of *leader* here means creating

Table 2.1 *Mintzberg's (1973) ten managerial roles*

Interpersonal roles	Information manager	Decision-maker
Figurehead	*Monitor*	*Entrepreneur*
Leader	*Disseminator*	*Disturbance handler*
Liaison	*Spokesperson*	*Resource allocator*
		Negotiator

a positive working climate and motivating and developing subordinates. This role is at the heart of the relationship between managers and subordinates. The manager must develop relationships with subordinates in such a way as to make them feel motivated and engaged. It is also about personnel questions such as promotion and reward systems. Management further involves creating networks and positive external links – in this, the manager is a *liaison*.

Management also means taking the role of information manager. One role of the manager in this is to *monitor*; this means gathering and processing information in order to identify problems and opportunities prior to decision-making. Another role is to be the information *disseminator*, in other words to distribute information to the organization. Here the manager must also be the *spokesperson* in contact with external stakeholders and inform them of the organization's results and progress.

A third group of roles involves decision-making. The manager must be an *entrepreneur* and initiate change. The role of *disturbance handler* involves dealing with unforeseen incidents and conflicts. In the role of *resource allocator*, the manager is occupied with allocating and authorizing resources and their use. Finally, in the role of *negotiator*, the manager negotiates with different stakeholders (usually superiors and subordinates, but also people from other departments and suppliers/customers) in all types of questions which arise in the course of business.

This frame of reference is intended to capture management in a more general sense. At the same time, it says more about managers at a slightly higher level in the organization. Many managers are also active in operational work: they participate in technical discussions and practical problem-solving, which is to say that they are involved in different kinds of very practical matters. Many managers at lower and middle levels have a fairly narrow field of activities within their part of the production chain.

The managerial roles described above are overlapping and can be performed in parallel. Which role is practised depends on a number of circumstances. The environment often plays a crucial role here – this applies to circumstances such as industrial logic, economic fluctuations or developments in technology. What is even more important is the nature of the actual work and the business. The managerial level and characteristics of the subordinates are often crucial in determining which roles are central. Research in this field shows that although personal traits are not insignificant when it comes to exercising different roles, it is generally the organizational demands which have the strongest influence. The research does not highlight individual variations. It does, however, state that managers develop slightly different modes of action based on their mandate and personal sympathies and check these against different types of situations.

Pointing to the diversity of managerial roles offers another perspective on the classical theorists' normative and rationalist characteristics. The different roles help us to understand the intensity, the fragmentation and the variation of managerial work.

MANAGEMENT – IDENTITY

As seen from the above, research into management in practice often tones down the personal aspect. It emphasizes patterns and tones down individual variation. However, it is not uncommon for managers to define their work in highly personal terms rather than describe it in terms of different roles based on external demands. We therefore often talk about the *personal management*, and sometimes about personal leadership (Mastrangelo et al. 2004). Many managers maintain (and wish) that their managerial work is (were) characterized by their own personality and their personal traits. They believe you should be yourself and authentic in your leadership. This tendency to psychologize implies a greater emphasis on how you understand yourself and your traits and abilities, for example the particular strengths you possess that make you suited to be a manager. It is not unusual for managers to declare that they have motivation, integrity, courage, a sense of responsibility and the ability to tackle difficult challenges. Managers like to describe their own style of management and leadership as something rather special and to base these descriptions on their perceived personality and self-view – their identity. This is in some contrast to adapting to the situation and to the demands and expectations of others.

The interest in questions of identity has grown in recent years, not only in the academic world but also in management and leader development contexts as well as among practising managers. There are many interpretations and definitions of identity (Alvesson 2010; Brown 2015; Kenny et al. 2011; Ybema et al. 2009). We see identity as a question of how you view yourself in a particular context. Identity is about seeking to build a self-view that is consistent and coherent and can provide a relatively stable platform for orienting oneself in life and organizations. Identity involves finding answers to questions such as "Who am I?", "In what ways am I similar to/different from other people?", "Which groups do I identify with?", "What do I stand for?" and "What is important for me?" In working life, identity is always work related – themes of identity such as father of four, football fanatic or (even) transvestite do not necessarily have any great influence on managerial identity – and generally become an amalgamation of certain personal orientations and how you, partly in interplay with others, develop a particular self-view in relation to your work.

In this book, identity represents a particular personal subjectivity which forms emotions, thoughts and values in a particular direction. People sometimes also talk about what they are *not*, almost as a kind of anti-identity. In other words, identity has not only to do with something positive, since a distinctiveness requires a contrast. Managers thus often point out what they are and what they can do indirectly, by pointing out what they are not and what they cannot do (Sveningsson & Alvesson 2003). They frequently stress that they are not authoritarian, that they do not interfere or that they are no longer a technical expert. Sometimes identities are well crafted, and some managers can give a coherent and consistent description of who they are and what they stand for. In many other cases, the question of identity is less integrated, consistent and clear. In a complicated and fragmented world, with ideals and demands which are at times contradictory, individuals struggle with identity problems (Sennett 1998).

In the book, we portray the efforts of managers to actively shape and form a managerial identity. We wish to stress that management is by no means a given, not even in cases where there are explicit mandates and demands. The latter are always interpreted and shaped by managers, and, as we mentioned earlier, this is based on many different circumstances, which may be determined by organizational or environmental factors, although personal experience and interests can also be central. In this respect, we can talk about identity work (see below for more about this), which implies that people strive to create a sense of a positive self-view as a platform for their work and relationships. These identities are created, negotiated and developed in relation to others (Watson 2009). Yet it is also in these relations that identities are at times threatened and undermined (Sluss & Ashforth 2007). A central element in these relations is, of course, the occurrence of feedback and confirmation of the identity claims; a lack, or questioning, of claims and ideas may lead to the feeling that the identity is being questioned, which may in turn lead to an intensification of the identity work. We will discuss this topic in detail in the book.

Identities vary somewhat since the answers to these questions of who we are and what capabilities we believe we have change over time and depending on the context in which they are formulated. This also applies, of course, to one's own image of oneself as manager: the answer to the question of who you are as a manager varies with time and context (Watson 2009). One's view of management changes slightly depending on the situation. It is possible, for example, to have one view of management when you first become a manager, only for this view to change as you work with this in practice, are given a new managerial job, deal with a radically different co-worker constellation or see new leadership ideals becoming popular. In other words, the "personal leadership" changes frequently with time, as managers struggle with questions of who they are, can be and will be. As we mentioned above, this change and development in the managerial identity often occurs in relation to other people, who frequently have a major influence on how one sees oneself as a manager. Work tasks, educators, senior managers, colleagues, management literature about what it means to be a good manager (such as coach, moral authority, visionary), company cultures, career and much more – all influence attempts to define identity to some degree. Changing and developing managerial identity is often said to be particularly salient in modern working life with its complexity and turbulence. These are central themes in this book.

Managerial identity in modern organizations

Working life in many organizations today is often described as being changeable, unstable, confusing and contradictory. Even if the degree of change and instability is at times greatly exaggerated, it appears that demands for rapid and conflicting changes, and consequently some fragmentation of working conditions, are rather noticeable elements of modern working life. These often involve introducing change efforts which subsequently come to nothing, or managers being exposed in the media or education to new ideals of how things should be: perhaps that the coaching manager is on the way in (or out) while the firm (more controlling and authoritarian) manager is on the way out (or in). Demands for change are rarely made or objectively based on qualified knowledge – what is seen is often a collection of separate ideas, uncertain interpretations, fear of not doing the same as everyone else (according to the media or consultants). The "evidence" for the latest fashion is often weak or totally lacking. Yet trends, fashions and ideas with regard to other types of changes still have consequences.

These might include demands for renewal and development alongside demands to downsize. Or efforts to make organizations flatter, reduce bureaucracy and create faster decision paths – or contrasting trends, in which the number of standards, regulations and procedures and other routines increases. Neither is it unusual for the manager to be expected to exercise overall leadership of a more grandiose kind, while at the same time being an administrator, in charge of everyday matters, budgets, sick leave and holiday schedules. The manager is a communicator of visions and a controller who checks that forms have been filled in correctly, an innovation leader and a janitor, someone who creates a pleasant atmosphere and the person who sets salaries (at least on the fringes). Much managerial work involves matters that may not be seen as being in line with a managerial position. Some managers may even prefer these – they are practical, not very complicated and must be done. Communicating visions or developing values can make them feel they are rather vague – or bring a suspicion that subordinates may see the managers as fluffy.

Turbulence and conflicting demands for change have a strong impact on managers since they have assumed a position as the person responsible for the progress, result and change within an organization or working group. They also have a relatively strong position in terms of resources, compared with many other co-workers, and can be expected to take a firmer grasp on the management and development of organizations (departments). Many of those who influence public opinion and who talk about the development of modern organizations – consulting firms, management and leadership gurus, the media, business publications, company executives, politicians and business schools – also target managers when it comes to questions of development and renewal. The general view is that managers must be able to both plan change and at the same time respond to changes in their environment.

Generally speaking, managers thus face many different demands and expectations, and the majority of individuals live in an imperfect world where ideals and reality, what is said to apply and what actually applies, complicate the picture. In fact, idealized descriptions of an attractive organizational and managerial world frequently collide with what is often a grey, bureaucratic and disorganized daily life (Tengblad 2012a).

Management in modern organizations is thus complex and problematic, something which busy people often say is hard work, perhaps, but particularly challenging and inspiring. However, some individuals experience uncertainty about the meaning of managerial work. Feelings of inadequacy are not unusual, and some managers see themselves almost as a modern victim of an increasingly high pace and the need to be present everywhere at the same time. Many ask themselves what management is all about and also try to work actively to develop a managerial identity which can serve as a relatively safe and secure platform in a working life which is characterized by contradictions (Hill 1992). Given, not least, the contradictions between ideals and practice, between wanting and being able, it does seem, however, to be increasingly difficult to develop a managerial identity which can serve as a stable platform for more long-term managerial work.

The managerial tools and models which are continuously being launched seem to make it difficult at times for managers to know where to stand, and they thus also find it difficult to maintain stability in the managerial work and its various tasks. Against the background of the changes and need for flexibility it almost seems necessary to constantly adopt a new identity rather than find a secure and more long-term identity which will function as a platform in times of turbulence and uncertainty. Fluctuating fashions also play a part. One day managers are expected to be a coach or a visionary, only to be met the next day by a speaker who says that they should avoid quasi-therapy or empty rhetoric, and be clear, assertive and willing to make demands! We could, perhaps, say that work with managerial identity is continuous and ongoing – it is, after all, often suggested that identity should be updated according to the latest management and leadership models. In the previous chapter, we said that identity is often referred to as a kind of ongoing project, with all the flexibility and variability that brings. Demonstrating flexibility when it comes to self-view and identity is described as the key to success in modern working life. At least, many people want to give the impression that they are updated in various respects by using and expressing themselves in the latest fashionable terms. Adopting the current management vocabulary is important in order to show themselves and others that they are a modern manager. Whether the talk has any deeper meaning is, of course, another matter, but it can be difficult, in the long term at least, to maintain a facade which does not affect one's own identity on a slightly deeper level.[1]

It is, however, also true to say that continuously working to adjust and modify your own identity might lead to a certain fragility and uncertainty about who you are and what you can do, something which might, in the long term, undermine self-esteem and self-confidence. This seems to be common in modern working life. Managers are, of course, not the only ones who struggle with the question of stability/ variability and self-view/expectations of others, but they are among those who are the most vulnerable. According to the heroic ideal, which has to some extent dominated the view of leadership in recent years, managers are expected to be independent and decisive and to leave a strong imprint on others, but at the same time there are other ideals, such as participation, sensitivity to others, humility and the ability to

[1] One question is whether it is possible to be authentic in working life and in the managerial job in particular. Authenticity is frequently described as an ideal, an obvious platform. Good managers are themselves. There is a counter-view that impression management is central in the modern working life, not least for managers. Being able and willing to adapt and get on with many people, not least customers and others, and flexibility are central. Those who insist on authenticity may not always be successful. Integrity is laudable, but in practice this quality is difficult to maintain (Jackall 1988).

promote others rather than oneself. Taking centre stage and standing for visions, values and ways of thinking demonstrates power, but may be seen as self-glorification and as sidelining others. Excessive participation and listening may seem attractive, but can also be seen as passive and weak. However, it can be difficult to combine apparently contradictory ideals within the framework of a stable view of one's identity in a way which will last.

Identity work

Shaping an identity in organizations is, more than in life in general, about attempting to balance different forces. Some researchers believe that managerial identity is primarily a result of external forces, such as role expectations, which are an intrinsic part of managerial work. The role makes the person, rather than the other way around. Others, however, claim that the personal experiences an individual embodies are more important for the way in which management is developed. There is, however, reason to believe that the personal management that many people talk about is a result of both external forces, such as expectations linked to the specific role, general ideas and recipes for what, for example, leadership should look like, and the personality traits and individual experiences which leave their imprint on all individuals and which help us to understand the world in different ways. Identities are thus the result both of external expectations of the role and actual work situations, and of internal forces related to personality, life history, appropriated ideas about work and leadership, and more (McAdams 1996; Watson 2008, 2009).

People shape and revise their identity in relation to these forces by means of *identity work*. Identity work refers to the way in which human beings more or less continuously shape, repair, maintain and revise interpretations that facilitate the creation of relatively coherent views of who they are and what they can do (Alvesson & Willmott 2002; Brown 2015; Sveningsson & Alvesson 2003). As has been mentioned earlier, people engage in identity work primarily in two situations. The first is when they have to develop an identity in relation to a radically new situation, for example when they take their first steps into working life, make a career change, take up a managerial job (for the first time) or retire. The second is in situations where their own self-view is challenged. This might be the result of this view being threatened or undermined in some respect, such as when confirmation or feedback at work is not forthcoming. Being overlooked for promotion, negative feedback in co-worker surveys, a conflict with your manager, difficult decisions, conflicting demands, and so on, can trigger identity work. The challenge might also arise from more positive opportunities, for example new leadership ideals or the opportunity for new and different work. A previously held self-view will then need to be revised. As we will see in the book, it can be difficult to create a coherent, positive picture of yourself as a manager if those around you do not confirm some aspects of this picture. The degree of such confirmation varies. We normally also engage in identity work when we experience uncertainty, anxiety, questioning or doubt, circumstances which are accentuated more frequently in times of turbulence and change. In more stable situations, it is often easier to uphold a fairly fixed view of ourselves and our abilities. But here, too, there are traps. Spending a long time in the same job or as an employee in the same company can lead to doubt both on your own part and on the part of others; perhaps, it indicates a lack of energy and willingness to learn – appearing to be a security addict with a low level of employability is not good for your self-view.

It is not unusual for people to create stories about themselves which form a meaningful context and which integrate the past, present and future in a time context (Giddens 1991; McAdams 1996). In our case, you could say that managers talk about the past, present and future in such a way that they shape a context which gives meaning to their work. If these stories are then confirmed by those around them, their claim to who they are as a manager is, of course, reinforced. As we have also mentioned, there are, however, occasions when such claims are not always confirmed by the environment; the stories you tell about yourself may be challenged, rejected or simply ignored by others. Inventing self-boosting stories may consequently be associated with a high degree of uncertainty and anxiety, since they may be challenged at any time (Sims 2003). Middle managers, in particular, are not left in peace with their descriptions of themselves – others may make claims which offer conflicting descriptions. A manager may, for example, happily describe him or herself as a central leading figure, while a more senior manager sees the person in question as someone who implements orders from above, and the manager's co-workers see him or her as having little involvement in the business. At the same time, the need for confirmation varies. For a new manager, the situation is often fragile, and uncertainty about who they are is common. In such a situation, they are hugely dependent on confirmation from their environment. Attempts to establish, maintain and gain acknowledgement for a particular leadership style often fail, which can be very obvious, and very upsetting (Wenglén 2005).

It is, thus, not always easy to maintain the high status we normally associate with managerial work, at least with that above the lowest managerial level (section manager, supervisor). This applies not least to new managers working in an environment, such as in a knowledge-intensive business with many independent co-workers, where the manager's tasks may be vague and unclear (it is difficult to know what "managerial substance" is). Managers in such situations sometimes have to struggle to maintain a positive self-view. The need for confirmation is often strong; in other words, managers rely on feedback which tells them whether they are doing the right thing and which can increase their self-confidence. If this is not forthcoming, it can lead to insecurity and doubt, and to weak self-esteem and self-confidence. Naturally, this applies to people in general and not only to managers. Yet many people find some stability at work thanks to their professional competence and technical skills. While, for example, craftsmen or nurses perform something tangible which, it is hoped, will lead to visible, positive results, this can be more difficult for a manager who spends more time planning and talking to people in meetings. It is not always easy to see tangible results of leadership efforts. Managers' relations dependency and the often fragmented, insecure and fluctuating nature of managerial work mean that it can be difficult to achieve and uphold a stable, growing feeling of competence and respect. This subject requires a close-up study, and the reader is lucky enough to have the result of one such study at hand. In-depth illustrations of managers' identity questions are given in the following chapters. But first, let us have a brief discussion on the increasingly popular topic of leadership, something else which is central for our managers.

LEADERSHIP

Many managers stress leadership as the most central aspect of management. "I am a leader, not a manager", some declare, thereby implying that their efforts are particularly effective and that they are different, in a positive sense, from the more boring types who are "just a manager". In a sequel to his 1973 classic on managerial work, Mintzberg (2009) critically maintains that leadership has, unfortunately and misleadingly, forced out the significance and value of other managerial activities, in education and management development as well as in descriptions of managerial work in general. The importance attached to leadership nourishes many people's desire to become managers. In other words, the idea usually advocated is that being a manager is no longer good enough; you must be a leader too (or even instead).

One consequence of the popularization of leadership in recent years is that many people believe that regularly recurring organizational problems to do with productivity, quality, innovation, morals and strategies can be dealt with by means of more and better leadership. When things go wrong, one of the first measures taken by the board of directors is to look for new leadership. Even organizations which have traditionally toned down leadership and emphasized professional competence and effective systems, structures and routines are now assigning it more importance. Today, administrations which run schools, hospitals and universities routinely encourage leadership in their own ranks. Pious hopes are placed in pedagogical and academic leadership.

Given our faith in leadership, we might assume that it has a clear and distinct substance. Unfortunately, that is not the case. The only thing that can be said with certainty about literature on leadership is that the majority of authors in the field appear to disagree on most things, including how to define leadership.

Leadership research usually includes five approaches. Three of these – trait theory, style/behaviour theory and situational theory – dominated the research for many years and are seen as the classics. They deal primarily with managerial supervision, with the focus on a mix of task and relationship orientation as well as the degree of control and delegation. As a contrast to this, a transformational view of leadership emerged in the 1980s, placing greater emphasis on, among other things, the emotional exchange between the leader and follower. Transformational leadership places great importance on the leader as the central source of inspiration with influence on values, identification and commitment. This approach has been criticized in recent times with the emergence of alternative theories, which, among other things, emphasize the relational aspects of leadership and where leadership is seen more as an integrated part of the daily activities (Uhl-Bien 2006). We sometimes talk about post-heroism (Grint 2005a). Here follows a brief account of the five approaches.

Leadership traits

The trait theory emerged at the beginning of the twentieth century and still holds a strong attraction for scholars, leadership developers, the media, business publications and managers. Leadership here is about innate qualities. You either have these natural traits, or you do not, in which case you are less suited to be a leader. Typical traits include a sense of responsibility, perseverance, goal orientation, persistence, boldness, originality in problem-solving, self-confidence and strong self-esteem (Stogdill 1974). Despite countless studies to find these traits – so-called *trait spotting* – it has not been possible to establish any clear links between personality traits and successful leadership (Wright 1996). The trait theory, with its strong psychological profile, has haunted leadership research for over a hundred years, and experienced a renaissance with the establishment of transformational leadership in the 1980s, when traits such as drive, motivation, honesty, integrity, cognitive ability and industry knowledge were emphasized as being central. The outcome is often a number of very general positive traits, which might be as relevant for dentists, shop assistants and product developers as for managers. As we will see in the study at hand, trait theory is also popular among practising managers.

Style and behaviour

The absence of conclusive evidence of the importance of traits for leadership led researchers in the 1940s to take an interest in behaviour or style. This approach is an attempt to define the behaviour of managers, primarily in relationship to subordinates. Studies of leadership behaviour have included asking subordinates to respond to a number of statements about their managers. The results of these have then been analysed based on two or four dimensions which were considered to be an expression of different forms of effective leadership (Blake & Mouton 1964). Common dimensions in these studies have been task orientation, relationship orientation, controlling/authoritarian or participating leadership (Katz & Kahn 1978). However, results of studies of styles have also been rather meagre and unclear. A more consistent result from these studies is that relations-oriented managers appear to enhance the mood – although not the productivity – of their co-workers. One problem in both the trait and style studies is the universal ambitions, that is to say the idea of finding the most effective leadership, *the one best way*, regardless of context.

The importance of situation

The idea behind this theory is to formulate the best leadership, taking a starting point in different situations. One popular version is Hersey and Blanchard's (1982) situational theory. In this, the situation is the relationship between the manager and subordinate. This is understood as the ability of the co-worker to take responsibility for and perform their tasks independently. They talk about a co-worker's maturity – willingness and skill – in relation to the task, and describe four leadership styles which involve a higher degree of participation and engagement on the part of the co-worker, from clear direction and control to delegation and independent participation. Researchers in general agree that it is important to recognize the situation in which the leadership is being exercised, but difficulties in implementing the concept in the majority of quantitative studies has meant that it has not been possible to deliver any firm conclusions (Wright 1996). One problem is that it is difficult to say something universal about what is situation-specific: type of business, size of organization, organizational culture, the organization's situation (recession or boom), co-workers' varying characteristics (age, gender, ethnicity, experience, education), the degree of uniformity and variation among these (homogeneous or heterogeneous group) and more can play a part. Situations are not necessarily "fixed", say in the form of co-workers' stable age, skills and level of engagement, but may also vary at different times: during a working day, a manager can meet a range of situations with different co-workers whose skills, attitudes, and so on, can vary depending on the task. Someone who is in general committed may, for example, be unwilling to perform certain tasks, and even well-qualified people can have gaps in their competence.

Transformational leadership

Transformational leadership emerged partly as a reaction to the type of simple and emotionally sterile exchange which characterizes the transactional styles above (Burns 1978). Here the exchange, or rather the relationship, between the leader and follower is described as a question of inspiration, emotions, loyalty and strong commitment (Bass & Riggio 2006). Management is contrasted with leadership, with the former being about traditional administration, including managing the exchange between the organization and co-worker, and the latter about overall and inspiring leadership, which is intended to make people less instrumentally oriented and more dedicated to the leaders and the organization. Transformational leadership focuses more explicitly than other forms of leadership on change. Strategies, visions and overall principles are also seen as central (Conger & Kanungo 1998). One idea is that a manager should not be solely occupied with the traditional, mundane drudgery of keeping things moving in pace with the demands of the organizational machinery, but should also infuse a feeling of passion, commitment and participation. The latter is something which can form the basis for learning, developing and renewal. (All good things – as is usually the case in popular contexts – go hand in hand.)

Transformational leadership in terms of the leader's importance for the overall questions – strategy and visions – and organizational change has contributed to the strong popularity of this approach and its major breakthrough among consultants and managers. It makes the leader a central figure and the answer to many of the problems – such as globalization, technological development and innovations – that modern organizations encounter, which contributes to its strength as a source of identity. We sometimes talk of the heroic status of the leader (Meindl et al. 1985; Pearce & Manz 2005) – as do several of the managers in this book.

Yet when it comes to the importance of charisma and inspirational leadership for change processes, the results are unclear here too. However, some people say that charismatic and transformational leadership is important for co-worker engagement, job satisfaction and sense of role insecurity (Niehoff et al. 1990). Charisma can, however, easily become counterproductive, since a charismatic leader is a dominating force and the co-workers may allow themselves to be influenced too strongly, stop thinking for themselves and become severely dependent. In this respect, there is some conflict between charisma and certain aspects of transformational leadership (Shamir 2007). The essence of the latter is that the leader tries to encourage not only a sense of community and engagement beyond a focus on self-interest, but also independence and development. Transformational leadership is then partly inconsistent with and undermined by charisma, which implies being spellbound by and dependent on the leader. One problem is, of course, that it is not particularly easy to realize transformational leadership. Convincing individuals to tone down the importance of salary, working situation, interesting work and career and instead be inspired by the manager's ability to build commitment to the person and to the organization can be very difficult.

Post-heroic leadership

Post-heroic leadership is an umbrella term for a number of slightly varying styles which are all sceptical to the heroic view of leadership. The post-heroic school considers leadership to be not about the big, all-embracing questions, but, on the contrary, about the more every-day questions which make up part of the ongoing managerial work (Badaracco 2002). In some cases, the relational and processual aspects of leadership are emphasized, and leadership is stressed as being something which can potentially be exercised by everyone in an organization (Uhl-Bien 2006). Many people hold the view that leadership is primarily a collective and mutual process which includes not only supposed managers but also other co-workers, who are normally considered as passive supporters (Crevani et al. 2007). Against this background, there are many who maintain that leadership should be seen as something which is shared or spread among several individuals (Gronn 2002). They also talk about a more socially competent, progressive or participating leadership – some emphasize a feminization of leadership (Huey 1994). This is a form of leadership which is often said to encourage humanistic and democratic working relations and conditions (Collinson 2005). Even when leadership is applied to more mundane activities, these can be charged with meaning, which has great significance for enthusiasm and motivation, and thereby co-worker performance.

Post-heroism is said to promote humanism and an improved working climate as managers encourage co-workers and enable participation. This implies highlighting and also developing reciprocity and dependence between leaders and followers with the aim of developing more fruitful relations (Fletcher & Käufer 2003). Managers who walk around and talk to co-workers are considered to have positive influences on the working climate and creativity (Mintzberg 1998). At the same time, there is some criticism of the post-heroic ideal, such as that it is more a question of influence in general rather than of leadership. Sveningsson and Blom (2011) further suggest that many "post-heroic" activities, such as listening to and constantly acknowledging people through the use of what are, on the surface, small gestures – greetings, glances and generally being friendly – may have more to do with the manager's own well-being and identity than about involving the co-worker in the business to any great degree (see also Alvesson & Sveningsson 2003c; Western 2008).

So what is leadership?

The traditions above give an indication of the complexity of this field, and this is underlined by an examination of how the term is defined. One of the leading figures in the field, Gary Yukl (1989), points out that the numerous definitions of leadership which have been proposed seem to have little in common other than that they are about an influencing process. Yukl himself has tried to bring some clarity to the field by defining leadership thus:

> leadership is defined broadly in this article to include influencing
> task objectives and strategies, influencing commitment and
> compliance in task behavior to achieve these objectives,
> influencing group maintenance and identification, and influencing
> the culture of an organization.
>
> *(Yukl 1989, p. 253)*

The definition seems reasonable but it does not actually say very much – leadership is about influencing a range of different things. It would appear that even the best definitions of leadership are often so broad and vague that they are of limited value, if not meaningless (Bolden et al. 2011). It is difficult to fully understand a notoriously ambiguous term such as leadership. (The same applies equally to many other frequently used terms, but leadership is possibly one of the trickiest.) It is more effective through the associations it awakens. Yet these can pull in different directions and make people think of everything from Martin Luther King, Jr., or General Patton to their own kindly, good-natured manager who trusts his co-workers and is not bothered if they take a nap during the working day.

We can see just how vague typical definitions of leadership are if we ask ourselves: Do leaders have to exhibit all the characteristics Yukl lists? Or are one or two enough? If the former, then leadership is undoubtedly something very rare. It is, despite everything, very difficult for even the most superhuman "company clan chiefs" to exercise such a broad and far-reaching influence. But if the latter is true, then leadership is something very common. Who does not, then, exercise leadership at least some of the time? We all influence each other's work. People who take it easy at work, take long coffee breaks, take every opportunity to tell entertaining stories and create a pleasant atmosphere and a feeling of indolence may be central norm-setters in the workplace. Maybe they are engaged in "country club management" or some other post-heroic activity? In other words, "leadership" can easily become everything or nothing. And the use of the term often swings between what everyone does and what a very small group of "real leaders" does. This makes it difficult to determine what leadership is and what it is not.

Despite what the majority of many contemporary managers and authors on the subject of leadership claim, leadership is rarely something obvious and uniform (Alvesson & Sveningsson 2012). Examples of leadership are open to interpretation, and people often attribute different levels of importance to what the leader does and its potential consequences. Listening carefully to people in organizations and finding out when and why they talk about leadership, what they mean by it, their convictions, values and emotions with regard to leadership, as well as different versions and expressions of it, often gives the impression of a high degree of diversity and variation. We will show this later in this book.

It is important to note that even if fashions and national cultures create conformity and similar discussions on a broad front, there are also significant differences between industries and organizations. It is undoubtedly possible, for example, to identify some groups and organizational cultures which are more "leadership-oriented" and others which are more "leadership-free" (Blom & Alvesson 2014). It may also be possible to identify organizational cultures which have less interest in heroic leaders or other types of leadership. The term may seem strange or have less relevance in certain contexts. Organizations with strong professional ideologies – such as universities – may be examples of this, even though the interest in leadership currently appears to be increasing in these organizations too. We should remember that leadership can, in fact, be a rather negative phenomenon for some groups. An emphasis on leadership may be synonymous with an authoritarian approach, elitism and non-professionalism. If the leader is held up as being central, then others become less important, and this is not, of course, something which is universally popular. In general, there is a tension between the ideal of leadership as something important and the view that all co-workers are important and that hierarchy is old-fashioned. This gives rise to a plethora of efforts to deal with conflicting norms in practice (Lundholm 2011). Perhaps we can talk about leader acrobatics, since it is a question of finding a balance between the importance of the leader and the minimizing of hierarchy.

Some of the lack of clarity in the question of leadership is related to the difficulties of identifying specific leadership behaviour. Does "leadership" refer to different types of people and/or actions in different organizations? Depending on the group, it may refer to the strong, assertive decision-maker, the leading expert or practitioner, the team-builder and coach, the person who educates and develops people or the result-driven number cruncher who rigorously monitors and pushes people to make them perform. How people talk about leadership bears witness to the broader cultural patterns in an organization or industry. When the idea of what constitutes good leadership is so diverse, it is very difficult to formulate a definition of leadership which can be applied to all times and places. Instead, it is the sensitivity to people's opinions – which are upheld by groups, organizations, professions, industries and society– that is important for understanding how people relate to leadership.

Management and leadership

As we have shown, it is not entirely easy to determine the significance of leadership. Researchers in the tradition of transformational leadership have attempted to do so by contrasting leadership with management (Burns 1978). They often claim that managers rely on their formal position and work with bureaucratic processes such as planning, budgeting, organizing and controlling. Leaders, on the other hand, rely on their personal ability, work with visions and agenda, build coalitions and use mainly non-coercive means to influence people's emotions and thoughts (e.g. Kotter 1996). It is further usually said that management is often about carrying out administrative work in stable conditions, while leadership is a question of establishing an overall style through inspirational communication and action. It is sometimes said that managers are people who "do things right" and that leaders are people who "do the right things". According to Zaleznik (1977, p. 71):

> The influence a leader exerts in altering moods, evoking images and expectations, and in establishing specific desires and objectives deter- mines the direction a business takes. The net result of this influence is to change the way people think about what is desirable, possible, and necessary.

To put it another way: leaders are heavily engaged in symbolic management, while managers are more engaged in administrative processes.

There appears to be an attraction in the division between leaders who influence interpretations and managers who administer. It makes leadership sound like a glamorous, challenging, almost magical occupation. Management, on the other hand, appears to involve tedious administrative duties. Both these stereotypes seem to be highly charged with an ideology that glorifies leadership as an indispensable component in the creation of uninterrupted and radical change and of seriously committed co-workers who give their all, or at least perform well. Leadership is considered to be a good thing in itself, and essential for all dynamic organizations. Almost all the definitions of management and leadership favour the latter: leadership is much more dynamic, important and effective, something which benefits both co-workers and the results. Presented with such an alluring picture, people find it easy to identify with leadership and happily describe themselves as leaders. "I'm a leader, I could never be a manager", as a financial manager in a small municipality put it at a seminar. (Is he really in the right place? You ask yourself.) Most people do, in fact, take their starting point in a managerial position – it is not normally easy for an ordinary co-worker to claim to be the leader at work and attempt to limit the manager to simply being a manager. But the managerial job is only a formal platform and resource base; you can use your personality and your persuasive efforts to exercise leadership and in that way become both manager and leader, or possibly leader rather than manager. That is what many people seem to want to believe.

Yet this generally widespread talk of managers as leaders does not always correspond particularly well with what actually happens in many organizations. All the talk of leadership does not necessarily mean that leadership is also actually exercised in the way it is described in various situations. A number of studies which are more critical of leadership have shown that much of the talk about leadership is not practised, at least not in terms of the more strategic and change-oriented questions which are usually referred to when leadership is contrasted with management. Many people talk a great deal about how they exercise leadership, but a closer look shows that the majority seem to be occupied with administrative managerial work (Alvesson & Sveningsson 2003a). This is generally because, in reality, the organizational machinery requires the managers to pay attention to everyday operational circumstances which lie beyond questions of strategies and visions; this is, of course, particularly true of middle managers. Even if everyone talks about the importance of leadership, it is given lower priority in favour of what they actually do – yet the idea of leadership can hold particular significance for the individual's self-view and the capacities they believe they have: in other words, for the individual's identity (Alvesson & Sveningsson 2003b; Sveningsson & Larsson 2006). We will return to this on a number of occasions in this book.

Against this background, you could say that the rigid distinction between leaders and managers is popular, but controversial. Most people who claim, or are assumed, to exercise leadership in organizations hold a formal position – in general as a manager, but it might also be as chair of the board or union representative. People in such formal positions often take advantage of our deeply rooted conviction that people who are in formal positions of authority have the right to exercise influence on us. We respect those who hold a formal mandate – and not least in the case of the person who employs us. It is difficult for an ordinary co-worker to be a leader, although there are often informal leaders. The managerial job is an important resource base for the individual seeking to exercise leadership. It is not easy to exercise leadership when you do not have a big room, higher salary, more expensive clothes, the right/opportunity to set salaries for others and to ask them to undertake specific tasks (Grint 2005b). In fact, people often gain access to these formal positions based on what is seen as an "informal" leadership skill – those who are seen as leadership material often become managers. The people who are promoted to managerial positions are expected to have certain qualities which are usually associated with "leadership", such as experience, education and intelligence. They are also expected to look like leaders, which often means wearing a suit and looking clean, smart and reliable, appearing busy and serious, talking more than others in meetings, going to many meetings, not going on sick leave without good reason and staying reasonably sober at the office party.

In practice, managers often manage with the help of planning, they coordinate, they control and they work with bureaucracy. But they also strive to create commitment to, or at least acceptance for, plans, rules, procedures and instructions. Managers who work with these more formal mechanisms, without any real interest in what people think and feel, usually accomplish little, other than possibly in organizations that are strongly characterized by routines and strictly controlled, where thoughts and commitment are not considered to be important. The mechanics behind stimulus and response only function in simple and rare cases. There are, of course, some simple tasks which can be communicated directly and which result in behaviour which is easy to monitor and adjust, but task instructions require some understanding and acceptance. Helping people to understand the purpose of an instruction or to follow a rule without too much grumbling, and to make it meaningful (or at least less unappealing), which is difficult at times, often cuts across the distinctions between management and leadership. It therefore appears to be more helpful if we consider management and leadership as discreetly interwoven phenomena. In doing so, we can also develop a more realistic account of how leadership is in fact exercised, in most cases linked to managerial work. Mundane leadership differs from both the heroic and post-heroic views of leadership (Sveningsson et al. 2012). Here it is about influencing meaning and expectations of what it is possible and desirable to achieve. What are important above all are activities which are an integral part of daily life, such as conversation and solving routine problems. As will be shown and developed later in the book, this "realistic", moderate way of looking at leadership is not particularly widespread among our managers.

We do not claim that all management is leadership, and vice versa. Rather, we claim that leadership is often interwoven with management. There are, however, many examples of managerial work which does not in any way involve leadership. Administration and pure managerial work such as tight and detailed supervision and monitoring of work progress and performance, for example, are not leadership. Everything which does not involve interaction or indirect communication with subordinates falls outside leadership, even where these activities can be considered to be managerial work. Neither is a careful monitoring of behaviour or performance usually described as leadership. The latter has a strong element of creating and clarifying meaning (Ladkin 2010; Smircich & Morgan 1982), which includes the shaping of ideas, values, understandings and emotions, but it can also include elements of force (in the sense of legitimate force). To understand this process, it is important that we consider not only what the manager does, but also how the action taken is formed by the whole context in which he or she attempts to lead. The importance of reciprocity for how leadership is understood in various contexts is central (yet often marginalized). Those who participate in leadership processes – leaders and followers – should be seen as co-creators of the relations created and formed in the interaction between people (Crevani et al. 2010). They are interwoven with and define each other. Andersson and Tengblad (2009, p. 250) state, for example: "Without a leadership and co-workership in constructive collaboration there is not much an individual manager can do." The co-workers are, of course, just as central as the manager here, but if talking about leadership is to be meaningful, the manager must have a stronger influence than others. The centrality of the co-workers is linked to the willingness to take up a role as follower; in other words, to give the manager/leader the authority and allow themselves to be influenced. ("Follower positioning" is a crucial element of leadership.)

CONCLUDING DISCUSSION

In this chapter, we have addressed the conventional ideas of what managerial work is about: planning, leading, allocating and following up the work. The often fragmented and varying nature of managerial life in organizations makes it difficult to work with clear principles and explicit ideals and modes of action. We have therefore also stressed the importance of identity for understanding managers' work and behaviour. Identity questions are central in working life: Who am I; what is distinctive, coherent and continuous in my self-understanding? This influences reactions, experiences, choices, motivation and modes of action. In a changeable world – with reorganizations, new organizational ideals, new trends in leadership, new co-workers who may have different expectations and reactions from the old – it is often difficult to adhere to a particular identity and thereby achieve a more lasting stability. Identity becomes something of a project, something you have to work with in order to actively form through identity work. It involves acquiring self-affirmation and some positive response from others, and stitching together what are often varying and conflicting demands and signals about how you should be in order to make your situation at work fairly stable. Attempting to sustain a positive and stable self-esteem is essential for this.

What is central for the majority of managers today is leadership – or, at least, claims to do leadership. Not only it is a part of the work being done, but it is also an important source of identity. It is (all too) convenient to identify with popular ideas of leadership. Yet at the same time, it is not altogether easy to appropriate new ideas about management and leadership. Leadership often appears to be simple and direct on paper and in conversation. People talk about values, styles, and so on, as if they were objects. In reality, leadership is often vague and unclear, and not always easy to exercise in practice either. Compromises and deviations occur on a large scale. Many people are flexible and adaptable. It is not uncommon for managers to be better at talking about leadership and tying their self-view to fine ideals of leadership than at actually allowing these to break through in tangible actions.

PORTRAIT GALLERY AND ORGANIZATIONAL CONTEXT

In the following chapters, the reader will meet and become acquainted with a number of managers who work in different types of organizations. We have interviewed the majority of them on one or, in the majority of cases, several occasion(s), and they constitute our primary material. They are flanked by managerial voices from secondary data material, which is taken from various media, trade and industry journals as well as research literature. Of the thirty-one managers who make up our primary material, thirteen are the main actors and the remaining eighteen secondary actors.

The main actors lend themselves to both in-depth study and slightly wider interpretations. As our account of the methods used (see Appendix) shows, they have been the objects of particularly intensive study: they have been interviewed on a number of occasions over a period of time. They are of particular interest as case studies, since they are faced with working situations and challenges that actualize identity work in ways which are both typical and insightful. The reader will become very familiar with the main actors and meet them to varying degrees in all the chapters where we report the result of our interviews and observations. The remaining eighteen, our secondary actors, turn up here and there in the chapters, but we do not follow them as deeply, intensively or thoroughly as the main actors. The secondary actors help to further illustrate our interpretations, and not only make the portrayals of managerial work more varied, and in some cases richer, but also increase the breadth of our study. This allows us to draw further conclusions, reducing the risk that a single, untypical case will give a misleading impression.

Our main aim is not to overgeneralize, but most of what we take up here appears to characterize large parts of management and managerial life today. If we find that our material includes at least two examples on a particular theme, we estimate that it is of a certain general interest since it shows that the phenomenon exists, and an analysis can provide wider insights. (There are some exceptions where we also take up questions where we only have only example, if we see this as particularly interesting or it provides a strong contrast to other cases.) The names of all our managers have been changed to guarantee anonymity, and we have inserted a number of smokescreens to prevent identification. We give the managers names that facilitate the reader's identification through hinting at their affiliation or their self-understandings.

Below follows a list of the main actors (in alphabetical order). The secondary actors are named throughout the book – as managers A to Q – in the order in which they appear.

MAIN ACTORS

Bert Bacon

We meet Bacon just after he has taken up a managerial position in logistics at International Foods Ltd. Bacon has worked his way up through the company and has been promoted six times since he started. He has studied economics and leadership and considers this education as a platform for managerial life. Bacon's statements indicate that he has serious problems and a high level of anxiety at work.

Benjamin Book

Book is a former newspaper director who has just been appointed CEO of Big Publishers Ltd. In the newspaper world, Book took a great interest in personnel questions, which made him very popular among the staff. This was part of the platform for his move to CEO of the company. He has gained an academic qualification by taking evening classes through which he has also learned about the modern view of company management and, above all, leadership.

Charlie Chase

Chase began his career at Big Technology Ltd. as an engineer and has since been promoted to manager. We meet Chase at the point when he has just been promoted from a lower middle management position to a more senior one with responsibility for staff. This has been an ambition for Chase, who has long wanted to break free from the role of engineer. Chase has taken part in several training courses and also taken an MBA.

Carol Courage

We meet Courage just after she has taken up the position as the manager of an R&D department at Global Pharmaceuticals Ltd. After several years in a research career, she has become increasingly interested in leadership questions. She has taken part in several leadership development programmes which have strengthened her interest in leadership questions, in particular in relation to culture and development. Courage describes herself as a humanist.

David Dean

Dean has recently been appointed principal of a private school, The School Ltd. Dean has previous managerial experience, albeit not from the world of education. He maintains, however, that his previous managerial experience qualifies him to be a school manager. Dean views management as a question of coaching and often talks about delegating responsibility to those he says are most competent. He is very familiar with modern literature on leadership.

Gary Gardener

Gardener is a department manager at Advanced Technology Ltd., where he is responsible for customer support. Coming from a "technocratic family", as he puts it, he chose to become a project leader in an electronics company when he graduated with a degree in engineering. Gardener describes himself as a leader who does not enjoy exercising leadership which is too direct – he prefers to let people take their own responsibility. He often talks about "management by walking around".

Gerald Goodman

Goodman works at International Construction Ltd. He often stresses his upbringing in everything from Sunday school to a range of societies as the key to his ability to take responsibility for people. Like Courage, he sees himself as a humanist and frequently refers to himself as something of a Samaritan in his desire to see that people are happy. Goodman feels that his managerial style does not always suit his environment, so he is careful to make sure he does not dominate too much.

Henry Harding

When Big Technology Ltd. was established, Harding was offered the role as head of the project organization. He is an engineer and has worked mainly with development questions in various technology products. Harding is often very direct in meetings and in conversations with co-workers. He likes to push his co-workers hard, so they will deliver successfully and meet deadlines. Performing well and working hard are central for Harding.

Matt Mooney

Mooney is a middle manager at Bank Ltd. He has taken part in several leadership development programmes and has nothing but praise for them. He has gradually become increasingly interested in leadership. He talks often and at length about coaching, about allowing co-workers to take responsibility and about helping them to develop by coaching rather than directing. He also enjoys planning and establishing predictability in most aspects of working life.

Nora Noble

Noble works in regional public services, with labour market questions. Like many other managers, Noble is interested in development questions and leadership, sometimes as a result of the leadership development programmes she has taken part in during her career in management. She sees herself as someone who is good at building networks of people who contribute to projects and business development. Noble is married and has four children. She is a reflective, cheerful person who enjoys the outdoor life.

Stuart Smart

Smart is a middle manager at Big Technology Ltd., where he has spent most of his working life. When we meet Smart, he is manager of a department which works with advanced product development. Smart believes he has the potential for a more senior managerial job and is disappointed that his managers in the organization have not seen this. He makes it clear that he would like more overall responsibility and to work more with strategy, markets and customers.

Steven Stone

Stone works at Global Industrial Products Ltd. and describes himself as a natural manager. He has taken several courses in leadership through the company but did not have an academic education when he started in the organization. Like Bacon above, Stone has taken the long road through the company. Internal company courses and promotions within the company have gone hand in hand.

William White

White has recently joined Advanced Technology Ltd. as manager of a product development department. We meet him when he is about to define the department's area of responsibility and business. White has a master's degree in business and economics and began his career at a global telecom company. He left because he felt anonymous and was not happy with his managers.

ORGANIZATIONAL CONTEXT

As the above shows, we will meet people from different areas of working life in the book. They are almost exclusively people who hold some form of middle management position. Some are managers on slightly lower levels, and others on slightly higher levels, such as senior middle managers, yet still in a traditional position between managerial levels. In one case, we follow a manager (Book) during a transitional phase from a middle management position (in a newspaper company) to an executive management position (at a publishing company).

The managers come from companies which cover a wide range of activities in completely different industries. We will meet managers from the high-technology industry – Advanced Technology Ltd. (William White, Gary Gardener and other, secondary actors), Global Industrial Products Ltd. (Steven Stone) and Big Technology Ltd. (Henry Harding, Charlie Chase and Stuart Smart)

the pharmaceutical industry – Global Pharmaceuticals Ltd. (Carol Courage and other, secondary actors)

the biotechnology industry – Biotech Ltd. (secondary actors)

the construction and projecting industry – International Construction Ltd. (Gerald Goodman and other, secondary actors)

the consumer industry – International Foods Ltd. (Bert Bacon)

the publishing business – Big Publishers Ltd. (Benjamin Book)

banking and financial services – Bank Ltd. (Matt Mooney) and Financial Services Ltd. (secondary actors)

private education – The School Ltd. (David Dean)

regional public services (Nora Noble and other, secondary actors).

Many of the companies represented are knowledge-intensive. They are organizations which offer relatively sophisticated or knowledge-based products and services. These include plans, prototypes or products for which R&D stands for the greatest share of the cost. The majority of people working in such organizations are primarily engaged in various forms of product and service development. The literature often describes knowledge-intensive firms as alternatives to more classic bureaucracies, in which more traditional forms of behavioural control are common. In contrast, knowledge-intensive organizations typically employ normative control, which involves methods such as socialization, recruitment and identity regulation. Desirable behaviour is obtained as a result of regulating and controlling co-workers' experience and ideas, rather than as a result of direct behaviour control.

These circumstances frame managerial work in alternative directions. Since the work in these organizations is complex, senior managers are often incapable of understanding in detail what actually is going on, and are also unable to control the process with the help of simple quantified performance indicators. The co-workers who are involved and informed thus have a high degree of independence. Furthermore, knowledge workers often see their own profession as a strong source of identification. This can weaken the position of their own organization and its management as the central authority and someone by whom they will allow themselves to be led. Professional knowledge workers also frequently expect relatively equitable social relations. They dislike strong hierarchies, which are less likely to be accepted. All this means that management is more complicated and often relatively weaker in knowledge-intensive organizations.

It is often said that management in these organizations focuses on overall circumstances such as norms and, more generally, organizational culture and identity. It is not uncommon to hear that management in knowledge-intensive businesses must be aimed first and foremost at supporting learning, progress and renewal. Highly qualified co-workers who have a fair degree of autonomy in more flexible organizations with high demands for learning require a style of management which is directed towards supporting the growth of strategies and overall orientation, rather than strictly traditional and analytical strategic planning (Løwendahl 1997).

Although we have a slight predominance of knowledge-intensive organizations, our material is fairly varied. We do not have any basis for comparisons such as private/public, knowledge-intensive/routine, higher-/lower-level manager, older/younger, male/female, since the basis is mixed, rather than having been selected for the purpose of making comparisons. We have prioritized in-depth cases (the thirteen main actors) and studied their specific situations, rather than making structured comparisons. As we see it, there are no simple, approximate correlations. There are undoubtedly some subtle ones, but they are of less interest to us than the deeper insights that rich case studies point to, which is the reason we have concentrated on these.

PART II Managerial life: roles and identities

3   Why management?

Judging by the enormous amount of leadership literature, the interest in management training and career ambitions, there are many people who want to become managers and – thereby, they seem to think – leaders. Some claim emphatically that they are leaders – not managers. (At times it seems as though leadership can be captured without a supporting managerial position, but things can become complicated if the Leader and the Manager in a workplace are two different people. Anyone who thinks that a managerial position means that they will be able to work solely with leadership and not with any managerial tasks will not last long in the job.) But what exactly is the attraction of being a manager? How do people reason about their future managerial role, and what exactly is it that makes them believe they are well suited to management? In this chapter, we meet people who talk about why they wanted to become a manager and their view of what being a manager means. They also talk about why they have the essential qualities for management – none of those we studied appears to have any doubt about that.[1] Many describe management as a stimulating challenge, which carries an element of excitement. Yet it is also associated with a large dose of uncertainty, partly because they do not really know what the managerial job involves. Many ask themselves whether they are managers or not, and what being a manager actually involves. One important question is what you actually need to know in order to exhibit credibility when you say you are a manager. It is about how to develop your identity as a manager, or begin to

---

[1]   We meet here newly appointed managers, some of whom have had a certain managerial supervisory responsibility as project leader or supervisor for a smaller, defined unit. The new position brings more traditional responsibility for the business. One of these managers, Bacon, describes his promotion as having taken the step up to a "real" managerial position, unlike his earlier role as project leader.

identify with the title and the idea of being a manager, in this transitional phase. How do you start working with this?

We begin the chapter with a discussion of the view of management as a means of self-development. In the section which follows, we address the way in which managers describe different types of personal traits as a natural platform for their managerial work. Most of them see themselves as natural driving forces in some way. We then discuss specific topics which the managers highlight as being important to work with, specifically strategy, change and organizational culture. Our interviewees leave us in no doubt that the opportunity to work with these questions is a major reason they are interested in a career in management. These questions are given a great deal of attention in leadership education, and the chapter ends with a look at the significance of this for some of the managers.

MANAGEMENT AS PERSONAL AND CAREER DEVELOPMENT

Many people see managerial positions as an alternative to other kinds of jobs. Someone who is genuinely interested in working as a professional may not view management as something positive. But this is not how the managers we studied see their career paths. In some of our cases, they are people who no longer feel that their occupational work or professional identity offers the opportunity for development. Their professional work conflicts with the way in which they understand their personality and their capacity. One of the managers, Bert Bacon, says that he no longer wants to be a "logistics expert" but to be a "leader":

> Leadership is a fascinating area, and I believe this is the direction my thoughts and my career are heading in, rather than being a logistics expert. I need to concentrate more on being a manager, and then I'll be free to move around as I like. Management is what I'm concentrating on, and I believe it's what many people here don't have. They're promoted through the ranks as engineers and work their way up through the engineering hierarchy and then threaten to

leave, so someone makes them a manager, but that doesn't mean they're good managers, it just means they're good engineers. And they're not good at managing people.

Bacon's fascination with leadership means he is re-evaluating his view of professional work. He wants to be a manager in order to facilitate both his mobility within the organization and his opportunity to exercise leadership. His somewhat idealized view of management portrays the role of expert as something of a stalemate, as a point of stagnation in his career. In contrast, managerial work represents development and freedom (as a manager "I'll be free to move around as I like"). In line with his idea of leadership within management, he points out that the professional role does not provide any scope for a people-oriented approach. He believes that, unlike other many other experts, he is well suited to managerial work because he understands how people work. Management is a way of expressing this knowledge.

Charlie Chase, a department manager at Big Technology Ltd., feels the same way. He talks about leaving his technical role, but the problem is that his manager does not fully appreciate him:

> Harding[2] sees me in a particular way. I have several years'
> experience in product development, I have a master's in engineering
> and I've got an MBA, but he sees me as a technical guru, someone
> who knows about technical design. But there are four people here
> who're much better at that than I am. Harding has a view of my role
> which doesn't match the way I work. I'm the one who facilitates and
> helps others to make things work, but Harding sees me as the
> expert, the specialist. I'm the technical gnome, and have been for so
> long that it's what I'll be forever. But that's not how I see myself,
> that's not my strength, I don't enjoy it.

Chase describes the role of expert as a profession-based lock-in, partly due to his own manager (Harding) and his lack of insight into Chase's true qualities. This restricts his mobility (upwards) and his

[2]   Henry Harding, another of our main actors, is one of Charlie Chase's superiors.

opportunities to help and support people, which is his strength and what he sees as central in management. His MBA qualification has reinforced his view of himself as a leader. Those around him, on the other hand, see him primarily as a technical expert, which makes it more difficult for him to identify fully with the ideals and recipes for success offered by the media, lecturers and management training. There is often a contrast between the latter and what is not expressed in the work environment.

Another main actor, Carol Courage, says that her interest in management emerged when her professional career as a researcher moved from specialist questions towards a greater interest in broader organizational questions:

> I started here as a researcher, a specialist. My personal development at the company has made me more interested in other things and I was able to make the choice to become a manager. I think that's what lots of people do in research organizations, you try to get more resources for your research and become interested in an organization, how it works, how you can effectivize the value, how people can motivate themselves, how you create growth. And now I'm in this position which doesn't really have anything to do with research.

Management here becomes a question of personal development. Courage also says:

> It's a long and twisty road but, as I've discovered here, a very positive one. I've been able to fulfil my own personal development, because I haven't been stuck in a position ... It's not at all a case of my career driving this, it's because it's what I'm interested in.

For Courage, the managerial job is thus a step in a longer process, an aspect of self-fulfilment.

Courage does not experience the same feeling of being stuck in one place as Chase, since she has always been given the opportunity to participate in management development programmes which have allowed her to form and develop her interest in management. She was hand-picked at an early stage to take part in a leadership development programme and thereby given an early opportunity to form an interest in – as well as indirect promises of – management in a more advanced meaning. She particularly stresses the importance of training which placed a strong emphasis on leadership and other "soft values" such as "culture, meaning, identity" and empowering co-workers. Leadership quickly became central to her understanding of her own role in the organization as a result of development activities on the part of the company, in which the idea of management is also formed in the individual's self-view. In the case of Courage, this formation or regulation found a willing subject. The regulation reinforced the interest in leadership questions in general, while at the same time the expert career became less interesting.

Another of our main actors, William White, says:

> It used to be about being a specialist, that was the natural path. So I began to think about what I'd do when I'd had this base for three years. I thought things were slow – the leadership closest to me wasn't what I'd expected. They weren't very good at seeing us as individuals, but saw people more as just another resource.

Unlike Chase, who suffers because his environment (at least, his superior manager) has the "wrong" view of him, the question here is of a lack of confirmation, which gives rise to identity insecurity. White wants to be seen and to receive clear confirmation from his managers about who he is and what he can do, and this leads to his interest in management. Having a poor first manager does not appear to be unusual, and it seems to influence many people when they themselves are given a managerial job (Wenglén 2005). They can do better, they are certainly not going to do the same stupid things as their own former manager, and they want to demonstrate this.

In conclusion, these people find the future managerial work attractive because they increasingly view their career as a professional expert as stagnation, a dead end, a straitjacket or a source of dissatisfaction for some other reason. It does not provide the opportunities for development they want, which is often a question of working positively with other individuals, for example to help (Chase), motivate and create opportunities for development (Courage) or acknowledge and confirm individuals (White). A "boy scout or social worker spirit" appears to be what drives many managerial candidates – they want the best for others. At least, this is what they say – we have not fallen into the trap of believing that what our interviewees say is necessarily a reflection of the truth, or even of any deeper conviction. The entire field is characterized by people following social scripts (cultural standards) for what they want, what they are like and how they see leadership (Alvesson 2011a). These are important, and express the norms and ideals which they say they follow, but it is important to be aware of the complexity and inconsistencies between what they say, what they actually believe, what they feel deep down and how they act.

The desire for management is also described more explicitly as a career issue. Some of the managers say that the role of expert does not provide the same opportunity to move upwards in the organization. Perhaps Bacon expresses this most clearly when he describes himself as "a careerist" and "ambitious" and says he has more to give:

> I've realized I've got more to give. I left school with some very low grades, and I was something of an under-achiever at school. But I always felt that I had more to give than I actually did.

Here, he himself is the person the managerial career can help or develop. It becomes a form of compensation for earlier failings.

The managerial interest is in contrast to a certain lack of interest in the former specialist area. Among the managers above, the interest in following the knowledge progression within their own expert areas appears to have faded considerably, partly because they had found themselves in a leadership position – responsible for leading projects – in the group in which they had most recently worked as a technician or researcher before taking up the more administrative managerial jobs. Some say that they are no longer the most knowledgeable when it comes to having the right expertise; they have been overtaken by other co-workers. A lack of specialist knowledge is seen by some as a virtue, confirming their suitability as a manager. Chase expresses this explicitly. White, too, sees the job of engineer as frustrating because he feels he was not confirmed by his manager, which suggests that as an expert he was not regarded as particularly important. Management becomes a way of being seen – and may also make it easier for others to be seen and confirmed. This is because the "expert" identity no longer boosts self-esteem and status as it did earlier in their career. The managerial career can then appear as an alternative in which self-esteem and self-confidence can be repaired and restored. This is perhaps particularly true in large organizations, where people are more likely to disappear or feel invisible, and where it is easy to feel that you are just a small cog in the machine.

What is interesting is how many people in our study appear to find it easy to give up their specialist area – at least in the context of management and the managerial career. But there are also examples of the reverse conflict between managerial and professional work. The former, rather than the latter, can become a dead end. As we mentioned in Chapter 1, many people see the managerial job as a diversion from their main career path. Few research stars, for example, see the job of head of department or dean of faculty as the ultimate goal or high point, unless it is a final move before retirement. In a law firm, advertising agency or consulting firm, it is not always those considered to be the best in the profession who are expected to take a greater formal leadership responsibility. Here, the power to influence is often gained via a partnership, high earning capacity or a natural authority, rather than via a formal managerial position. For example, a study of female managers in one pharmaceutical company showed that a number of them saw their managerial positions as temporary assignments which they would hold for around three years (Billing 2006). They saw research as their main task and central source of identity, and the risk of losing touch with this was a source of worry – and not, as in the above examples, a source of joy. But for the majority of managers – almost all of those we have studied – management, without doubt, ranks higher than other jobs in terms of importance, opportunity and status.

SOME TRAITS AS NATURAL PLATFORMS FOR MANAGEMENT

The managers studied claim to have what it takes. They want to be managers because they can lead others. In some cases this is something they believe they were born with, in others it is described as something they have learned through experience and sometimes it is a combination of both. They want to be managers because they are good at getting people to go along with them in different directions – it is about influencing and controlling, even if this is not always expressed so explicitly. Here we would like to point to four approaches. The first stresses psychological consciousness and the ability to act as a dialogue partner. In the second, it is the natural authority and clarity that is central, and in the third it is the managers' energy and ability to take action which guides them to a managerial career. In the fourth and final approach, it is the capacity for, and interest in, change which is central.

Dialogue partner, driving force and understander of human nature

Many of our managers see themselves as highly competent psychologists. They have a good understanding of human nature and help individuals and groups perform well by being good coaches or having the ability to elicit and stimulate the best in their co-workers in other ways. Recently appointed school principal David Dean – one of our main actors – has worked as a manager in different organizations and now wants to do the same in the world of education. He stresses that he wants to be a manager because he is focused on how his co-workers act, think and feel. He describes himself as a coach who wants to form his leadership as a "constructive dialogue" and help others to improve their performance. Dean describes himself as "less of a manager and decision-maker and more of a coach". He says he is "very staff oriented". He also talks more about releasing work potential and empowering co-workers than about authority and responsibility. In the case of Dean, what emerges is largely a personal, rather than formal, style of management, and we might ask ourselves why Dean wants to hold a formal managerial position – are there not other jobs where an interest in dialogue and personnel can find an expression (personnel manager, consultant, social worker)?

In addition to seeing themselves as more restrained speaking partners, like Dean, the managers often emphasize their own traits as active motivators. Let us return to Chase, who wants to become a manager because it suits his personality:

> I make groups work. I make other people act. I'm not the one who designs the solution, we have others who're much better at that. My style is empathetic, I don't like steamrolling over people. I want us to have the same view of what we do so everyone's on board and knows where we're going – that's my style of leadership.

Chase also says that it's about influence and power, although "not for the sake of power, but because you make things happen more quickly, and it's easier to make your ideas heard". Chase sees himself as an active motivator who is good at activating and engaging others. As a more senior manager, he would have the power to get things done more quickly and to have his ideas heard more easily. Like all the others who talk about influence, he (naturally) sees it as just one way of being able to achieve improvement: better response and increased tempo. It is also a less important aspect compared to his capacity for empathy and making people work well.

The combination of empathy and drive is also expressed by Benjamin Book, who stresses that it was his naturally positive disposition and interest in people, his ability to be persuasive and convincing and his feeling for motivational questions and engagement on behalf of the employees that were the driving forces behind his ambition to become a manager. He describes this as a natural talent, but also as a result of his upbringing in a family where there was always a strong emphasis on taking responsibility, showing consideration and getting things done. Book says:

> I actually come from a family of entrepreneurs, and that's always been a driving force, but so has the desire to create something good and to do good for people. I wanted to be a manager because it suited me. I knew how to deal with people and how to drive the business.

In this variant, natural management sounds like a rare idealistic combination of result-oriented and relations-oriented management. In later chapters, however, we will see that the organizational environments in which these managers operate are not as friction-free as they sound.

Natural authority and clarity

Another of our main actors, Gerald Goodman, stresses his natural authority as a driving force:

> I've always wanted to be a manager. I want to be a leader, I can't get away from that, I'm always the leader and I'm always myself. It's not something I go round thinking about, it's just the way I am. In my opinion, a good manager and leader must be clear and visible, people should know what he stands for, he should give information without necessarily knowing everything. I don't believe just anyone can be a leader. You can learn to use some tools and become a good leader through education, but it's also about inherited qualities like being present and being socially competent.

Goodman emphasizes that he is what he is, nothing more nothing less, and that being himself means, in this case, being a leader. Management is presented here as a natural result of personality traits, not something that you can choose to be or not to be. Nature, rather than individual desire, determines who will or will not be a manager; that you are both called and chosen is what Gerald, like the majority of our managers, appears to think. (On the other hand, many of them are open to the idea that they are not automatically *good* managers in all respects; that takes something more, which can be acquired through education.) In answer to the question of exactly what the attraction of managerial work is, Goodman goes on:

> Actually doing the work myself, that's not Gerald Goodman. I want to influence, listen, delegate, make it work. People find it easy to approach me, talk to me, feel safe – I give a lot back. That's when I'm happiest, when I can help and be part of something.

Another of our main actors, Steven Stone from Global Industrial Products Ltd., also emphasizes his innate capacity, which makes it natural for him to be the manager, while implying that it is equally natural for others to be his subordinates:

> I must admit I've got something, people listen to me. I've always had it, and it's always been natural for me to want to be a manager. People take an interest in what I say – I'm visible. I don't really know what it is, but it has to be said, I've got some kind of ability.

Carol Courage, who is another main actor in our gallery of managers, also sees herself as someone who has always "taken the role of leader and forced the pace in different questions" in most situations. She says that she would undoubtedly have had a managerial position regardless of what organization she had found herself in:

> [In other organizations] I would still have had pretty much the same kind of tasks, I'd have been on committees and boards and things like that, taking decisions is part of my personality.

Goodman, Stone and Courage see management as being related to what you do and how you are – clear and visible. Training can help you to refine your managerial work towards a moral direction, but management is based on natural leadership skills which control people's desires and guide them into management. As Goodman points out, this is not something you can escape, since it is an integral part of your personality.

Stuart Smart, another of our main actors, is a manager on a lower level and, like Chase above, works at Big Technology Ltd. Like Chase, Smart feels that he is stuck in his position and aspires to become a more senior manager because, as he puts it, he has potential. He points out that he can be very persuasive when it comes to questions of an overall nature, but that he has not yet had any real opportunity to show this:

> I could do so much more in this company than I'm allowed to do at
> the moment, if I was in the right place and was given the right tasks.
> I see myself as a resource which is very poorly used in this company.

Smart describes himself as someone who takes charge and persuades others of the goals and purpose of the business. This ability to understand the bigger picture is one of his strengths and what makes him suitable for management at a higher level. In a more senior managerial position, he would be able to express and fulfil himself. Smart, like Chase, is dissatisfied and frustrated by his lack of confirmation. Their view of themselves as good managerial material is not being confirmed by (understanding) superiors; instead, they are being held back in lower-level project leader roles.

One of our main actors, Gary Gardener, also describes the ambition to become a manager as a question of being a natural driving force. His leadership is effective because he takes responsibility:

> It's the drive to be responsible for something, rather than to be a
> leader. And the fact is that my leadership has been seen to work
> well. I think I'm very clear, and because of that, people go along with
> me. I've never really felt the need to be a manager, it's just
> something that's happened because I've pushed things through and
> had responsibility.

Gardener stresses that he wants neither to be a manager or leader, nor to appear as too much of a careerist. Yet at the same time, he claims to have the traits, the ability to influence and control (clarity and getting people to go along with him), which appear to characterize and suit managerial work. He possesses personal traits which more or less guide him into management. It is natural for these leadership traits to be formalized as management.

Drive and ability to take action

Another variant of profound traits providing strong motivation and a foundation for management is the ability to take action and the drive to control and get results. One of our main actors who expresses this view is Matt Mooney, who works at Bank Ltd. He points out that he wanted to become a manager because he was the natural leader who took command and made decisions:

> I learned early on to take decisions, capture the situation and deal with people. So I learned to be a leader early, and I took decisions without having much information – I learned how to do that in any kind of situation. I'm used to taking decisions and leading. I'm very impatient and so I need to make decisions – I'm the kind of person who takes charge. And I get a real kick out of taking charge in a bigger context.

This action approach is a consequence of his personality:

> I'm very driven and clear about what I feel and think. It's easy for me to control and to capture things that happen. I live on those things. That's the basis of my leadership and my entire personality.

Mooney also says that there are probably many people who think that his drive is about wanting to make a career, but he himself stresses, not unlike Goodman above, that he is simply being himself all the time and that his personality determines his behaviour. Becoming a manager is not something he has consciously striven for, but, rather, he has found himself there as a result of his natural driving force. This articulates his view of himself – his identity – and contributes to reinforcing his self-esteem.

The personal ability to take action as a source of managerial aspiration is also articulated by White, whom we met above, when he says: "I have always wanted to express myself and have an influence and have more of the whole picture."

He emphasizes that he grew into the role of manager gradually and naturally when he was a subordinate. White became "the manager's right hand there quite quickly" (at Advanced Technology Ltd.); he had already established a good relationship with a senior manager in the company, Susan, during the recruitment process. There was, however, a tier of management between himself and Susan – Anna – with whom he worked closely:

> I had an informal role with a lot of work on Anna's level, and things just rolled along. I was given more and more responsibility and I felt I was in the right position. That was the level I wanted to tackle problems on, it was about talking to people, taking part in meetings, making things happen, not burying myself in technical questions. I felt I was doing something useful, although I noticed that the people around me just thought, "He's in the right place".

White describes himself as someone who wants to have a voice, to influence and control in questions of an overall nature. As a subordinate, he was comfortable with being given more responsibility because that was in line with his traits.[3] It is interesting to note that White sees the managerial job as taking action, as opposed to technical work. As a manager you are outgoing, you are on a level where things happen – you tackle problems, talk to people, take part in meetings, all of which is apparently viewed by White as real action. The opposite is "burying yourself in technical questions", which comes across as somewhat primitive, tedious, narrow and not particularly important. Yet again, the sense of being confined is stressed – the managerial job becomes something of a liberation from the specialist's routine, fixed

[3] We can note that White has also had some confirmation of his style, and this leads to self-esteem and self-confidence, which strengthens him in his role. White, like Gardener, states that positive confirmation is a driving force behind his desire to have (more senior) managerial jobs. As we have seen, Smart, in contrast, is disappointed that this has not been forthcoming.

existence. As a manager, you are no longer an engineer slaving away to earn your money, but at (or close to) the centre of power, where you can go to meetings and make things happen. Similar views are expressed by other managers in our study, not least Chase above. They seem to be saying that technical work is for cavemen, while those who are more advanced move in the sphere of leadership.

Of all our main actors, Henry Harding is perhaps the one who most clearly stresses management as the natural outcome of having the ability to influence and control people. Harding says that this has been a recurring theme throughout his life, partly as a result of his innate personality, but also as a result of his upbringing; he had to learn to take responsibility for his family at an early age. This helped him understand that it was important to push things forward and know what was going on, something he sees as playing a decisive role in his ambitions to become a manager. Consequently, in answer to the question why he wanted to become a manager, he replies that he has always been the driving force:

> I've always been the one who organized all the big things which needed organizing. I organized wine festivals, demonstrations and all kinds of things. Take the wine festival, it hadn't been properly run before, so I took charge of things and within three years it was the biggest in the whole region. So I had managerial experience early on.

Harding has worked in a large number of organizations, most of them fairly technical, often in a demanding project leader role but also at times as a line manager. Challenges and problems are driving forces which motivate his management:

> I took on the role of manager in the production company because they were facing extremely tough challenges which needed a lot of motivation and a special ability to deal with them.

A recurring theme in Harding's description of his career is how often he comes into an organization which he quickly realizes needs a strong hand because of financial and organizational mismanagement and neglect. With a strong and determined hand, he transforms a downward trend into something positive and constructive. Harding's self-view is that he, more than anyone else, constitutes the driving force in difficult and vulnerable organizational situations. He is – in his own eyes – the hero.

This variant lies close to the natural authority variant, but places less emphasis on obvious charisma and the willingness of other people to listen and follow without question, and more on the controlling activity, the strong action he willingly engages in. The ability to take action and the ability to take charge are different from the authority that makes people listen. What is underlined is the doing rather than the being, even if it is not possible to separate them completely.

Natural desire (and ability) for change

A slightly different variant is to stress that you are a dynamic person who is willing to change. Management is an obvious consequence of the willingness and ability to work with development and change. A couple of our main actors stress that the change traits – exhibiting a dynamic personality – were crucial for their move into management. One of these, Nora Noble, who is a manager in the public sector, tells us that she began her managerial career because she wanted to change and develop the business in which she began her career. She talks about how she applied for a managerial post with a focus on development:

> I saw an advert about developing the public services of the future. That was what I wanted to do, and it was exciting. But I was young and naïve and thought I could change things in a big state monster where it wasn't really possible. So because of that I started in another public service.

Change is the central element in Noble's view of herself as a manager:

> I want to work with development. And it's easy for me to do that, because I think it's such fun. But the other part, administration, that's not my thing.

We can note that development and change themes regulate the self-view in a positive way, while administration constitutes a kind of anti-identity. Administration, which Noble finds so alien and boring, reinforces her positive self-view as a person who works with development, which implies that she is creative and dynamic. She further describes herself as a natural manager because people listen to her. Her natural influence means that decisions are accepted without grumbles and protests:

> The management comes from your employer and the leadership from your co-workers. It's simple. If you've got a mandate to lead then it's quite natural to weave management into the leadership. Nobody questions that, nobody questions me when I make decisions. My co-workers see me as the obvious manager. I think they trust me, that when I say something, that's how it is. Then things happen, and they know that I can influence things. It motivates them, it inspires them.

The implication here is that everything is friction-free. The inherent leadership traits form the platform for management, which is also confirmed by co-workers.

Courage sees herself as a natural authority, but also stresses her strong interest and skills in handling change. She points out that it was natural for her to take a step up and become manager of several functions in conjunction with a large organizational change since she is someone who understands overall questions and also has a more dynamic and change-oriented mindset:

> I see myself as someone who usually understands change and sees it coming a little before other people do.

This view of oneself as a natural leader is not unusual. People want to believe that they possess something positive which shows that they have something that distinguishes them as managerial material – why would they otherwise be considered? This reasoning is in line with the reasoning in the trait theory about what distinguishes a classic manager or leader. In Courage's case in particular it is about an exceptional ability to understand and manage change.

*

Now that we have introduced all our thirteen main actors, a short summary is motivated. We could say that Dean wants to coach – this is how his essence or true identity is expressed. Chase and Book make others act. Chase and Smart, who were both somewhat frustrated when we interviewed them, stress that management would give them opportunities to influence which they have naturally but lack formally – and which the lack of a sufficiently senior formal position denies them. Book says he has the right character and personality for management. Goodman and Stone appear to be clear driving forces as a result of their personalities. Smart, too, describes himself as having a natural talent for persuading others of the whole and the goals. Gardener is another person who influences, gets people to go along with him (by convincing and persuading) and takes responsibility. Mooney describes a personality which is suited to taking command and making decisions, which many people would see as being typical managerial behaviour. White and Harding are also individuals who convince, influence and command in questions of an overall nature. In the case of Harding, this is very explicit and distinct. Noble and Courage are individuals who drive change naturally; they have a natural style, which means that when they talk, people listen and allow themselves to be influenced. Several of these people connect to some of the four trait variants which we have identified, but in the majority of cases they stress a particular core aspect of their obvious aptitude for management. With the exception of Harding, they have a great deal in common; the differences are mainly in their personal qualities and how these make them cut out for managerial jobs – and leadership jobs in particular. Bacon differs from the others by not stressing any obvious "essential" quality which in itself makes him managerial material. He is more prepared for the fact that he must work his way up to his managerial capacity.

It can be noted that no one mentions title, salary, formal responsibility and powers or the spectrum of managerial tasks which are typically included. Status and career are stressed mainly by Bacon – although Chase and Smart are keen for promotion, they do not stress this as an intrinsic value, but more as a way of being able to express their innate leadership qualities. It is the self, rather than the desire for status, which is crying out for promotion.

NATURAL TRAITS AND LEARNING

All our main actors, with the exception of Bacon, make it very clear that they have the right personality to become managers. They want to become managers because their personality in effect "guides" them into such positions. They are born to the task – at least, in their own minds. Although some of them tone down the formal managerial position as such, they find it natural to hold one, given their personality. Others stress the significance of the managerial position and say that this is central if their leadership ability is to be expressed fully. Several say that they need a more senior managerial job in order to exercise leadership correctly. This would suggest that leadership resides in the job rather than in the person, but at the same time the personal traits are stressed as being central, which makes the question of the relationship between the person and the (formal) position rather unclear in many cases. It is possible that they see the "wrong" job – including a junior managerial position – as a barrier which must be overcome if the natural leadership traits are to find expression.

Gary Gardener is open to the idea that it is difficult to know whether his leadership resides in his genes or if it has been formed over time, but, like the others, it is he himself who is the actor behind this:

> Leadership is moving more towards symbolic leadership, which
> means not micro managing but rather having goals and strategic
> frames, more freedom. That's how I see it, and that's how I work. If
> I'm honest, it's because it suits who I am. Whether this is something
> I realized through analysis, or whether it's how I am, is something
> we can discuss.

What is interesting is the lack of emphasis on education, learning, experience, role models and suchlike which stress personal development, change and maturity. It is the managers' inherent nature rather than any "external" factors which makes them suited to managerial work. With the exception of Bacon, it is certainly not hard work, effort and learning which makes them managerial material. Some stress the fixed aspects of their traits which are already in place. Book says that "it has always been a driving force", Goodman that he is "always the leader", Stone stresses that he has "always had it" and Harding that he has "always been the one who organized all the big things". Mooney and White mention learning, but this seems to be a question of something fairly quick, simple and natural ("I learned early on take decisions", says Mooney, for example). It is all rather ironic given the fact that several stress the responsiveness and development of co-workers in relation to their own efforts. The managers we have studied appear to be saying that this has no equivalent that applies to them to any great degree.

They also appear to see themselves as such by nature, or possibly self-made, while views that fashions in leadership, imitating one's own manager, company cultures or co-workers' demands and expectations play any role worth mentioning are conspicuous by their absence. Given the somewhat standardized ideas of their own management and leadership, it is perhaps natural for them to emphasize the importance of social and cultural – rather than personal and unique – circumstances. One interesting link between the social and the individual is leadership education.

LEADERSHIP EDUCATION AS A SOURCE OF IDENTITY

While many people describe management as a question of dealing with challenges, there is, of course, also some uncertainty as to what the job actually involves. Most of the managers we studied had already been engaged in some form of management prior to their first "real" managerial job, albeit often at a slightly lower level and in the rather more limited sense of supervisory responsibility. Now they are suddenly "a real manager", as Bacon puts it, and with this comes a certain doubt as to whether they are up to the job. A new job or a major change can cause problems even for those who see themselves as natural leaders. Do they have the right personal traits and the right knowledge? Do they have what it takes and can they shoulder the responsibility for the challenges which are often painted as the driving force for managerial work? Our managers spend a lot of time thinking about these questions. In a sense, this is a paradox, because, as we have seen, the majority of them have stressed how natural it is for them to take on the role of leader. They point out traits and interests which show they are suited to the managerial job like a duck to water. Yet, at the same time, they do have doubts. This becomes clear to the external observer who looks beyond the interviewees' statements describing themselves as natural and obvious leaders. And as we will see throughout this book, there is no consistency when managers describe what they are, do, prioritize and achieve. This is often even more salient when managers' statements are compared with those of co-workers or our own observations. Consistency and clarity are often conspicuous by their absence.

But when managers initially – before or when they start a managerial job – describe themselves in relation to the (future) job, the doubt is less evident. They deal with, and reduce, this doubt in a number of ways. In many cases, leadership education appears to have had an active role in creating clarity and certainty. Many of our actors appear to see such training as central to their interest and engagement in management. This might be because having the opportunity to take part in leadership development programmes, which are often expensive, makes them feel special and like a real leader. Another example is the content of the training, which highlights leadership, reinforcing the participants as real managers and leaders and encouraging identification with senior management and leadership in particular.

Carol Courage says that leadership education developed her understanding of leadership but that it also made her realize how important it is to develop and motivate people in businesses where creativity is paramount. The fact that she was hand-picked for several courses in leadership made her feel that she was being both recognized and chosen for more important tasks. The training has allowed her to recognize new sides of her personality, and this has contributed to making the managerial role increasingly attractive:

> What I've been able to do is take care of my own personal development, because I haven't been stuck in a position.

The training has allowed Courage to develop her personal interests and position herself for leadership of an ambitious, not to say high-flying, nature:

> When I took the job, I thought I was going to shape culture. I believe that a global organization needs a cultural glue. Research is done in environments where people come together – people are local. We may have a global network but we need a local everyday life. One role I think is interesting is when we local managers are given responsibility for the culture. I can see that the strategic thinking takes place in a different way and that the role, the responsibility, is to see the whole picture: If you make a particular decision, what will the consequences be?

Management thus triggers Courage's interest in and ambition to shape an organizational culture. The idea is that the competent and ambitious leader also creates a culture.

The person who stresses the importance of management training more than any other is perhaps Bert Bacon. He points out that in his job, a traditional education in engineering is not enough: "I've got that, but it's completely worthless." Instead, he says that what is important is management training:

> An MBA and management training, that's what make a manager the manager, that and experience. My MBA has opened my eyes to different ways of thinking. I've worked here all my working life, but there are other ways of doing things. And it's not just the MBA itself – you need to talk to people with an MBA and pick up tips and ideas. It's one thing to be able to put MBA after your name. But it's quite another thing to learn things and take on new ideas.

Bacon also says:

> I'm glad I've got an MBA. It gives me a base, and I wouldn't be where I am now, because I don't have the technology and the tools that managers use. So the only way I could play this is the way I did. But I can see from the reading I've done and from talking to other people with an MBA that this is a credible way to do it. It gives me a platform from which I can move forward.

The MBA education, with its formal and informal elements, is presented here as an almost revolutionary qualification for Bacon and as something essential for his ability to do his managerial job successfully.

A lengthy managerial education has also had a deep impact on Charlie Chase. In his case, managerial life is a question of being able to express his identity, how he sees himself, through more comprehensive tasks. Compared with Bacon, who stresses the knowledge/technical qualifications in the education (MBA), Chase appears to see the content as being more about clarifying identity.[4] This has contributed

---

4   Yet again, we underline that this is his view. The fact that someone sees something as providing an explanation, qualification or insight does not mean it will withstand closer scrutiny.

to him seeing himself not primarily as an engineer but as a manager, and experiencing the relationship between elements of the engineer and the manager as a disadvantage and not the right thing in relation to his identity (desires and qualities). Until a more senior managerial position comes up, he is doing something which others can do better and which he no longer wants to do. He has an urgent need to fulfil himself, and says that managerial work makes this possible:

> I want to have a better overview and have more opportunities to influence, more challenges. I've been in the same type of job since I started here but feel I need to develop.

The keywords are challenge, change, influence and power. We can see that this career ambition has been triggered and reinforced by the content of the MBA programme.

Matt Mooney, too, says that he wants to work more strategically after his leadership education:

> After the leadership education I want to be a manager who drives the development forwards and takes responsibility for planning, budgeting and future direction. The market is changing in a way that means changes in the way we work, and here I can see myself in the role of strategist, of manager. They sent me [on the course], I didn't tell my manager I wanted to go. It was HR who sent me. And they must have had a reason. So it's obvious they expect me to do other things too. Strategic business management is on the level above me, and I could imagine having that role, the total responsibility. Not the operational, but an overall responsibility.

Mooney talks about how he developed during the management training as a result of being put into difficult situations, something he stresses was useful for his future leadership:

> I feel like I want to be in control of what's going to happen and prepare myself for what I'm going to answer and what I'm going to do, but there wasn't time for that in the activities we did, so you had

to go outside the box to test yourself. For me, the box is the control zone, what you're used to doing. I think you need to step outside the box and feel uncomfortable, that's when you learn something new about yourself. Something you can use in your future leadership. It was very exciting, euphoric.

Education is, thus, not only about reinforcing career ambitions and making people see themselves as company leaders in the making rather than lower-level managers. It also includes a great deal of psychology, and many people say that they have become better at understanding themselves in relation to others. This can apparently evoke euphoria. Mooney talks about how he gained an insight into how he works in relation to others, in particular his tendency to talk too much and to dominate. The leadership development programme showed him the importance of having a coaching managerial style which is about

letting people take responsibility and being a janitor who provides a toolbox for the employees. But at the same time, being focused on the goals when it comes to direction. I don't want to be the authoritarian leader, I want to practise a coaching leadership.

We can see here, yet again, how important it is to say what you do *not* want to be when you define your position as manager. Being the person who provides the toolbox which allows other people to take responsibility clearly sounds more attractive than acting as the person who always calls the shots and decides over others. The rejection of the idea of being authoritarian and making decisions is combined, in some contradiction, with the ideal of the manager's centrality and crucial importance – in management training as well as in real life – and we will return to this on several occasions in the book.

One might imagine that expensive leadership development programmes are an expression of a company's conscious and systematic investment in carefully selected "coming men and women". Carol

Courage appears to have interpreted the number of leadership development courses she has attended in this way. But it is not always experienced thus. Charlie Chase is not sure why he was chosen for a leadership development programme. In answer to the question of why he was selected, he says:

> I don't know. The right question at the right time to the right person, maybe. It's hard to believe there aren't a hundred people with the same qualifications as me who could take that course – and what determines that it's me?

Even if the feeling of being chosen is clouded somewhat by his uncertainty about the reasons for this, the experience only serves to reinforce his interest in management and its substance. The training offers security in the face of his managerial assignment:

> I've worked with technical questions and felt that I wanted to know how a company works. It's good to be able to hang what you do and how it works on a theoretical framework. And what do the people who work with management, strategy, marketing and leadership say? I've been in the same company and environment for a long time, and it makes me feel confined.

Chase underlines the narrow scope and limitations of the professional role and how leadership development programmes offer the opportunity to talk and learn about strategy, leadership and external questions such as marketing. The courses open up new views and lead to high expectations:

> They are very important. The question is how to show what you use in a tangible way, but that's part of the attraction.

Chase points out that the vagueness and uncertainty about what is actually learned on the leadership development programmes is part of the attraction of managerial work. Put more directly, we could say that the "fluffiness" of managerial work is in sharp contrast to the practicality and constraints of technical work. Leadership appears to be a central attraction of managerial work.

Nora Noble also points to the importance of managerial training for confirming identity, even if it is hard to say exactly what that is:

> You do develop, but I can't say that a particular exercise or residential centre or activity led me to where I am today. My insights changed over a year. But I can't point to anything in particular. It had a lot to do with the confirmation of me as a manager, with the fact that when I talk, people listen.

We see here yet another confirmation and reinforcement of the self-view as manager. Noble says that the management training was not at all about challenging her self-view or problematizing managerial identity, but that it was, rather, a question of infusing her managerial ambitions with a little more passion, even though it is difficult to give practical examples of how it happened.

Gary Gardener, as we mentioned earlier, sees management/leadership as something which suits him well, and he has also acquired more knowledge in the subject. His speech is clearly influenced by management literature, and he also stresses the fact that he has an MBA:

> Over the years I have been lucky enough to attend many courses. I have gained an MBA, and the college there has a strong focus on leadership. And it has been a journey, and the various angles of approach have undoubtedly contributed greatly to the process.

We initially identified several former "experts" who had found themselves in professional dead ends. This dead end manifests itself partly through various forms of training. You are – for some reason – selected for management training and discover that there are alternatives to the role of expert. The alternatives – managerial and senior managerial jobs – may be presented in idealistic, not to say PR, terms, and they clearly go home. Managerial careers are seen as attractive. Expectations rise and hopes are raised. The professional role may not be much fun any longer – you feel you are no longer the person who knows best when it comes to particulars and you no longer follow the knowledge trends in the field in which you are an expert. Some of our managers seem to find the latter unimportant. When they talk about becoming a manager, many distance themselves from the role of expert and their professional career. The role becomes almost an anti-identity, something they do not want to be, a kind of counter-view through which management suddenly appears to be particularly attractive. Put another way, the education causes a shift in identity from professional to manager, where you identify with the manage-ment sphere, and leadership, strategy, company management and upward career moves become important elements in your identity project. Set against the rather neutral and thus somewhat grey tech-nology is the rather splendid world of leadership, which some clearly find seductive.

As several of the people we have studied make clear, the training is viewed as an extremely effective injection and platform for the managerial career. Two elements are worth noting:

- Attractive courses present what managers do. Managers have an overview, act as leaders, control, influence and determine strategies and shape the organizational culture. Managers are seen as central norm-setters, or the hub around which the organizational life revolves.
- The communication of a strong feeling that there is a natural harmony between this leadership and the training participants' own self-views. The managers generally express a view of themselves as natural leaders; they are influential opinion leaders, they have an overall understanding and ability to deal with people, they are good people who like people – in short, they have a view of themselves as strategists and leaders. The training courses confirm, emphasize and reinforce this view, even if it is not entirely possible to show what the education is actually about.

This may appear to be stating the obvious – that management education stresses the positive aspects of being a manager – but one personnel manager (interviewed in another context than the one reported in this book) told us that her internal management training contained a great deal about the more negative side of the managerial position: learning how to say no to people and realizing that the job is largely about things which are not instantly enjoyable or positive. The more external and, therefore, strongly "customer-oriented" training in which our interviewees took part appears, however, to have had a strong emphasis on the brighter side of managerial work. It has a seductive effect.

In the cases above, the question of working with matters that are considered to be important recurs frequently. It is expressed as something more overall, strategic and long-term. For technicians, it also includes guiding the business towards the markets and helping to decide which direction to take in relation to these. We can also note, once again, that leadership education contributes to reinforcing the self-view as a leader with a more all-embracing responsibility. The training thus creates "company leader wannabes". "Non-expert wannabes" are created or reinforced indirectly. We are not saying that this can only be explained by management training, but it does appear to have contributed to the slightly derogatory view several people (Chase, Bacon and White) have of engineering work (their own background), at least for their own part.

We can describe this as identity regulation which is encouraged by companies through leadership development programmes, and observe a reinforced leadership or strategic identity as a result (Alvesson & Willmott 2002). From a company viewpoint, it may not be such a good thing if the training encourages *too* high ambitions and expectations.[5] Many are called but few are chosen, as they say. At all events, it will no doubt be a while before our managers can expect to have a job where they formulate strategies – as, no doubt, is the case for the majority of managers, for that matter.

---

5   This probably does not affect the education providers directly as they often are focused on satisfied participants, the latter also often being a main criteria among HR staff and senior managers who take decisions on various leader education programmes for what are seen as coming managers.

CONCLUDING DISCUSSION

In this chapter, we have primarily addressed the progress towards, and driving force behind, the desire to become a manager and work with leadership. It is not adaptability, learning or a difficult and messy road to a particular capacity which has made them the good managers and/ or leadership material they understand themselves to be. Neither do they place much importance on unlimited energy, a large capacity for work and actual hard work. It is, rather, an inner essence which calls out to find expression and confirmation in the form of a (senior) managerial position.

In the question of why they are attracted by managerial work and what they want to do, we can broadly discern three related themes.

One theme is personnel management: motivating and encouraging people to act and develop – sometimes directly, by convincing or persuading, and sometimes indirectly, by supporting and inspiring. Here we can discern a classic and somewhat idealized leadership role.

A second theme is having influence on the overall and strategic questions. Here we can discern a managerial role as a company leader-like strategist, with a strong overtone of overview, force and meaning. As a strategist, you stand over and above the operational and technical drudgery. You are a member of the elite. It is very clear that, as far as our interviewees are concerned, the technical expert (engineer, researcher) and the manager are far from being on an equal footing.

A third management theme which attracts and motivates is the opportunity to work with value questions and create shared values and views. This offers the opportunity to work with and control over-all approaches. We can discern a managerial role as culture bearer/ agent of change.

These themes are the antithesis of simply "doing management". There seems here to be an interplay between will, role and identity. For some of those who have not been promoted highly enough or given a "pure" managerial job, but still find themselves, for example, close to the operational activities and needing to work as a technical expert, this is a source of frustration. There is something wrong with their environment, in particular senior managers, who do not understand their capacity. What they want is to work with something which is purely leadership oriented.

There appear to be five significant driving forces behind the desire to have a specifically managerial job (which may be a couple of steps higher up in the hierarchy):

1 There is a discrepancy between the person they are or what they should be doing naturally, and what their current/previous job (non-managerial job, or too junior managerial job) involved. The person and (senior) managerial work (leadership) are, however, well matched. The motivation for the managerial job is thus to correct a frustrating imbalance between the individual and the job. It is a bit like wearing shoes that are too small. When you are in the right managerial job, you (finally) have the right shoe size – and can move around without any unnatural constraints.
2 Managerial work is part of a natural development. As a person, you change gradually, you become increasingly competent, you tire of some tasks after a while, want more and have other ambitions. You become curious about and interested in a wider (organizational) horizon than the one you are offered as an ordinary co-worker (engineer, salesperson, etc.). Managerial work then becomes as natural as the sequence of seasons, or the apprentice eventually becoming an independent craftsman, the junior doctor becoming a consultant, and so on.
3 Managerial work is fun, satisfying in terms of tasks and/or results. Talking to people, engaging in dialogues, taking part in meetings and making things happen are more enjoyable than "burying yourself" in the specifications of some gadget.
4 Managerial work is something big and important. As a manager, you work with important questions and make a difference. You also make a stronger and more positive contribution, and since you yourself are seen as being better at this (more naturally suited to the job) than others, it is a good thing if you have a strong influence yourself.
5 As a manager you can make positive efforts on behalf of other people. You are good at dealing with people, making relationships work and making

people feel comfortable. While other people, and also some managers, lack the ability to see and confirm individuals, you see yourself as an excellent people manager. The ability to talk to people, to listen, see and generally make them feel comfortable, means that you see yourself as being cut out for managerial work.

These five motives frequently overlap, but different people emphasize them in different ways and to differing degrees. What distinguishes all the people we have studied closely is that they express little doubt about their suitability, they have the strongest reasons and they can make the unsuspecting listener believe that they are without doubt the "coming men" (or women) heading for a more senior managerial career. The majority also believe that (senior) managerial jobs are mainly full of causes for rejoicing, as should be the case when you are cut out for the job.

It is worth noting how little talk there is of the negative aspects of managerial work. For most people, managerial work will undoubtedly include being exposed to a high workload and pressure, being forced to make decisions with negative consequences for co-workers and accepting high demands for loyalty and subordination in relation to senior managers and top management. It also involves a great deal of administration. The people we have studied express a rather one-sided and somewhat idealized view of the managerial job, one which, on the whole, only stresses positive opportunities to influence things for the shared benefit of the company and co-workers. The view of managerial work presented is, without exception, extremely one-sided. This gives the impression that our managers have a very positive view of this work prior to taking up their managerial jobs, and on a general level, and that they themselves – in the question of ability and reason – are virtually cut out for managerial work.

But as we will see later, it is not always easy to be successful in a managerial position. As they say, "Shit happens".

4 The manager as change agent, strategist and networker

In the previous chapter, we described our managers' view of what it means to be a manager – in some cases a more senior manager – and pointed out that many see it as something deeply personal which allows them to express themselves and to work with leadership that is positive and develops their co-workers, as well as with cultural change and overall strategic questions. The themes highlighted seem important and prestigious. But how do they view what they do and what they want to do once they have reached a managerial position? What do they think influences and controls their work, and how do they see their own opportunities to form their managerial work?

In this chapter, our managers talk about what they want to do and what they actually do as managers. What they say they do does not always correlate very well with what they actually do. Here, we will return to the roles that attracted them to management, but also relate these to authenticity and morals. As we will see, the people in our study stress the latter in their managerial work. We saw in the previous chapter that the managers see management as an expression of their natural behaviour – self-view and management go hand in hand. The management styles discussed in this chapter are an expression of how they view themselves. The managers do not describe the managerial job as something neutral, but as strongly value-charged, with moral overtones.

We begin by discussing the fact that many managers who are at the beginning of their managerial career highlight the importance of managers for the organization, in particular in questions to do with change, values, strategies, visions and networks. This is followed by a section on the manager as change agent, with a particular significance for the organizational culture, and also the importance of the manager as a role model. We continue with two sections on the manager's significance as strategist/visionary and networker, respectively. In our cases, many of these views of management can be seen as strongly value-charged expressions of transformational leadership, which we described briefly in Chapter 2. This is a style of leadership which the managers believe has a moral foundation; they frequently state that it is right and proper that they work with overall questions and do not bother co-workers unnecessarily by intervening too often. We discuss this moral aspect of management before the chapter ends with a brief critical conclusion.

As in other chapters in the second part of this book, we discuss primarily the way in which managers talk about themselves and their world, which tells us a great deal about their interpretations. We have a more critical discussion about possible differences between talk, interpretations and practice in Part III.

STRENGTHENING MANAGERIAL IDENTITY – THE MANAGEMENT TEAM

Many newly appointed managers want to emphasize their role, and thereby their importance for the organization. Many talk about strengthening the function of management and allowing managers to be managers – or, preferably, "leaders". Exactly what this means is often vague and unclear, but sometimes they do express a clear idea. In many organizations it means standing for renewal and development, but also creating a pleasant atmosphere and opportunities for growth and generally making life agreeable for the employees. The impression given is that the managers feel they were limited and restrained in previous managerial or other jobs by overly narrow and operational tasks. Some say they lacked a forum where they could hone and develop their managerial work beyond a limited focus on the function (cf. Watson 2001). It becomes important to clarify, streamline and strengthen the managerial work. Carol Courage says:

One thing that's important is to identify the managers and make them feel like managers, that they're not just a member of a strategic management team and responsible for a function, but also to have the senior management team. So the managers can feel like managers.

Charlie Chase likewise stresses the importance of a management forum for questions of a more overall nature:

I develop my local managers. I don't have a recipe for it but I like to have meetings where we talk about our processes. The important thing is how we can become more effective and talk about what works well and what doesn't. I work with questions which are difficult to formulate, like how we can learn, how we can be better at what we do, how we can be more cross-functional, how to make people more aware of what other people do, how we can work in a more structured way and create forums for this.

Here we see activities which are intended to influence the understanding of the managerial role and its importance for the organization. Many have, like Courage and Chase, stressed the importance of including the managers in discussions about the organization's status in the questions of values and processes.

The idea here is that managers must take responsibility for questions about the organizational direction, which often means working with visions and strategies, with the aim of inspiring co-workers to change and renewal. Our managers believe that without managerial initiatives little will happen in an organization, and that it is therefore necessary to have, for example, management teams in order to confirm the management and help to build up the managers' identity as managers and, specifically, leaders. Another of our main actors, Benjamin Book, told us that when he became a senior manager, he would create a management team for his closest managers purely to "give them a bit of a boost", as he put it: in other words, to make them feel important and motivated. We can talk here about control efforts which are aimed directly at the managers' self-view and social identity (that is to say, the group and the social category constitute the base for identification). Such attempts at identity regulation are often intended to have an effect on common sense, emotions and behaviour. You should consider yourself as a manager and act accordingly.

The customary use of "fine titles", which often stress the word "manager" even when there are no subordinates, illustrates this wish to reinforce identities, but sometimes causes confusion. An interesting example of this is a leadership training course where a senior manager wanted to reinforce what he called section managers in their "managerial role". However, the co-workers in question did not see themselves as managers, but rather as one of the group, so they did not understand the point of the course and some dropped out (Borgert 1992). They did not like the idea of appearing to be superior to, and thereby visibly apart from, the rest of the co-workers.

It is not uncommon to try to clarify the managerial work by setting up different kinds of management teams. The idea is to establish forms of consultation for managers in which the managerial work in central questions can be sustained and strengthened. Forming groups means drawing up boundaries and including people in circles which are largely exclusive, and which provide a basis for making people feel they are involved – but above all chosen. The manager as social identity – distinct from belonging to a professional group or being one of the gang in the group or department – then becomes an important ambition. This is intended to raise status and, in the longer term, lead to a stronger sense of engagement – and loyalty to the company – in line with the view of management held by the selected members. The identity regulation takes place here through the processes of forming groups, and the aim is to make people identify themselves as belonging more to the managerial group than to other groups (co-workers, subordinates, and so on).

Management teams tend, perhaps, to be less a question of direct and coherent leadership than of confirmation of belonging, identity and loyalty to other senior managers. To some extent, much of the managerial work is about having a slightly more central role than subordinates in meetings and regularly taking part in meetings with other managers. The rituals of managerial meetings are a central activity in most organizations. What managers do in relation to others is perhaps not always apparent in the daily business (Alvesson & Sveningsson 2003c; Lundholm 2011), which is why these rituals of managerial confirmation can be extremely significant in pointing out the difference between managers and others.

It is interesting to note that while nearly all the managers we studied in depth see themselves as natural and undisputed managers with good leadership skills, they do not always credit other managers with having this natural "managerial essence". The quotes above show clearly that Courage and Book believe that they have to do something special in order for other managers to really see themselves as managers.

ORGANIZATIONAL CHANGE – THE MANAGER AS CHANGE AGENT

As we have mentioned earlier, it is popular to highlight different kinds of change. It is often said that organizations must learn to adapt to change, and the art of managing this has grown into an industry which includes consulting firms, management and leadership gurus, the media, industrial journals and business schools. In general, change is seen as something positive or necessary, and the general perception is that managers must maintain an active approach to change (Beer & Nohria 2000). There is, however, a significant difference between all the talk of change and what takes place in organizations – the change industry has a tendency to exaggerate when it comes to the former (Alvesson 2013a) – which also affects the talk and interpretations within organizations.

Embarking on change efforts in organizations is a common occurrence and frequently requires a great deal of time and energy on the part of both managers and employees. Sometimes managers are appointed specifically to implement change, although it is also common for new managers to want to mark their arrival and presence by initiating change. This shows that they are doing something new and tangible – at least, that is the impression they give. It is about setting a new agenda, and new brooms sweep clean, if we are to believe many of the managers. It is often a question of *organizational culture* in some sense (Ogbonna & Wilkinson 2003). Culture is regarded either as the central factor which must be changed or as something which must be taken seriously in order to create conditions for change (Alvesson & Sveningsson 2015; Balogun & Johnson 2004). The term has the advantage of being able to capture many things – albeit in a rather vague sense. We will show that many managers see managerial work as a question of working to change the company's values, and attempt to clarify what this means. One expression of the ambition to change organizational culture is the establishment of discussion forums for managers. These mark a clear distancing from the business which is being conducted and what people do in their daily work. Talking about change becomes an important activity for managers.

Managers as cultural change agents

It is not unusual for newly appointed managers in an organization to point out a weak market or business orientation as a major problem and an obvious reason for making comprehensive changes within the organization. At Global Pharmaceuticals Ltd., an organizational change was initiated to reinforce the importance of the managers for innovation and to make the co-workers more business and market oriented. The aim was to reduce the traditional autonomy of the researchers and introduce stronger elements of market orientation, directed and controlled by the managers. One of our secondary actors, Manager A, is a senior manager at Global Pharmaceuticals Ltd. He says that the change in culture in favour of an increased market orientation which took place was crucial for the company's continued competitive advantage. The role of the managers here is central:

Developing new medicines is no longer a question of the village genius working alone and being creative, it's about mechanized processes where size and market muscle are crucial to success. We're a different company now, and we global managers are the ones who are controlling this development, guiding the culture towards a stronger market orientation.

When Carol Courage became manager of one of the local units at Global Pharmaceuticals Ltd., she pointed out that the lack of an over-all view was the result of an exaggerated role specialization and, like Manager A, "weak business orientation":

We've had a fragmented world and not seen the whole picture. We've come together for cake and parties, but we've had too little focus on the business. Now we gather round the core business. That's my aim, and there's a lot of support for it in the senior management team.

Her aim was also to clarify the role of the managers in new business valuations – from biscuits to business, you might say. As we mentioned above, Courage formed a management team with the aim of creating a discussion forum for questions to do with organizational culture:

We can only achieve cultural change through the managers. It's not enough, but the managers must back a change in culture, otherwise it won't happen. I used to believe that change can take place from the bottom-up, but I don't believe that any longer. Change must come from both directions. It needs a mature organization and people who are positive and open. And managers must want it, that's the only way to effect change. It's not enough if only the co-workers or the managers want it.

Here Courage expresses a more balanced view than is usual when leadership is emphasized, since she also stresses the co-workers' acceptance and willingness, not just as an effect of leadership.

Management here becomes a question of wanting, supporting and accepting a change in culture – changing fundamental values is not possible without management. The management team was expected to act for a change in values and thereby for a renewal of the business. The mandate also included administrative issues, but according to Courage, these were marginal compared with the aim of creating a cultural shared view and renewal:

> The role as chair of the senior management team holds a special attraction because it's difficult, and it's about making a group of managers reach consensus regarding what is important for this unit. It's also about administrative questions which we need to address together: the working environment, policy and salary setting. But it's also about being able to work for an organizational culture which is important for the business. The most important thing for this unit is to accept the whole and feel that that all the parts are important. In a research organization, it's the whole – how all the competencies from start to finish, how well they work together – that determines the quality of what is generated.

One of our secondary actors, Manager B, from Biotech Ltd., expresses herself in a similar way:

> At our management team meetings we talk about cultural and value initiatives. We discuss what values are important and what actions in our team best express them. This is something we can really use to establish the way the team works, and I encourage this at the meetings as a way of guiding these.

It is not unusual for the middle managers to be the key group in efforts to change and guide organizational culture. When Benjamin Book took up his management position at Big Publishers Ltd., he set up a management team where one important task was to identify and actively work with organizational culture:

One of the more important tasks for the management team is to work with the culture and develop it to create a sense of community and an understanding of the company. This has been unclear and weak in the past, the owners have frightened people, but this is where I can exercise my leadership and get the managers in the management team behind me. You can create a positive company culture, but you have to be genuine, that's absolutely the most important thing, that you're honest.

Gerald Goodman at International Construction Ltd. also stresses that the work of changing the company culture is an expression of his personality:

We've been very bad at corporate culture. We produce concrete, not leadership. Right back at our first big meetings I thought we should have values in the company, and so I found myself in the group which was drawing them up. People see and hear me. The old leadership which was still there was extremely hierarchical and there were different cultures in the company. Two big factories with two factory managers who couldn't stand each other. But I can control. That's why we need changes to take us towards the whole, and that's where I'm at my best: convincing, inspiring, manipulating, getting people on board and making them feel safe. I'm good at selling ideas and changing things. There may be someone who has different ideas, but once we've decided to do something we go for it. I'm good at that.

The middle managers are often seen as an important link between more senior managers and other co-workers, and are often held up as good examples for other members in the organization. In the case of school principal David Dean, the position of middle manager as a link between different levels is particularly accentuated, since in his case it is about implementing a business idea for how to run and lead a school with a team of relatively well-qualified teachers. Here, as in the majority of cases with middle managers, it is not a question of formulating visions and strategies but rather of communicating those already determined by management:

> The vision has been determined and it's obvious what we stand for, and I like the concept, which I think is very clear.

At the same time, it is, of course, not certain that discussions about organizational culture have any impact on other members of the organization other than, perhaps, those who are involved in the activities (see further below about Harding). Authors with a popular approach are generally optimistic in this respect, although research gives cause for some scepticism (Alvesson & Sveningsson 2015). We will not take a closer stance on this here, but for the time being would just point out that, in many cases, managers accept that discussions of values are important and can act as a clear contribution for how people should act. For many people, management thus means, at least to some extent, discussing and/or preaching values and norms associated with the company culture.

Culture and change are attractive concepts for managers to identify with, and quickly evoke the image of the manager as the central value- and norm-setter. It means they further position themselves as privileged in the question of having an overview, and almost always through progressive and attractive values. (Talk of "values" seems regularly to invite "good" values, often vague without much implication for specific practices, for example, being open or customer oriented.) The thinking is generally that "other people" – such as those who "bury themselves in technical matters" – should become more aware and change. What is interesting is that no one says that they themselves might need to gain an insight, reconsider values or make changes in order to achieve the right approach. They say they have seen the light and that the challenge is to enlighten others about good approaches.

Not everyone, however, is equally convinced of the importance of talking about values, as we will see in the next section.

Acting for cultural change – the position of role model

Some managers stress that talk of cultural change is simply talk and that it does not lead to any fundamental changes. Henry Harding at Big Technology Ltd. is critical of the value of talking about company culture:

> I don't believe you change anything by talking about it, you have to live it. If you don't live it as a manager, then you can try to change any programme you like, but in the end you won't have changed anything. I support my co-workers by doing things. I don't stand around chatting with the engineers. Show them the way instead, that you're making changes – make sure that we gain a market acceptance and that we're doing things properly. I don't talk about cultural change – if that's what we really want, then we have to do it and live it. I live cultural change and support it as best I can.

On another occasion he says:

> We change the culture through what we do. I don't believe in cultural change programmes, I believe the management team must be role models. They have to take the culture into their own hands and change the culture through their daily work. You shouldn't go to a consulting firm, you have to be the role model and show in your daily work that you really mean what you want to do. That's real cultural change.

Managerial life here is not a question about acting a role in a remote and "pretend" way; it is about identifying with the job in a way which makes others believe in you and have faith in the way you work. "Role" here refers to the fact that there is an external world – an audience – which observes and reacts to the manager, who is, it is understood, the central actor in this situation. But the leading actor must be one with the role, and through identification and commitment make sure that it is an expression of their true identity. It then becomes less of a role – rather, it is about the individual expressing what they stand for a little more clearly, more dramatically.

Harding has this to say when he describes an attempt to implement cultural change at Big Technology Ltd.:

> What I want to do here is to write a success story and drive through these cultural changes in the daily work and the daily role – to make it become reality. I believe you can make cultural changes here through your soul and by putting your heart into it. They're all intelligent and see through your motives, and if you have good motives they'll see you are good, but if you have the wrong motives they'll understand that it's only talk and that you don't mean anything by it.

We see here how managerial life is a question of being a role model who is central for the subordinates, which thereby has consequences for the organization. The manager's arena and medium of influence is the actual practice. This requires presence and the ability to participate in the practical work. Being a strategist or a generator of culture are thus not seen as distinct positions or separate elements of the managerial identity and managerial work.

Harding thus differs radically from others who take a more discursive, communicative and indirect position. He places himself in the centre and sees the practical action as central.

THE MANAGER AS LEADER AND STRATEGIST – OBJECTIVES, VISIONS AND STRATEGIES

It is popular to refer to questions which embrace the whole organization: purpose, general principles, strategies and visions. The term "strategy", as used to describe a company's overall approach to its environment – conventionally in terms of planning and positioning products and markets – was established in earnest in the 1960s and 1970s. Since then, the concept of strategy has been widened to include a number of terms – overall principles, objectives, policies, visions, missions – which all refer in some way to an organization's overall approach to its environment, the latter in a somewhat broad and often imprecise meaning. In practice, these terms are often used synonymously to describe the efforts of managers to control by high-lighting the broader organizational and environmental context within which they operate. It is about the purpose and direction of the work, sometimes referred to as "the bigger picture". There is much talk about raising questions such as where you are going and what you want to achieve.

Many of the expressions used convey an impression of power and a more or less conscious idea that they may contribute to shaping the understanding of managers and other members of the organization as to who is best suited to work with and decide over a company's development. The vocabulary is seductive. It establishes the manager, at least the manager on a more senior level, as, say, a strategist or visionary, which assigns to the managerial role a special privilege in relation to others. It conveys a kind of "supremacy" or superior position, without directly emphasizing a formal hierarchy or similar rather old-fashioned and boring matters. It is easy to see the attraction for managers, since they are assigned a particular legitimacy to pursue the overall, long-term and important questions. The expression supports managers' efforts to feel like Managers with a capital M, and more specifically like Leaders, as we mentioned at the beginning of the chapter.

Here, it is not about managerial supervision, dealing with the employees' problems and questions of well-being, or even about talking about values and trying to create awareness of these. Rather, it is the strategy which is central. We will continue more specifically with this.

Strategic leadership

As has been mentioned, "strategy" implies an importance and super-iority in relation to everyone else, and "leadership" accentuates the same. Combining these two to form strategic leadership creates a very strong base for identification (Hambrick & Mason 1984). It highlights the manager as the real key player. This is a form of leadership in which great emphasis is placed on controlling with the help of broad, general principles, rather than traditional micromanagement

(Hambrick & Pettigrew 2001). In many cases, this leadership style is motivated by the argument that the manager leads qualified employees who have relatively independent working tasks, and that they do not, therefore, need to be micromanaged. In other cases, it is claimed that this kind of leadership is always right because it is in line both with what individuals generally want and with a positive view of mankind.

Stuart Smart from Big Technology Ltd. points out that his personality leads him towards overall themes such as goals and context:

> It's about me as a person. I'm usually a bit top-down in meetings – I try to persuade other people that we should begin with the goals and purpose and then work down to the details. I point to the bigger picture. I think the discussion often starts on too low a level, and you always lose some people as a result.

Here we can see how the managerial role as leader and coordinator of the overall organization supports Smart's personal inclination to raise questions of detail to an overall level, which provides an overview of the context in which he works.

The role of leader as strategist is an attractive identity position. Bert Bacon from International Foods Ltd. answers the question of what he wants to get out of his management as follows:

> Definitely to try to be a leader. That's something to aspire to. Leadership. Everyone wants to be a leader. And to work more strategically.

General principles are preferred to control. One of the secondary actors, Manager C, says, for example:

> The people working in the project are senior people, and that means I don't have to give them daily direction, just guidelines.

Many managers, in particular in knowledge-intensive organizations, often work with issues of which they may have relatively little knowledge. Managerial control is often guided by sweeping arguments about the "overall", "the bigger picture", "strategic control", and so on.

> If you give them the bigger picture and there's a feeling that minor decisions are in line with that picture, then I think that's how to lead big organizations. That's where leadership comes in – we need to give them the bigger picture and the general principles.
>
> *(Manager D, R&D organization)*

> I have a much greater strategic focus now compared with the operational focus I had as manager of a smaller unit. Now it's about strategic assessments.
>
> *(Manager E, R&D organization)*

Strategic assessments refer here to long-term evaluations of recruitment questions and competency profiles in the organization. A strategic role means that you avoid having to absorb yourself in detail.

These descriptions suggest that while other people have an excessively narrow view of the business, the manager stands for a wider understanding and wisdom. Very few middle managers appear to deviate from these views. In many cases, this is related to what kind of person they are. People are keen to stress that they embrace positive values and give their co-workers freedom and encourage independence. One of our main actors, Gary Gardener from Advanced Technology Ltd., has this to say:

> The people I lead are self-reliant, strong, senior individuals, so my leadership is symbolic in terms of "Where are we going?" and "What do we want to achieve?" Leadership is moving towards a more symbolic leadership, not micromanaging but controlling more with goals and strategic frameworks, more freedom.

The content of "the strategic" is fairly broad, and our managers deviate noticeably from what is traditionally defined as company strategy, which focuses on the company's marketing and production focus – competitive strategies – rather than on planning within their own department, which is what the majority of managers do, including those quoted above. "Strategic" is almost the antithesis of behaviour which is participatory and close to the business. With Harding's action orientation in mind, and with a certain irony, we might, perhaps, talk here about "desk leadership". These managers are far from the everyday business in the sense of actual practice. This is seen as something special, since getting involved is often described as micromanagement.

At the same time, they make it very clear they do not see themselves as administrators. We note that middle managers like to identify with strategic, as opposed to operational and administrative, questions. This is often reinforced when the organization in question encourages the middle managers to work with what they call "strategic questions" and avoid what they call micromanagement. Yet there is also, of course, considerable pressure to keep the administration running smoothly – budgets, IT systems, the question of rooms, expenses approval, salary-setting, sick leave, temporary staff, and so on, all demand their due share of the working time. Much managerial work involves the practical conditions that enable people to work. We will return to this important topic – what managers actually do – in later chapters (specifically Chapter 6). Before that, we address visionary leadership, which is typically linked to the themes of both strategy and culture.

Visionary leadership

Another topic which recurs fairly frequently when discussing leadership is formulating visions. This is a central aspect of modern leadership and is about inspiring extraordinary engagement and commitment. The idea is to set out an overall ambition which will add a bit of excitement to the work and inspire and guide (Bass & Riggio 2006). All too often, this comes across as something vague, and the question is often whether it is enough. Yet many managers stress that this is at the heart of their managerial activities. We noted earlier that Book highlighted the importance of visions. It is also illustrated by a typical comment from one of the managers at Global Pharmaceuticals Ltd., Manager G, who says that the knowledge-intensive nature of the company makes its leadership special:

> Almost everyone in this company has a PhD and we have a lot of associate professors and many people who have the competence to become professors. This requires another kind of leadership, and here we must, together with others, create a vision and keep it alive and understand that what we do has a higher value.

A middle manager in the same organization, Manager H, answers thus when asked what leadership involves:

> What do we stand for? It's about values and making the values clear, for example that you see people and not just results. It's about communicating visions: what are our goals and what do they mean to us, what is our shared belief?

Even though it is difficult to give a precise definition, leadership here appears to be about how to ensure co-workers are included in and subordinate themselves to visions. It is understood that if the manager "makes clear" and "communicates" values, then everyone will think in more or less the same way. Another of our secondary actors, Manager I, stresses the importance of "making people move in the same direction":

> Leadership is about providing a vision and the values we want to work towards, which direction the group is going in. And as the manager, you have to live that vision.

Leadership is thus about sharing visions, values and understanding. We see here how management is expressed as a question of symbolic leadership and that this is about questions of a fairly overall and rather vague nature, distinct from managerial supervision, administration and other practical matters one might otherwise assume that managers work with. As has been shown, this interest in overall ideas and symbolism has gained ground among managers in recent years. This is to some extent related to a general loosening up of class and hierarchical differences, but in some cases also a consequence of managerial authority of knowledge being weakened. In knowledge-intensive organizations, the manager's role and opportunities to control in practice are often questioned, since managers lack a deeper understanding of what the co-workers do, which is why they risk losing authority. Leadership as defined above may possibly go some way in compensating for this. Yet societal ideological circumstances also play a part – there is a desire to highlight and associate oneself with what sounds attractive in many other people's ears. The popularization of leadership is in itself, needless to say, another important circumstance. Leadership is attractive because it privileges managers in relation to other groups in the organization in various ways. Managerial supervision appears as something trivial – leadership, or why not strategic leadership for that matter, holds a greater attraction.

The essence of meaningful work appears to be to follow the vision. But the question is how many people other than the "visionaries" actually value the vision as a driving force. Practical work tasks, specific work goals, salary, promotion, belonging to the group, among other things, may have greater importance, which does not, of course, mean that a credible vision cannot also have an impact on engagement and motivation.

THE MANAGER AS NETWORKER – STRATEGIC DEVELOPMENT

As we mentioned earlier, the meaning of "strategic" can be widened considerably, in particular when it is reinforced by the term leadership. In addition to the strategic leadership, which is here understood as coordination of the organization, above all internally (using strategies and visions, as described above), many managers also talk about the importance of being active in external networks in order to position their own organization and thereby facilitate strategic development of the organization.

Nora Noble, one of our main actors, stresses that she has found herself in managerial positions as a result of her ability to make others listen to her. This has led to her managerial work being dominated by two roles, namely administration and development. It is not unusual for managers in public services to feel that they have rather limited scope for action because they constitute a well-integrated part of institutional and political contexts. This may be linked to the fact that public services are often described as public *administrations*, which refers to the fact that they are about implementing political decisions in a neutral and legal way, rather than occupying themselves with developing activities in a more independent and comprehensive way. Noble says, however, that in addition to the administrative work, there is also plenty of scope "to do most things" and not be limited to only the administrative side of public services. On the subject of managerial work, she says:

> Management has a lot to do with development. It involves quite a lot of work with politicians, and then you have to make sure the business is keeping in step – I spend a lot of my time thinking about that. And working to make us all move in the same direction. There are a lot of development questions and overall questions. There are also a lot of collaboration questions to do with external collaboration and with other administrations.

She also talks about the managerial work as administration and about having a "door-opening" role. Opening doors here means building an external network of people who can help to support the strategic development of their own business:

> My role is to drive the business and open doors. Opening doors means making it possible for others to take a step up. Opening up doors nationally and to other public organizations, through my contacts. And trying to get the right representation in different situations. Networking is about finding and identifying key individuals. That's one of my success factors, what I'm good at.

> Identifying key individuals in administrations and politics. And
> keeping the relations alive, from having lunch to all kinds of things.

Networking takes place, of course, among almost all our managers and
is often described in personnel, marketing and ceremonial terms.
Benjamin Book, for example, talks about the importance of marketing
the company in different situations, but since he is not always able to
take part himself, he often sends his co-workers. This way he can
market the company and give the staff a little extra motivation at
the same time:

> I don't have time to go to everything and sometimes I give the staff
> the chance to take part in various ceremonial events and dinners. It
> does them good and increases their commitment and motivation, at
> the same time as it gives the company a chance to present itself, like
> a form of marketing.

Carol Courage talks about taking part in various ceremonial events,
which gives her the opportunity to strengthen the company's local
relations. She sees the external networking role as more symbolic
and describes herself as an ambassador for the company. We will
return to this later. For some people, like Noble, the external networking is not simply a question of ceremonial duties, but a substantial and central aspect of the managerial identity. Networking is
part of the opportunity for strategic development of the business; it
is about projects which may be in line with the business as a whole,
but which nonetheless do not normally belong to the day-to-day
administration of the business. The networking should enable a
certain level of entrepreneurship and strategic action over and
above the existing public machinery, which is considered to be
more autonomous. This emphasis on networking is also connected
to the general increased significance of making relations work
smoothly, inside and outside organizations. Relational skills and
social sensitivity are becoming increasingly important in contemporary working life.

THE ROLE OF LEADER – AVOIDING MICROMANAGEMENT

Positioning management in terms of the leadership roles above is often done through not getting too involved in what co-workers do, but remaining on an overall level. As we have said, this often has a certain moral undertone. There are, for example, those who stress the importance of clarifying the context in order to achieve a better understanding and participation on the part of the members of the organization. Others talk about the need to work with values, strategies and visions in many knowledge-intensive organizations in an effort to avoid micromanagement and thereby allow those who are most familiar with the details to make decisions. Understanding, delegation and participatory decision-making are seen here as morally superior to traditional bureaucratic control.

Gerald Goodman from International Construction Ltd. says, for example:

> It's about making sure the organization works without me controlling everything. I provide the conditions and look ahead and maybe see what others don't see. What we should do from now on. But the everyday things, things they have to make decisions about and have been given responsibility for, that needs to work without me. I need to be more of a leader. The co-workers get on with things and I haven't needed to go in and get involved in the daily work, but people know their role and they can rely on me as far as that's concerned. Some of my co-workers have really grown in that respect and that makes me really happy.

Here we can see a noticeable moral undertone: the manager should preferably deal with the long-term, strategic matters, and avoid bothering independent co-workers since that would hamper their development. Morality is also a central topic for many managers who describe the role of leader as a question of company culture, strategy and visions; in these cases, it is often about creating the conditions for delegating and motivating among professional co-workers. One of our main actors, Gary Gardener, has this to say on the subject of confidence:

> I'm someone who has integrity, which means I get irritated when my managers start getting too involved in the details. I try not to get involved in details when it comes to my co-workers.

One of our senior secondary actors, Manager J, says:

> Micro-leadership is when you take away the decision-making rights from those who should be making the decisions – when you ask for details which have no value for you personally or for your position. It might be a piece of information about a specific office, a budget question or if I go down to project level and ask: "How are things going in the project? And I really want to know." It's about not doing that, but delegating and having confidence in people.

Here we can observe the strongly value-charged language: having confidence in your co-workers and not taking the decision-making power away from those who should rightfully have it. Given the way in which the view of management is formed here, it is easy to understand the positioning of management which takes place – no one wants to say that they lack confidence in their co-workers or that they are taking away their decisions. The view seems to be that a manager who micromanages is a bad manager. Another of our secondary actors, Manager K, says this about his management:

> I try not to meddle too much in operational matters. That would be completely wrong, and no one would gain anything from it. I try to make myself indispensable in strategic questions, but dispensable in operational questions.

Likewise, many managers say that they try to avoid telling their subordinates what to do, as they put it, in questions of detail. They relate this to the idea of co-workers as independent, autonomous and proactive. For managers in both high-technology organizations (R&D organizations) and others (like Goodman's construction company), avoiding this means staying away from the laboratories and other areas where subordinates operate. Some of the managers in the R&D organizations talk about having a certain distance to the researchers, or at least avoiding distracting them with daily requirements to report details and managerial instructions. As one of our secondary actors puts it:

> It's not managers who discover new products, it's the researchers.
>
> *(Manager L)*

Another explains that a company in the same industry was unsuccessful as a result of the managers' inability to leave things alone:

> Their managers were terrible because they told people what they should be doing. If I told people what they should be doing then I'd be a failure. That's not the way I work as a manager.
>
> *(Manager M)*

The talk of avoiding micromanagement is thus in line with the managers' identification with strategies and visions. It is a managerial approach which is clearly made easier by the fact that in modern organizations, micromanagement is generally described as demotivating, as an expression of interference and lack of respect for co-workers and as a barrier to learning and development.

Such a view, however, raises questions around managers' involvement in and contribution to practical activities. The flip side of staying away from the operational activities is, of course, that managers can become peripheral and work primarily with things which are a little outside the productive core business and viewed as rather marginal. This, of course, carries the risk that managerial status will be undermined and that they feel excluded from the real, core business. As has been mentioned earlier, strategies and visions may possibly compensate for the lack of knowledge-based authority in such a situation. This argument is supported in popular management literature, which says, more often than not, that one should exercise authentic leadership, and where it is suggested that "behaving in the right way" (honest, decent) goes a long way in managerial work (George 2003). Sometimes it might even seem that managers, unlike others, do not really work. They do not contribute so much through practical activity but by radiating goodness and authenticity: they are polite and well meaning, have integrity, give freedom and go round trusting people. Leading well is not the same as micromanaging, but rather about making a nice impression on others and making them feel good.

CONCLUDING DISCUSSION

Organizational culture, strategies and visions for the business are topics which many managers today regard as central elements in their leadership role. Transformational leadership is generally broadly and vaguely regarded as the ideal, although the managers studied do not use this term. What they say with one voice is that as a manager you should avoid the traditional administrative and bureaucratic type of excessive micromanagement. This, too, is largely in line with much of the contemporary literature on managing organizations in change-able environments; it is often said that it is not possible to micro-manage or plan these to the same extent as previously. For this reason, members of an organization must be given a greater degree of freedom in their work. This all sounds very positive. Perhaps we should ask ourselves if it sounds too good to be true.

The illustrations in this chapter highlight this development, that is to say interpretations of it. They suggest there is a fairly strong awareness of what a modern view of management means and a certain general familiarity with modern leadership. We can therefore see this as a sign that theories regarding the role of leader and the importance of leadership for modern organizations are now well established and that our study confirms this. This is at least true as regards what the managers say, in other words when it comes to talking about it. Whether pop management and textbook-inspired statements present the whole picture of what managers do is something we will return to later. If that is the case, then the development in the way middle managers in our study view management appears to follow a some-what general trend, which means that they are developing into agents of cultural change, strategists and visionaries. Even if the demands which result from this are sometimes experienced as trying and chal-lenging, we note that the majority of managers experience these roles as close to the way in which they see themselves (Avolio & Gardner 2005). The roles appear to give many of the managers the opportunity to be themselves, which is to say authentic in terms of honesty and integrity (Bass & Steidlmeier 1999).

In a way, much of this sounds admirable. Management appears here to consist primarily of the role of leader, and since the managers in our study consider themselves to be natural leaders, they appear to have found a good balance between what they do and who they are. Most of them seem to construct a style of management based on how they construe their identity. They are given the opportunity to fulfil themselves within the framework of the role as leader. But is this really the whole picture? No, not exactly. Perhaps not even half of it, for in many cases an unruly reality puts a spoke in the wheel for a harmonious relationship between the self and the demands of the organization. Even if the managers dwell on the role of leader and this is encouraged by large numbers of actors both inside and outside the organizations in which our managers are active, there are a num-ber of circumstances which, in various ways, make this more difficult to exercise.

In this chapter we have pointed to a number of difficulties which are partly camouflaged by the accounts that many of our managers have given through rose-tinted glasses. It is hard to escape inconsis-tencies and dilemmas.

One dilemma is the relationship between managerial work as meetings, plans, discussions and overall, abstract matters – manage-rial work in the form of "meta-events" on the one hand – and manage-rial work which is made up of actions that are more specific, practical and rooted in the business, on the other. For the majority, what is central is leadership on a fairly high symbolic level, and this is in part justified by the negative aspects of being occupied with micromanagement, or "interfering". There are, however, those who distance themselves from this, in particular Harding. A central question is whether a manager can exercise much influence by getting involved on a meta level and generally communicating positive values. If we are to believe Harding, for example, being a strategist or bearer of culture does not function as a specific position or element in the managerial work, since you quite simply do not have so much impact on actual practice. Instead, effective influence is better exerted by demonstrating qualified and exemplary conduct as a clear role model. The managerial identity and the role are less marked here, but are fused with the activities as a senior professional. Leadership is then seen in terms of practical involvement and action.

There is a spectrum of possibilities where, at the one extreme, managers live in an abstract PowerPoint world – formulating visions and values – with relatively little support in or knowledge of the business and where, at the other, managers have a strong operative focus and are involved in the day-to-day business but do not have any real overview or contribute to the long-term perspective of the business.

In the first case, the manager is quite remote, while in the second, he or she stands for something which is distinctly different from others in the workplace. Almost all our managers place themselves at one of these extremes (in particular, the first), but in all probability such a pure approach is not always free of tension nor fruitful. Nonetheless, almost-pure extremes appear in most of the managerial talk and probably also in the way they understand themselves. Exactly what people then do may be more varied and mixed – and possibly also inconsistent and confused.

Another problem is what hides behind all the talk of strategy. This is not clear. Strategy is interesting as an indicator. It is often used to underline that they do not interfere or work with operational questions. At the same time, they want to avoid defining themselves as administrators. The term strategy is rewarding here too. Sometimes the term strategy is used to rewrite or enhance administrative work – the budget, for example, is sometimes described as a strategic matter. Talk of strategy can here be viewed as a simultaneous smokescreen and identity amplifier for managers. We will return to the importance of administration for managerial life, in particular in Chapter 6.

A third problem, which we will look at in more depth later, is the difficulty of achieving a natural, close link between the managers' personality and values on the one hand, and what the organizational life often demands on the other. There are a number of tensions, which many of our interviewees sidestep in their eagerness to stress their authenticity in the managerial work.

These conditions help to undermine much of what managers (and many others) often see as more positive associations with the role of leader. Even though many talk about being authentic, and also declare a harmony between the identity and role, they frequently say that they find some areas of managerial work difficult and that they do not always receive the identity confirmation which they also seek, some would say paradoxically, from their environment. Sometimes this undermining and the feeling of a lack of confirmation occur in such a way as to create frustration, a sense of powerlessness, and a certain paralysis of action. We will return to these circumstances, but before that we will describe another central element of management, namely the manager as humanist and moral authority.

5 The manager as humanist and moral example

According to many of our managers, management – as well as being about more overall questions – is about dealing with the constant stream of everyday demands and expectations. While the daily work varies considerably, it involves, among other things, managing relations with subordinates. This means listening, having an open dialogue with and being accessible for co-workers in order to support them in their efforts. In particular, the managers stress the importance of recognizing and acknowledging their co-workers, as well as creating a pleasant atmosphere. For many managers, this is a question of how they understand themselves in terms of morals. The managers describe themselves as open and honest, and as people who are not afraid to tackle sensitive or difficult questions. They also stress that it is important to defend and promote the interests of their subordinates *vis-à-vis* the senior managers in the organization, who all too often insist on getting involved in every little detail and do not understand the complexities of the business and natural demands for autonomy. The middle managers feel that they have an important role to play here in defending and protecting their co-workers' demands for independence. They themselves say that they are good at letting things be, and describe themselves as fair and as having a feeling for the real nature of the business. This approach to managerial work is described as being morally superior and is based on how the managers see themselves. In many cases, it is confirmed by co-workers, which contributes to sustaining and reinforcing the managerial identity.

We begin the chapter with a discussion of the manager as coach and continue with the importance of listening to and recognizing co-workers. We then discuss the manager as an authentic understander of human nature and people's friend and follow up with a longer discussion of the manager as a paragon of virtue and moral example.

MANAGEMENT AS COACHING

Many managers say they want to be a coach for their co-workers. Unlike an American sports trainer, who actively instructs and pushes, coaching in the managerial world commonly refers to some form of supporting leadership. Coaching is often defined as the "process of equipping people with the tools, knowledge, and opportunities they need to develop themselves and become more successful" (Peterson & Hicks 1996, p. 14). This view of coaching is also expressed by our managers, who take their starting point in the co-workers. This is very apparent when, for example, we look at where Charlie Chase positions himself as manager:

> I coach the project leaders, I talk to them and act as a sounding board. I'm their sounding board, so I ask people what they want to do rather than suggest what would work. My job is to help people screen out what's not important and think through what needs to be done. I'm good at getting the discussion going and using people for what they're good at. Being a sounding board, giving them a framework and structure. Creating something which means they can solve problems not just once but several times. People probably think I'm not very clear sometimes, that I don't give them the answers and say "that's the direction you need to go in". But there are often other people who know better than me.

Managerial work (leadership) is articulated here as a supportive discourse which will help people to structure their work. There are times when it does not work, mainly because the co-workers are not independent enough and ask for tangible instructions, something which Chase neither can nor wants to give, but he also admits that the fact they think he is not always clear is a problem. But what does being a sounding board actually involve? Chase answers:

> You need to have experience of projects, but it's difficult to be more precise about what's needed, it's about asking the right questions and making people think things through. But you don't want to take away their responsibility for setting priorities, so it's more about asking questions, making other people think for themselves. You do that by talking and asking them to give practical examples so that I can understand – being a sounding board is a critical competency. I'm good at that, I can make people think about things.

Chase stresses the importance of not telling people what they should do, but rather of making them think and act more independently as a result of his questions and demands for practical examples of problems. Managerial work (leadership) is about being a speaking partner.

Another of our main actors, Steven Stone from Global Industrial Products Ltd., makes his co-workers take personality tests so he knows how he should coach them:

> We do tests so we know what kind of people they are and what I should think about and how I should coach them.

The idea of the coaching is to bring out the positive aspects in his co-workers, according to Stone:

> I want to know what they're like so I can treat them in the right way and develop their strengths.

Another of our main actors, Matt Mooney from Bank Ltd., also stresses the role of coach in the interaction with his co-workers. He says that this means building relations which will contribute to co-workers taking greater individual responsibility:

> When I'm with the employees it's in the role of coach. They know I'm their manager but that I want to lead in a way that makes them take much more individual responsibility. Making my co-workers think – for themselves. How can we reach these goals? That's where I see myself more as a coach. Some of these financial matters are incredibly difficult, so I'm not the expert. They know more about it

than I do. But I'm still the coach, because they'll always want advice in the matters they're dealing with.

Gerald Goodman from International Construction Ltd. also describes the role of leader as a kind of coaching, but at the same time points out that leader is in fact a better word, even if you mean the same thing:

> Coaching is only a tool – it's about encouraging people to do things. Leader is a better word. Having conversations and making them take responsibility. And instructions – because they've come from a level where they didn't know anything and so we have to educate them. The more they've developed, the more conversations we've had, and I ask them how things are going: "What do you think?" Then we share ideas and discuss what we can do. That's how they grow in their role as leader. So it's moved on from giving instructions to standing on the sidelines and listening and offering good advice.

The organizational context is not unimportant, and in Goodman's case it is about working with a traditional industrial product rather than high-technology systems and co-workers with qualified specialist competence. But even in a low-technology context – where much of the work concerns instructions relating to specific production circumstances – we can see that management involves a large element of coaching, or being a leader, as Goodman prefers to call it.

Our school manager, David Dean at The School Ltd., also talks about making others, in his case experienced teachers, act in a well-considered and responsible manner:

> You can't tell people what to do. They have to come up with a solution by themselves. This will only work if they have self-insight. They must have the ability to reflect upon, and be open to, changes in themselves. It might look as though I don't make any demands, because I don't tell them which direction to go in. But my managerial work is built on commitment. Just because I'm the manager doesn't mean I solve other people's problems or decide

which project we're going to do. We have a dialogue, so everyone has to take responsibility.

Talking about his management at the school, Dean says that "the goal is that the work teams will make their own decisions" and that his own role is to "provide knowledge about group processes and help people get over individual barriers".

In the previous chapter, we met managers who emphasized that they worked with strategies and visions and allowed their co-workers to make their own decisions in matters where it was felt they knew best. What they called micromanagement should be avoided. The coaching manager also dislikes micromanagement and takes pride in staying well away from how people do their work.

Management appears here to be about achieving influence and co-determination by allowing people to decide the direction and make decisions for themselves. This sounds like a progressive form of management, but, at the same time, the managers strongly indicate that they often lack the necessary knowledge to be able to offer suggestions for solutions or direction. Their knowledge is more about how to bring about discussion and create processes which make it possible for people to express themselves and arrive at the correct solutions. Managerial work here is about showing openness and sensitivity.

Their "management" has more in common with the conversation leader, therapist or consultant, who uses gentle questioning, advice and input to develop greater wisdom, confidence or realism among co-workers who are uninformed, are uncertain or have lost their way.

MANAGERIAL WORK – BE OPEN, LISTEN AND MOTIVATE

Many of our managers describe managerial work as the ability to be open towards and listen to people, and thereby motivate them. That attentive listening instantly motivates people is what they seem to be saying. At the same time, it also offers a source of information which makes it easier to influence in other ways. Stuart Smart at Big Technology Ltd. says, among other things:

> I know all about being responsible for the staff. I can listen and pick
> up the atmosphere. I know how to motivate people.

Smart describes himself as not just a manager, but also "friends with everyone, even at work".

Charlie Chase, from the same company, also says that he is both friendly and someone who listens to his co-workers:

> I think I get on quite well with everyone, I understand how they
> think and feel. They feel they can tell me things that won't be held
> against them. People feel they can be honest with me. I get feedback
> about what I say – open communication.

Gerald Goodman from International Construction Ltd. fosters this aspect of his work situation, and possibly takes this humanistic aspect further than any of the others when he likens himself to Mother Teresa:

> You should be accessible and sociable. You shouldn't overdo it, as
> I'm in danger of doing sometimes, so that you become too
> accessible. You have to have the right kind of personality to like
> people, to work with people, see the potential in people but also be
> able to put your foot down. To like people and be able to face them
> and communicate. I come across as being hard, but I want to help
> everyone. I have a very strong altruistic streak. Even though I work
> with leadership and am a leader ninety-five to a hundred per cent of
> the time, I still have a very strong altruistic streak, there's a lot of
> Mother Teresa in me.

We can observe here how these managers appear to develop emotionally charged relationships with their co-workers. Managerial work here becomes a case of mutual and trusting relations, and sometimes even friendship. Some say that they are emotionally engaged and enthusiastic, which can result in them talking rather than listening, but they still want to emphasize that they are good listeners:

> I'm an emotional person, I go on intuition. I'm present, I take part in
> the meetings, and unfortunately have a tendency to take over. But
> I'm still not such a bad listener.
>
> *(Gardener)*

The ability to listen is something that many of our managers stress as
being particularly important if you want to be a good manager. One or
two people express a certain amount of self-criticism, such as
Manager B:

> I have to learn to listen to people, because one of my problems is
> that I can be too enthusiastic, and people can get tired of that.

Another manager, Manager C, says:

> Anyone can make suggestions, and they're discussed by everyone
> in the group. Everyone comments and listens. So everyone feels
> that "We're involved". I believe you have to listen to each
> person. Otherwise you're not a team, for one thing, and for
> another, it's incredibly important, because of the ideas that
> come up.

Listening in itself appears here to be something good: it is important to
listen to people since that is how you acknowledge others. You should
be careful not to be too enthusiastic and take over, since you then run
the risk of disregarding other people's opinions, and they might feel
marginalized by the manager. The result might then be that they lose
their motivation and feel discouraged. Listening is important in order
to make people feel involved and motivated, and leads to emotional
ties between managers and subordinates.

The personal conversation is often about making people feel
comfortable and included, but also about building an understanding
for where the business is going. This also means that the manager
must be accessible for the co-workers and easy to get hold of for an
informal conversation:

You have to work through symbolic leadership. In smaller groups you can do this in personal conversation and get the group to go along with you.

(Gardener)

Finding time to be available for people is the hardest thing and what you have to put most effort into. People want to see you and have an informal conversation.

(Manager N)

It seems to be specifically the manager's presence, or, if physical presence is not possible, accessibility, which is central. Benjamin Book, for example, says this when he describes his previous managerial job in the newspaper business:

People knew what I stood for and that I had things to do but that I always had time for them, even on Saturdays and Sundays.

It is interesting to note that so many of the managers in several of these knowledge-intensive companies with independent co-workers talk so much about the significance of being present and accessible. Here this seems *not* in the first instance to be a question of the substantial work – such as that the manager has information or access to resources which are needed to do the job – but about other questions of a more emotional and personal nature which in some way require the manager to be present in the sense of listening and conversing. The impression conveyed is that the manager has an important role when it comes to acknowledging people in the way they want to be seen. It suggests that the subordinates are heavily dependent on being acknowledged by the manager and that they may not be particularly confident, strong or mature. The manager appears here to be given the opportunity to form and control the co-workers' self-esteem and understanding of their identity using simple means, something which can, moreover, have considerable repercussions on the manager's own self-esteem and identity. We will return to this, as one of several paradoxes in the understanding of managerial work. An interesting question in this respect is who benefits most from the good listening: the co-workers or the managers themselves? Are independent co-workers so dependent on the twinkle in the manager's eye and the pricking of his or her ears? Is it really so essential for the manager to have time for co-workers?

THE MANAGER – UNDERSTANDING HUMAN NATURE

Managerial work, as we have seen above, is about, among other things, trying to empower workers, to make them think for themselves and make their own decisions. This can be understood as managers making themselves dispensable in many questions for which co-workers themselves can take responsibility. Yet it hardly makes the managers less important, or redundant; on the contrary, they become even more important when the full potential of the co-workers depends on the manager's ability to act as speaking partner, listen attentively and show restraint when it comes to offering suggestions for how to solve problems. The manager may appear to have a passive role, but is in fact the true central actor, as a result of the strong significance attributed to the manager's presence and ability to act as a sounding board. Behind the (apparently) independent co-worker is an independence-enabling manager. For many of our managers this independence needs to be fuelled and maintained by attention and support provided by the leadership.

The manager's significance is further reinforced in other areas, since managerial work is also about noticing and acknowledging co-workers and their potential. This requires openness, communication, listening to co-workers and not taking over. The manager must be present and accessible, preferably by walking around and having informal conversations with people. These conversations should not, however, be mainly about substantial situations, of the kind that concern work, but should, perhaps somewhat surprisingly, be focused on circumstances which do not demotivate or deprive co-workers of their own capacity for initiative and job satisfaction. In this respect, the work of the manager (leader) is a question of taking an interest in your co-workers' well-being and self-esteem in general.

Bank manager Matt Mooney is fairly typical. He says that the coaching manager must have a good understanding of human nature and describes this, perhaps somewhat paradoxically, as being a janitor:

> In appraisal interviews, I've tried to understand what kind of person they are. Some want support, others want to be led, so that's what you do. That's when they feel at their best. It's about building a relationship with each individual so you can coach them in the right way. And being a janitor suits me. I'm interested in people. I make sure they get the job done by giving them the tools.

The metaphors here are thick and varied. What Mooney is saying, however, is that, in general, his co-workers need either support or direct guidance. He has to gain an understanding of people, develop a personal relationship with them and provide the right tools for the job – then his co-workers will feel at their best. The manager here becomes something of an understander of human nature, supplying people with what they need to do the job. Mooney talks about coaching as a way of getting to know people properly:

> One of the leader's tasks is to get under the skin of each individual, to see them and ask, "How does he or she think in different situations? What effect will it have if I say that?" I spend a lot of time analysing this, and the fact is that the more you learn about a person, the easier it is to coach them.

Benjamin Book is another manager who knows what his co-workers want:

> I'm a good listener and a decent guy. When Ann was feeling a bit down and we received an invitation to a dinner, I sent her, and she really appreciated it. Things like that are important. Instead of just throwing it away without thinking, it's something you can use as a reward without upsetting anyone – so you win. Small, simple things which are important, regardless of whether you lead through other

managers. People need genuine thoughtfulness from the top person, and it costs peanuts.

Similarly, Gerald Goodman talks about soft values and standing for what he calls femininity:

> It's been extremely masculine here, but I represent a certain femininity. I'm not a female leader, but I value those sides more than my colleagues. I care about the soft values in the personal meetings with my co-workers. So they feel seen. You have to be able to have the difficult conversation.

In other words, it is important to demonstrate femininity, decency and friendship. The modern manager – regardless of gender – frequently appears to match the feministic idea of a caring rationality. Generally, many of the managers studied – despite most being men – score high on cultural femininity (Alvesson & Billing 2009) and can be said to exercise feminine leadership, for example being non-directive, relational and caring (Helgesen 1990). Bert Bacon says that he does not really know very much about the business and that if his co-workers disappeared the business would cease to exist. His own role is to provide support and care, rather than knowledge and technical support:

> If my team were to be run over by a bus then the business would cease to exist. It's run by teams, not individuals, and my job is to encourage them, not to know everything about the business. Strangely enough, my job is about not being good at certain things and accepting that. But I'm good at encouraging others, and I think they think that too. If they ask me what we should do in a factual matter, I say, "Don't ask me, I've no idea what you're talking about", but if they say, "Bert, my hamster's sick and I'm having a hard time right now", then I can give them a shoulder to cry on.

William White describes this caring style as central, even though his co-workers do not always see its value. Of course production is important and the ultimate goal, but, as a manager, he is required to use a psychological approach in his contacts with people and give them added motivation by taking an interest in their lives:

> As a manager I see that we must produce, we have targets. I expect these to be clear for my co-workers too. They get a salary and coffee and other things for that. But what I'm focused on is the package around the job. What is it that makes people give that little bit extra and makes them more motivated? The fact is that one person wants to go into something more deeply, someone else wants to be more of a generalist and someone wants more responsibility. That's the kind of thing I pick up on as manager. Not all engineers need a manager who picks that up and deals with it and pushes it forward. But I have a strong need to be involved in that kind of thinking: how we're going to work, not just be allocated a job and do it. And I understand that not all engineers are the same. Some don't want all the things round about but are focused on producing things. So you have to tweak things a bit and bring other things into their day which will make them take a step forwards. Having a candid, close dialogue is the way you win your co-workers' trust. Taking an interest in your co-workers' lives and not just in what you want them to produce.

White quite simply expects his co-workers to reach the work-related goals they have agreed on – this hardly seems to bother him. And there is no way he can properly assess what people do, or directly influence their work and the outcome – that is about specialized engineering tasks. It is more important to take an interest in their lives and relationships. Even if the co-workers themselves show little interest in this, White believes it is something that he should work with:

> Being open means they know that I'm on their side, I'm working for them, I pursue their interests and tell them about constraints. We can't spend all our time just on product development.

Management here means identifying the co-workers' interests and working to realize them. Being there for his co-workers sounds like a self-sacrifice but should perhaps also be seen as a question of securing the existence of the manager and management in a business in which the co-workers' actual work to some extent lies beyond the manager's understanding, focus and maybe even interest. Managers need to focus on the well-being of their co-workers for their own sake too – to have a platform for influence and self-confirmation.

For the majority of those we studied, their interventions are thus about making people feel good, but also about generally acting as their representative and friend.

On one level, we can see here how middle managers, first and foremost, shape their management in relation to their subordinates. These are important; in our interviews, far more emphasis is placed on them than on their own managers, and they sometimes appear to be more important than the business. Many managers give the impression that they believe that the business will take care of itself as long as they manage their co-workers satisfactorily. In a way, it could be said that the managers identify with their co-workers. The aspects which are stressed are, above all, being a speaking partner, letting people take responsibility and make decisions given that they know best, being accessible and taking an interest in the way people develop as co-workers. Being a leader is given a special meaning, almost distinct from leading in a more clear and direct way. That a leader is in the "make-people-feel-good" business is what many managers appear to think.

One of our secondary actors, Manager O, who works in a public organization, says for example:

> If my staff feel good, then both employers and job-seekers get the best service. I put my staff first in every respect. My door is always open. When I'm here, I'm here for them. I see my staff regularly and see when they're not feeling good. I keep my eyes and ears open for the general ambience – bad atmosphere, incidents – and I act accordingly.

The focus here is on personal relationships and having a generally pleasant manner, rather than laying down guidelines and following up what people do and accomplish. Management as administration, managerial supervision, a focus on following the rules and results and other business-related matters are conspicuous by their absence, and, when mentioned, they are done so separately from the role of leader and described as some necessary evil which they are forced to do (by circumstances and/or management).

This approach towards co-workers also reinforces this manager's view of herself as someone who understands human nature and is a good friend. She believes she is by nature a certain kind of person, with fine qualities, and that this finds expression in her leadership. The latter is, thus, not about adapting to expectations and demands, but comes from "within".

For many, making people "feel good" is, in other words, the core aspect of leadership. Manager O talks about an open door. Benjamin Book talks about giving generously of himself and being a decent guy. Matt Mooney talks about how he adapts his managerial style to suit the personalities of his various co-workers, because they are then at their best. Gerald Goodman describes how he takes questions on behalf of his co-workers higher up in the organization and always makes sure he takes care of their interests so they feel secure. The point is that they give of their attention, because in this situation it is specifically the attention of someone who is signified as manager which is important. It cannot be said that the people we interviewed can imagine a helpful colleague or considerate secretary standing for the feel-good efforts; this appears, rather, to be a core task for the manager. Many of the managers indeed believe that it is specifically their attention people need in order to feel good and – consequently– perform well. According to Zaleznik (1997), this a common focus for managers in contemporary working life. In Chapter 6 we will critically discuss the advantages and problems associated with the decent, considerate, "feel-good manager".

The focus on co-workers expressed by our managers is not formulated in a neutral manner, as one of many leadership styles they might consider, but often as something good, which includes moral superiority. The managers position themselves as good people who care about the health and well-being of others. It thus appears that it is not possible to make a choice between taking an interest in the work and the result, and taking an interest in the staff and their feelings – the general perception appears to be that the latter is almost without question the best.

THE MANAGER AS UNDERSTANDER OF HUMAN NATURE
AND FRIEND – A MORAL POSITIONING
AND IDENTITY REINFORCEMENT

The positive interest in their co-workers thus becomes for many managers the core in what they say is their contribution. This requires them to have noble personal qualities, such as giving generously of themselves. Matt Mooney stresses that taking an interest in his co-workers is central in his managerial work:

> My strength as a manager is that I'm empathetic and interested in people. I have coffee and a chat with my co-workers every day. Maybe not in person, but I try to talk with them all on the phone every day. I understand that people want to be seen and acknowledged. I know when all their birthdays are, and call them even if it's on a Saturday or Sunday. We've also put some thought into it beforehand, so it's not just "Hello, Happy Birthday", but I know a little about them. I know they appreciate it. It's the same when they come to me with a problem and ask for help. I remember what the problem was and ask them later how it went, and I know they appreciate that. Appraisal interviews and salary interviews are very difficult for exactly that reason – I think they should have a fair assessment and it's my job to lead people forwards, develop people and hear what they don't say outright. But I get something back, because it develops me too.

What is emphasized here initially is the importance of listening, paying attention to and taking an interest in activities which acknowledge co-workers in situations which are outside the actual business processes. This is partly a result of how Mooney understands himself as a person and his inherent capacities for leadership. But it is also a result of the fact that it is seen as a morally superior, and thereby attractive, way to lead people. It is difficult for today's managers to say that people do not want to be acknowledged or receive confirmation. Mooney is something of a specialist in this respect, calling people at weekends to congratulate them on special occasions, which indicates the significance of his own efforts and sacrifices to give confirmation. But more formal managerial tasks, such as appraisal and salary interviews, are also platforms for acknowledging people and making it possible for them to develop. According to Mooney, his co-workers really like this; he says that "they appreciate my attention". Furthermore, his own managerial identity is reinforced by the feedback from his co-workers:

MOONEY   I get feedback about what I need to work on from co-worker surveys and appraisal interviews. And in the health checks they also ask them how they feel at work, and I get feedback from that too.

INTERVIEWER   But is positive feedback meaningful?

MOONEY   Yes, of course, you feel they've got confidence in you. Everyone has a need to be seen, and it's me, their manager, who sees them. And when other people feel good, I feel good, that's my janitor role. It makes me feel damn good.

There is a sense of harmony and something "good" in these apparently mutual confirmations of identity and reinforcements of self-esteem. Mooney offers a style which confirms people and makes them feel good, and in return he receives confirmation of his identity, so that he too feels good, damn good. We will see later that this can be a problem and not as harmonious as it appears here, but first a little more about this humanistic and progressive style of management.

Another of our main actors, Charlie Chase, emphasizes, like Mooney, that in his new role it is important to try to take people along with him and build good relationships:

I'm empathetic, I don't like steamrolling over people, I want to have consensus for what we do so that everyone's on board and knows where we're going – that's my style of leadership. Making sure people support and accept the issues we discuss, and that even if it doesn't seem to be to everyone's advantage, they understand what we're doing. It's important that each person accepts the issue, and it can be difficult in some cases when you don't have time to explain why.

The majority of the managers we studied give a clear picture of their noble humanistic traits. Both Carol Courage and Gerald Goodman describe themselves as humanists with a genuine interest in people and wanting people to feel good. When Global Pharmaceuticals Ltd. and its new international organization were established, Courage talked often about the importance of people's need to feel local:

People need the local daily life and to feel secure, and I try to create that.

In other words, Courage is trying to take into account the human aspect at a time of global change by highlighting the importance people attach to having a local context. Goodman says that he is good at getting people to go along with him, and that his co-workers also trust him:

People trust me. I try not to deceive anyone. I keep my word. That's my trademark. It's also been made very clear to me that my co-workers agree.

Goodman portrays himself as candid and trustworthy in the way he deals with people, someone people can trust and who would not go behind a co-worker's back. The self-view created here is strongly charged with humanistic values.

Another of our main actors, William White, likes to see himself as a manager who is open and with whom it is possible to have a good, strong relationship:

> I'm open and give generously of myself. I talk about my private life and what I can and can't do. They've picked that up. I know that from the feedback. Lots of people at my previous workplaces said I'm very good at making myself accessible and listening. Then you sometimes had to tell people that while they had a good point, we also had constraints which meant we couldn't do anything. But I got a very clear response from my co-workers that I was good at that.

White emphasizes here the importance of building personal recipro-cal relationships with his co-workers. He believes that positioning himself as someone who understands human nature means that they can be more open with each other and talk about things which are not directly work related; we also saw this in the descriptions above. What is significant here, however, is that when White acts as some-one who understands human nature and a truly friendly person and makes himself available in different ways, this also has a bearing on how others see him. He receives feedback telling him that his style and person are right and that people like him. White's co-workers become important for the way his identity as the good manager is controlled: by stressing his personal traits as giving of himself, being open, accessible and a good listener, he makes himself a competent leader.

This type of simple reasoning is only complicated on the odd occasion. Gary Gardener is, however, perhaps a little more self-critical and balanced when he says the following:

> I'm a structural fascist but still very flexible. I don't have a problem changing my mind in the short term, I'm pretty fearless and I don't mind admitting I've made a mistake. In that respect, I'm an easy person to deal with. I don't get mad at people who make mistakes, but I do get mad at people who're not honest and are clearly arguing so they won't have to do something they don't want to do.

The suggestion here is that some individuals have a rather unclear moral calibre, which makes it difficult to be seen to be good all the time. There are occasions when it is acceptable to be angry, but his anger at people's moral failings reinforces his own superior morals.

We can note that this positioning has consistently strong moral tones. Matt Mooney describes himself as empathetic and interested in developing people, Gerald Goodman says he is empathetic and interested in people while Carol Courage repeatedly emphasizes her profound interest in how people create meaning in their daily lives. Charlie Chase also says he is empathetic, but, in addition, he wants to reach consensus, and indicates that he has a democratic view of leadership. William White describes himself as open and a person who gives of himself. Gary Gardener says he accepts the blame when someone makes a mistake, he takes responsibility and is honest. And he gets upset when others demonstrate moral failings, such as dishonesty and attempts at manipulation (like Noble below). Distancing oneself from all things political seems to be particularly important for our managers – they want to appear apolitical. In this, they express a humanistic view of management and leadership: it is about being open and creating a shared view in important questions.

We have earlier seen that the management in these portrayals is formed primarily on the basis of a softer view of management, in which the role of leader is prominent, and where it is largely about being empathetic and humanistic. The picture of management appears, however, to be fairly one-sided, since only the positive sides are presented, those that can create a feeling of mutual identity confirmation. There are, of course, other sides to management – administrative problems, operational tasks, leadership challenges and a generally disorganized daily life – which are not obviously apparent here, and we will return to these circumstances in the next chapter.

AUTHENTICITY AND INTEGRITY – BEING YOURSELF IN MANAGERIAL WORK

As in the previous chapter, we can observe here that our interviewees describe their work as an expression of their personalities. The man or woman does the job, rather than the other way round. It is their inner self, rather than expectations and demands or the need to think through their impression management carefully, which is central. They stress that it is not possible to fake it, or to play a role as manager. The managers describe themselves as emotional and intuitive. Nora Noble says:

> I am emotional. What upsets me as a manager is dishonesty. Dishonesty can really upset me, and I find that very difficult.

Benjamin Book emphasizes that leadership is a question of building trust by making the odd joke and being sensitive to people:

> We can joke with each other. Leadership is built on being able to stand by what you say, having principles and backing up your employees. If they've made a mistake, you sort it out, nice and calm, face to face. That builds trust, and it takes a number of meetings to find the right way and know where you stand so they'll dare to open up. In the first phase, I don't push as hard as I usually do, perhaps I'm less severe in discussions, I can be more flexible by saying that it's interesting. I always try to be like that in discussions, but you can be a little more generous at the beginning. I mean, it's obvious, we can't do something we don't agree with.

You should stand for what you say but at the same time be a little flexible and perhaps sometimes appear more interested than you actually are. It is not always easy to maintain your principles and be categorical when it comes to honesty. We will return to this later. For the time being, we note that many appear to see the humanistic approach which we described above as an expression for how they understand themselves. Book says:

> The key qualities of a good leader are that you can show your feelings and never pretend to be someone you're not. I see myself as honest and straight – I'd never go back on my word. If I make a promise, it's worth more than just the paper it's written on. I'm

> meeting someone today and he's checked up on who I am with some people he knows and he said: "Yes, you had a good reputation, you're a big name and they knew who you were." That was nice to hear, positive, and I said: "Yes, you can believe what I say."

We can see here the interplay between identity and image. Book's self-view is reinforced by what he believes is confirmation from those around him. Another of our main actors, Bert Bacon, says that he has no desire to pretend that he knows everything as a manager, and has learned to admit ignorance:

> I've seen leaders come in and pretend they know everything, like: "I've worked for different companies and this is how I did things and now we're all going to do it the same way." That's not what I've done. These people have experience, they have knowledge, and I appreciate them for that – and trust them because of it. I don't try to answer questions. If senior management asks something, then I ask my co-workers: "Tony, what's the answer?" And I'm very careful not to take the credit for it. I take the credit when it's due, but if others do the work then I make sure that comes across. That's how I am. I'm a facilitator between them and senior management. They feel good because they have a voice in the other tiers. But I make sure they get the recognition.

The managers describe themselves here as managers who have reflected over themselves as managers and who act with honesty and integrity. As we saw in the previous chapter, this is a central element in what many today talk about as leadership (Avolio & Gardner 2005; George 2003). Our managers' own superior managers (and in one case successor) do not appear to possess the same good traits. Book, for example, has the following to say about his successor:

> I can see now that it's turned into a circus there [at the newspaper]. Peter has been there for a month and a half and he hasn't greeted the staff, and that's not a positive sign. Ten members of the staff sit ten metres away from him and he can't even say hello to them. That's a

common mistake. You should be generous with yourself, and why wouldn't you? Perhaps it's because he isn't familiar with the company and maybe he feels insecure and maybe it's a question of prestige and he wants to be a bit cocky.

Bert Bacon compares other managers' non-authentic and arrogant behaviour with his own honesty, modesty and respect for others:

> I've seen managers claim to know everything. I haven't done that. Those managers' subordinates have all the experience, they have the knowledge.

As the following quote suggests, Gary Gardener's superiors are another example of those who do not always show any great respect when they interfere in minor questions and cause confusion, something which he himself never does:

> I've got integrity. I get irritated when my superiors start confusing things with details. I try to avoid doing that with my co-workers.

Even if managers other than those we studied frequently do not come up to scratch as far as morals are concerned, they themselves do, in their own minds. They do not dissemble, but their managerial work becomes a straightforward expression of their authentic identities. They behave in a particular way, which appears mainly to include positive traits which are extremely valuable in leadership. You do not have to be a cynic to have some doubts about whether it can be such a good thing and so straightforward.

So we can say that managers, to a great extent, construe management as a question of having a good understanding of human nature and putting the spotlight on the person behind the working roles and the instrumental tasks. They try to avoid involving themselves in the details of their subordinates' work, partly perhaps because they do not understand it, but also because to do so would be morally unacceptable and alien to how they see themselves. This is also seen as increasingly central in, for example, the project leader role, according to Bredin and Söderlund (2012, p. 282), who cite a senior project leader's view of the development of the role of project leader:

> I think the project leader is moving more towards being a non-specialist and being even better at running projects, and taking care of people. I usually always make that point – you have to take care of your people, because if you don't, you'll have problems. This is a very big part which is often forgotten, and then you can't make it work, it doesn't work the way it should. Then, of course, you have other bits too, you have to know how to control, and all the traditional things that are involved in project management. But I think people often forget about taking care of the human capital, and I think that will become more and more important.

There is possibly a complication here: a lack of time, interest or ability to take an interest in both the work itself and the individuals. In project management, delivery often comes first.

However, many view this matter as mainly a question of not forgetting to take the personnel ("human capital") and relationships seriously enough. As long as management is described as a question of leading in a relations-oriented sense, management appears naturally harmonious, an extension of one's personality. Relational leadership does the trick, both for practitioners in our case and for many leadership researchers (e.g. Cunliffe & Eriksen 2011). In some cases, however, managers make a distinction between being a manager and being a leader, even if they all see management mainly as a question of doing leadership. The managers sometimes talk about what they describe as the darker sides of management, which include, among other things, the need to be tough and firm in a way which may be seen as negative. This might, for example, refer to difficult changes in the organization, or mergers, the winding down or cutting back of business or other things which involve negative consequences for large numbers of people. This is, naturally, an element of management, but it is not something with which our managers want to identify. This darker aspect of management is therefore described as a necessary evil, something which they are almost forced into by other, often more senior, managers or overall management/corporate systems. It means doing something which is in direct contrast to how they see themselves as leaders, and which can constitute a kind of anti-identity. Some managers describe performing such activities as being forced to "manage" as opposed to lead. Gerald Goodman gives a good illustration of this:

> There are times when you have to get into the managerial role and give very clear direction. Then I act according to that role, the responsibility I have – there's something I have to do. So I have to do it, and then I'm a manager. In many situations you're a leader, because there are a lot of teams, there are people who have a higher level of competence than me. They lead different projects, and then it's about leading and making sure things work. You need a manager when things are distinctly uncomfortable, when it's stormy, when we need to change direction, because that's what senior management has decided. Then I need to be a manager too and stand behind what my manager has said. There have been times when I haven't agreed with him and we've discussed it, but I have to accept it. I have to see it through and then I have to be a proper manager. Show them I have a heart, but still make it clear that this is my role.

As is apparent above, management also involves activities which risk undermining the claim of being an authentic and morally superior manager (leader). In such situations, you risk appearing insensitive and ruthless, which can undermine your identity. Better then to talk about these aspects of management as something forced on you from the outside, and try to maintain a certain level of self-esteem by saying that you do not necessarily agree with what senior managers decide and trying to show some sympathy, even when the decisions to be made are difficult. In such cases you are forced to play a role – to be non-authentic rather than authentic. It can be noted that this description of the managerial role as some enforced evil makes it possible to maintain your integrity and continue to hold your head high when you do things which do not match the way you see yourself and want others to see you as manager.

For one of our main actors, Henry Harding, this is, however, a minor problem. For Harding, taking a close interest in the business – focusing on fact – and the substantial managerial influence are central aspects of management, even if many people experience this as meddling and authoritarian, something which Harding is at times accused of. Harding is not particularly concerned to appear as a relations-oriented and sympathetic friend. On the contrary, he wants to avoid too much talk outside the core tasks and instead let his actions show what he can accomplish. Harding therefore describes himself as a role model, as we could see in the previous chapter. He says:

> As a manager you must be a role model, and that must be evident in every problem you meet. When I'm a role model for my co-workers they will show themselves as role models for their co-workers, and so on. It acts as a positive example which spreads through the organization.

Like other managers, Harding is, of course, keen to have positive feedback, but in his case it is about what he accomplishes in terms of result and outcome, rather than how humanistic his personality is.

The majority of our managers emphasize, however, things other than actual practice. We can see that the humanistic interest which has emerged works with the "strategic" interest to the extent that they "circumvent" what people do and accomplish, and focus on the individuals and the bigger picture, respectively.

THE MANAGER AS PARAGON OF VIRTUE

As has already been mentioned, we can see that the managers in our study position their management in moral terms. They portray themselves as true humanists. They reason that by being helpful, supportive and friendly, and acting as a speaking partner, they will be able to encourage others. Their co-workers are empowered to take responsibility. The manager should listen and hold informal conversations and not push too hard – it is, above all, about acknowledging your co-workers. If this is to work, you must be accessible. The manager's importance in the substantial sense, in other words in making a more direct contribution to the actual business, appears to play a less important role. Instead, the spotlight is on being someone who has a good understanding of people and is relations oriented.

For many people, the moral qualities also involve being honest and trustworthy. For the virtuous manager, dissembling is out of the question. Henry Harding has this to say about being a role model:

> Being a role model is not about acting but about really putting your heart and soul into it. Being a role model means more than just playing a superficial game. It's a question of identifying with what you do, you have to believe in what you're doing if you are going to be an effective role model.

Benjamin Book is another of our main actors who frequently returns to the importance of authenticity:

> You have to be authentic in your management, or you won't be credible. You can't fake an interest in people because they'll see through you.

Gerald Goodman also stresses the importance of being yourself. When asked if he is acting the role of leader, he answers: "No, I'm very much myself", and says he does not distinguish between himself as a person and the role of leader but instead identifies strongly with being a leader.

For Carol Courage, too, honesty and credibility are in contrast to the political and manipulative:

> When you represent the employees you can't ever be accused of being political, you have to be credible. If there was a change that affected our department it would be important that I didn't pretend. That I didn't make it political, which would reduce my credibility.

> What I say has to be based on what I really believe and not what I think is best in a particular situation. There are two things I think I've learned: to act in a way which is not political and actually to have the courage to stand up for what I really believe in. I don't shake in my shoes, I have the courage to stand up for what I believe.

Nora Noble also emphasizes her authenticity, and claims about her work and herself that:

> It's about leading, and that means living leadership. And that's what my closest co-workers expect me to do.

Here she is positioning her leadership in terms of authenticity and the highest moral calibre. It is not about playing a role or dissembling, but about actually believing in and living what you say. There are no hints of issues of power, politics or the need to navigate smoothly among various interests and egos and deal with dilemmas about being one's true self and adapting to the demands and feelings of others. Many managers say that they identify strongly with their managerial work, which they see as an expression of their true nature.

They describe how their behaviour as managers is based on their understanding of themselves as good individuals. They know themselves and modify their self-view in accordance with what they understand to be authentic in terms of integrity and honesty. In the eyes of these managers, being authentic and being a good leader are to all extents and purposes the same. In this context (as in the previous chapter), authentic refers almost by definition to what are here seen as positive – humanistic – traits. They believe that they are this kind of manager because they believe in allowing people to develop, to speak freely, to be honest and to feel they are appreciated. This is a strong moral positioning, the opposite of which seems primitive – acting a role, giving in and meddling are quite clearly inferior in terms of values. The opposite picture is one of managers who talk a lot and often take over, who give clear direction for what other people should do, who are authoritative in their manner and pretend to know everything. Our managers describe the authoritative, power-hungry, political manager as false and non-authentic. This is in line with both popular and academic literature on authentic leadership, where it is said that managers who achieve results by putting the fear of death into their co-workers are bad managers because they themselves feel inadequate – they are said to be non-authentic (Fairhurst 2007; George 2003).

Their strong moral positioning means our managers can portray themselves as paragons of virtue and good examples. After all, they are helping to establish what is for them the good leadership, that which encourages co-determination, confirmation of people, development and learning. Through this, the managers become the main actors in the development and renewal of modern organizations. It is the managers, more than others, who contribute to organizations developing and producing innovations. It is through this positive influence exercised by the humanistic managers that the creative potential is released.

It can be noted that external demands and expectations, adapted to socially dominant norms and procedures for how managers should be, behave and speak, are not mentioned as being particularly central in this context – at least, not as conditions which severely restrict the opportunities to form their work according to how they see themselves and their capacity. That the person does the managerial job is the dominant impression gained from listening to our (mainly Swedish) managers – whose integrity, high moral standards and reliability appear to be firmly rooted. This is almost inevitable – you cannot be anything but the way you are. Your own nature, and your environment's ability to see through any deception, make morals and genuineness the central managerial qualities. Exercising your own positive traits – honesty, openness, authenticity, not being political – result in a leadership where all good things go hand in hand, to the benefit of the company, the co-workers and possibly even the general good. There is almost a feeling of Sunday school about it.

CONCLUDING DISCUSSION

In this chapter, we have shown how the managers, without exception, have emphasized their qualities as good understanders of human nature and moral examples. It is striking how strongly they stress their admirable ambitions and traits, as well as the positive consequences of these – first and foremost for their co-workers, but also, indirectly, for the business.

Although the managers portray themselves as moral examples and claim that management is primarily characterized by the role of leader, we are talking about fairly mundane activities. It is about listening, having informal conversations, and generally paying co-workers some attention. What makes these activities remarkable in this context is, of course, that it is the manager who performs them. It is the person who is designated manager who listens, takes part in the informal conversation and is the speaking partner. When the managers say that they actually perform these daily activities, it is made to look like something exceptional – it lends a special aura to the activities. When managers perform them, they become almost mystical. Here we can talk about leadership as the extraordinarization of the mundane (Alvesson & Sveningsson 2003c). If anyone else – outside the therapy or preschool fields – were to stress these efforts as the main contribution in their work, we would probably wonder what they actually do at work and whether they should be highly paid for it. But for managers, it is central and fitting, at least in their own view of the world.

The fact that managers make huge efforts to adjust to the psychological needs and demands of others seems central, at least in the western world, which is increasingly sensitive to human relations and people's need for gratification and support (Alvesson 2013a; Foley 2010; Lasch 1978). Zaleznik (1997), identifying these orientations in US companies, refers to this as "psychopolitics", which often dominates in workplaces.

If this is accepted by others, the idea that the manager's small talk and listening, seeing, openness, honesty and other virtues have magical effects is reinforced. The manager is upheld as a main actor in circumstances in which the manager perhaps neither is (nor needs to be) so important for the actual core business – which other people understand better. If managers in this type of organization are merely sidelined to an administrative and ceremonial role, there is of course a risk (or possibility, if you prefer to see it that way) that the importance of the management for the development and renewal of organizations is marginalized. The manager is no longer seen as the obvious central actor for the organization's survival and development. The manager risks becoming a secondary figure occupied primarily with treasury and managerial supervision activities. But this is not attractive – it does not sound impressive in other people's (or one's own) ears and is not something it is desirable to identify with. Better, then, to stress the role of leader and its therapeutic approach, even if this is expressed in slightly different terms, such as coaching (Western 2008). It is easy to understand why literature about the significance of the manager in a more rational and emotional meaning is becoming increasingly popular. It highlights emotional intelligence, and managers become almost quasi-therapists, skilled at interpreting their own feelings and those of others (George 2000; Western 2008). This is celebrated by many, but others are worried about an exaggerated focus on psychology at the expense of "real work" (Zaleznik 1997). Whether or not this really works as well as the managers themselves believe and much of the literature claims is a more open question, to which we will return.

PART III Management: ironies, labyrinths and pitfalls

6 Self-view and managerial ideals meet reality

Managerial work in practice

We have so far addressed people's expectations of managerial work and what they want to accomplish as a manager. This has mainly been about how managers understand themselves and their leadership. In this chapter, we take a closer look at the managerial work by examining what happens to people in managerial jobs in practice. What happens to the aspirations and claims to work with strategy and to listen to and communicate with co-workers to make them feel good and develop? As we will see, it is not necessarily the case that the managers' views of themselves and what they do in their work – their identity claims and leadership ideals – are matched by what they actually work with. Although many managers want to work with overall questions, influence culture and boost co-workers by listening to and engaging in dialogue with them, they are faced with problems and challenges in their daily life which make these ambitions difficult to achieve. Complications which arise can make it difficult to work as planned, and sometimes the manager and/or others feel that they are failing in their management.

The chapter is structured in two comprehensive sections. The first describes the problem of working as change agent, strategist and networker, the leadership roles we described in Chapter 4. The second section describes problems associated with the role of being someone who understands human nature and likes people, described in Chapter 5. We begin with a discussion of the problem of exercising the strategic role and point to the difficulties managers face in maintaining a coherent view of what they do, not least because they do not always receive confirmation from other people for the strategic and/or authentic elements of the managerial identity. Here we also discuss how managers are exposed and vulnerable – to complexities and contradictory demands. We then discuss problems in practising the role of someone who understands and likes people in relation to the fact that many see themselves as natural and authentic managers. Here, too, we discover that ideals and self-view are not always clearly expressed in practice – the latter is determined by a multitude of circumstances. Demands from the environment – including demands from senior managers and the organizational machinery for an effective administration – frequently collide with the individual's leadership interests. It can also be difficult to make sense of one's own values and ideals. In particular, it appears to be difficult to reconcile the views of oneself as both a natural driving force and a sympathetic and unconditional listener. This is another breeding ground for uncertainty, problems and conflicts of identity. We end with a discussion of the importance of leadership as a way of attempting to achieve stability in the managerial work. We develop and discuss these conditions in the following two Chapters 7 and 8, with the help of the identity concept (see Chapter 2) and with a particular focus on what regulates and controls identities (Alvesson & Willmott 2002).

MANAGERIAL IDEALS AND ORGANIZATIONAL REALITY

Many of the participants in this study have become managers in part because they have wanted to move on from what they regarded as confined professional working roles and tasks. This is particularly true for Charlie Chase, Carol Courage and Bert Bacon. In their cases, the managerial role offered an opportunity to express and further develop their personal qualities. Many have also seen the role as an opportunity to realize the managerial capacities they believe they possess and thereby fulfil themselves, as it is sometimes called. So far so good. Yet one common problem is that managers are exposed to demands which they find difficult to deal with in a way which corresponds to how they see themselves. In many cases, they are forced into issues which conflict with their expectations of the managerial job, such as working with strategy, visions, cultural questions and organizational change.

It can hardly come as a surprise to anyone that there are times when managers have no choice but to do things they neither want nor have expected to do. Most see this as an inevitable element of managerial work, as it is of any other job. What is meant here is, rather, that a large proportion of the tasks are at variance with what they understood to be the core of the managerial work. If they then also lack the opportunity to work with questions they had expected would constitute the core of the managerial work, the situation becomes complicated. The question is, what happens then?

As was pointed out in Chapter 4, many believe that working with strategies and visions is an important part of leadership, and also that it is in line with their personalities. Further, many pointed out how important it is to avoid micromanaging co-workers. On the surface, this sounds convincing and correct. But what does it mean in practice?

The reader may remember that our main actor Stuart Smart talked a great deal about the value of elevating discussions to cover the big, overall questions. However, when we ask what this means in terms of interaction with his closest co-workers, it turns out to include a lot of other things:

> It's mostly a matter of discussing the schedule, project staffing and resource consumption.

Smart also feels that the latter questions do not match his self-view:

> I'm the kind of person who should be working with overall questions, have a helicopter perspective and give people the whole picture, our goals and direction.

Gary Gardener stressed the importance of the symbolic leadership and staying away from the details, since getting involved would limit the freedom of his co-workers. Yet, in a closer explanation of the symbolic leadership, he says:

> I spend a lot of time following up the operational work and making sure we don't diverge too much from the time plan and schedules that have been agreed.

Manager G pointed out that it is important to have a common vision and purpose. But when this manager is more specific about what working with the vision means, his reasoning becomes somewhat operational:

> I get very involved in the technical work.

Another manager, E, talked in Chapter 4 about the importance of the strategic questions in management, which he means is exercised primarily in meetings. However, when clarifying these, it becomes apparent that he and his managers often discuss quite different things in meetings:

> Budgets, capital budgets, revenue budgets, project budgets. But also absence due to training, and operational questions, like our website. These questions are frustrating, and especially when we spend so much time discussing them. I'm also frustrated that we don't discuss central questions – we have a lot of experience in the group.

Here we observe the struggle between devoting yourself to strategic and overall questions on the one hand, and being tied up by administrative and operational questions on the other. It is clear that the administrative questions are a pitfall it is difficult to avoid – together with the operational questions, they force out the overall questions. This is a leading theme in Carol Courage's (frustrating) work situation, among others, and one we will return to in the next section.

In Chapter 4, we also met Manager E, who described how his managerial work has gone from being operational to being more strategic. However, when we ask him to explain this at a later stage, he says, among other things:

> As a manager here you have to apply considerably more controlling ways when dealing with people. You have to tell people that "For

the next month you'll be working with this development and learning about it".

It thus appears to be fairly common to stress the big, long-term, overall questions and distance oneself from operational and controlling work, while in reality frequently working with the latter – which possibly even makes up the biggest part of the work.

The mystery of managers who like – but do not practise – leadership

Taking our starting point in these examples, we can say that many managers are good at expressing and identifying with leadership, as in "I'm a manager who practises leadership" (as we saw in Chapter 4), but much worse at exercising it in practice, at least if we believe what they say they actually work with. Again, we meet managers who are stuck between a very popular and attractive image of leadership which demands work with visions and strategy, on the one hand, and practical, mundane circumstances which require traditional administrative managerial work, on the other. Here, the managerial ideal meets reality, and for the most part the latter appears to take over and, in practice, to marginalize the ideal of the strategic leadership.

The managers stress that this is partly because the administrative questions force out the strategic. This is common in modern organizations. Despite a great deal of popular literature about flexibility and learning, classic bureaucracy with its formal hierarchies and rules still appears to have an impact on current-day organizations, at least on large ones (Alvesson & Thompson 2005; McSweeney 2006; Tengblad 2003). There are many structures, systems and procedures which must be in place in order for large organizations, in particular, to work. HR, financial and performance management, IT and other control systems generally mean far-reaching standardization, and a great deal of work in general to make the organizational machinery run smoothly has already been done.

This means that we see continued high, and often increasing, administrative demands on managers in modern organizations. As we have mentioned earlier, many of the organizations included in our study are knowledge-intensive, which normally means organizations that are primarily intellectual in nature, unlike other businesses which are based on physical labour or capital. Knowledge-intensive organizations are understood to motivate normative control which is directed towards norms, ideas, values and views of how things should be, and be done. Traditional forms of control, such as behavioural control and performance measurement, are toned down or supplemented with normative control. It is sometimes said that the culture replaces the structure as the organizing principle, since the culture both explains and controls behaviour (Wilkins & Ouchi 1983). One could say that desirable behaviour is achieved as a result of the regulation and control of co-workers' experience, approach and ideas, rather than as the result of direct control of behaviour. People's identity, that is to say, how they understand themselves in relation to their work, is increasingly often an object of control. We also observe that many of our managers frequently emphasize that they work with values and approaches because they are managers in knowledge-intensive organizations where the need and opportunity for direct managerial control is often limited, since co-workers know more about factual matters than the manager (this was expressed by Manager G, among others, in Chapter 4; see also Alvesson 2004; Rennstam 2007).

Many organizations have a greater degree of standardization and centralization, with stronger bureaucratic control as a result (Kärreman et al. 2002). Global Pharmaceuticals Ltd. – where Courage and Managers A, C and N work – has implemented organizational changes intended to increase efficiency and development capability. From having been a fairly decentralized and informal organization, they have attempted to tighten up processes such as time consumption, reporting, and so on (Kärreman et al. 2002).

This development is one reason the role of the middle manager in particular is becoming one of communicating strategic decisions to the rest of the organization rather than of being involved in their formulation (Watson 2004). Many of the strategic ideas which are to be implemented put pressure on the managers to exercise fairly detailed management control downwards in organizations. With the lack of a deeper insight into what people actually do, the focus moves to attempts to regulate things such as sub-reports and the like. To this is added an expectation among senior managers that lower-middle managers will demonstrate a willingness to follow initiatives which come from higher levels of the organization. This is, of course, nothing new; it has always been a key aspect of management, where it has often been a question of implementing policies and strategies, as well as the demands and expectations of top management. What is new is, perhaps, the widespread communicated views and expectations of managers as leaders, rather than cogs in the organizational machinery.

Nonetheless, the talk of strategy formulation and leadership appears to be just talk. All talk and no action, if you like.

We saw earlier that Carol Courage is keen to shape culture and work with long-term questions of an overall nature. This is a job that corresponds well with how she sees herself. But there are other things which are in urgent need of her attention:

> There's still an incredible amount to do, and the thing I find really hard is that you're supposed to widen your perspectives at the same time as you have to report small details. We meet once a month, my manager Bibbi and the site managers. But our group doesn't work. That's because Bibbi has a role where she only wants information, and she uses our meetings as a kind of cross-examination, which I think is terrible. The best thing is when we're left our own and try to work with things to do with our role and how we can control this strategically. But now we have these awful senior co-ordination meetings where we're interrogated in front of Bibbi and asked if we've fed this project, the synergy project, into our database. It's on a level of detail I don't like.

As we have also seen above, this development causes frustration among many middle managers, even those on a senior level (such as Courage), since it places them in a contradictory situation. They are expected to work with both "strategic" leadership and control-oriented operational managerial activities. In Courage's case, it is not only about having to exercise micromanagement, but also about being micromanaged. The ideologically coloured talk of the need for strategic leadership in management clashes here with the demand at group level for micromanagement and control, which is rather far from the more development-oriented leadership many identify with. Instead of being acknowledged and recognized as the real manager – in this case a strategic leader – they are regularly held responsible for the delivery of administrative details as a part of the daily maintenance and control of the organizational machinery. They are called upon in the capacity of subordinate and follower, rather than independent manager and leader, which makes it hard for them to identify with the managerial work and see it as a natural extension of their own personality.

The general impression gained from our managers is, thus, that a considerable amount of their work involves what they all describe as micromanagement in administrative and operational questions. In other words, the ideal image of the strategic, network-building, visionary manager appears rather fragile, to the extent that it becomes weaker rather than stronger when our managers are asked to be more precise about what they do. The strategic leadership appears, so far, to be mainly a question of a facade behind which there does not always appear to be much substance.

When the managerial work is directed towards administrative control, follow-ups and rivalry regarding resources, a strategy and culture-oriented view of oneself as manager – and even more as leader – is undermined. The self-view is in danger of being rocked. In some cases, managers attempt to hold on to the leader identity and the self-esteem it bestows by stressing situations where it does not risk being undermined by tasks which strongly deviate from their self-view. In others, this is difficult, and the contradictory demands made on managerial work form a breeding ground for identity conflicts. If the manager's platform for leadership is regularly undermined– as we saw in the case of Courage above – it can, of course, lead to a loss of credibility among co-workers or other key individuals, as well as a corrosion of identity. It is sometimes said that managers are cut off by other actors in their environment. We will see next how this can play out in a highly tangible case for one of our main actors, Benjamin Book.

Wing-clipped managers

Despite his formal position as CEO, Benjamin Book is a clear example of how difficult it can be for managers to sustain a view of themselves as a leader and strategist in the eyes of others. He is by no means the only person in our study with this problem – Courage, Dean and Chase are other noticeable examples of how management and organizational structure restrict the scope for action – but in this section we focus on Book, not least because of the fact that his senior official position should give him the freedom and opportunity to exercise his leadership to the full. Yet this is not the case. Book's co-workers say that the company's management team has very little to do with the company's overall direction. One of them says this:

> I think we should discuss strategies and visions in the management team, questions to do with business ideas and goals: What's going to happen with the firm, and how are we going to develop in the future – are we going to publish just any old rubbish? I've had opinions on this. Why are we publishing things which are no good? But this isn't done in the management team, it's done in the boardroom, and the owners have different values from us in the management team. We seldom discuss important publishing decisions, they're taken on the level above us.

Book describes the situation as frustrating and says that the owners' interventions are destructive:

> We have an informal and external interaction which can strike at
> any time and which we have to fight off. It's incredibly annoying.
> There have been times when I've decided on a course for the
> organization which the owners demolish. They intervene and say
> that we're going to do it this way, and I say we're not. The situation
> with them is incredibly difficult, really annoying.

The owners interfere with his management, and their behaviour is
not in line with his person or his values of acting in a direct, honest
and trustworthy manner – authentically, as Book repeatedly calls it.
We can see here how difficult it is to sustain the ideal view of oneself
in practice. Describing oneself as authentic sounds good – the
opposite is considerably less appealing – but actually realizing it in
an imperfect reality is, of course, quite another matter. In the latter
case, there are instead a large number of situations to be taken into
account, from material limitations and conflicts of interest to
social and cultural norms and obligations. In Book's case, this
means that he often has to compromise and subordinate himself to
the demands and expectations of others – in this case, specifically
the owners:

> In the management team we've talked about how the owners
> intervene in the wrong way. My co-workers make a decision, and
> the owners come in and shuffle the cards and the result is crazy.
> Then I have to go in and put things right, like Bob the Builder. I say,
> "Now the wall's fallen down and now we have to build it up again",
> and tell the owners, "You can't say these things or do that".

Book describes the situation as a challenge, a kind of "mission impossible", which can be a learning experience, and makes comparisons
with other managers who have been forced to work with strong owners. In doing so, he tries to generalize and thereby "normalize" the
situation, in order to maintain his identity – "we all have to compromise sometimes, and it doesn't make me a worse person" – but in
the long term, of course, this risks undermining his self-esteem and

self-confidence, not least because his self-understanding is not confirmed by his co-workers. He loses their respect. One co-worker says:

> He [one of the owners] is slightly above both Benjamin and me. I've asked Benjamin who the hell actually makes the decisions, I mean, if he's the biggest shareholder, or he wants to call himself chairman of the board ... He isn't, but he acts as if he is, and you can't pretend he isn't there, either.

INTERVIEWER So in a critical situation, he's the one with the power?

> Yes, and I think that's when Benjamin gives in.

Another co-worker says, "It's obvious, he's had his wings clipped", meaning that Book does not protest but is far too weak. This is confirmed by yet another co-worker:

> Book is in a difficult situation. His problem is that his opinions don't count if the owners have a different view. If you're the company CEO, you shouldn't change your position every second minute. You shouldn't have people above you who intervene and change the decisions you've made. You can't just be a yes-man, that's no good.

Book is described here as weak and pliable in relation to the actors above him, a manager whose wings have been clipped, making it difficult for him to act as a manager, which in turn creates credibility problems. The comments above express a powerful expectation of the manager as someone who makes the decisions in questions of an overall nature, and then allows others to implement these, not someone who makes compromises and subordinates himself to the will of others in a way that makes him appear as a puppet. The added fact that he is also officially the CEO makes the problem worse, because he is perhaps expected to stand up for, or stick to, his decisions even more. In practice, he is reduced to a kind of middle manager and executor, as are many managers in the majority of organizations. His co-workers also say that Book involves himself too much in details, as in "He goes in and pokes around in too many small things", instead of being firm with the owners in strategic questions. Even Book himself says that he has a tendency to become too involved in operational matters at times, and that this makes it difficult for him to exercise real leadership, which is understood here as being focused on the overall parts of the business. On one occasion, before a meeting with his co-workers, Book told us that he was going to exercise leadership by talking about strategy and other overall circumstances. But strategies were barely mentioned at the meeting, and when we asked him afterwards how it had gone, he said:

> Well, there wasn't much leadership really, but we still had a good discussion about important matters in the company.

It is interesting to note that Book appears to think that practical tasks and activities which are close to the business – often administrative and operational – make it more difficult to exercise leadership. He appears to consider leadership as something which is, by definition, outside the everyday questions which affect the substantial business. Although these questions might be crucial for good outcomes, they are not considered to be part of strategy or leadership. Strategy and leadership are not seen as an integrated part of the ongoing business, but as something which you have to exercise and occupy yourself with outside the ongoing and daily activities.

We can also note here that Book often stresses that he is characterized by virtues such as honesty and reliability, although these are traits which his co-workers do not recognize in his behaviour, since he frequently adapts and subordinates himself to the interventions of the owners. This indicates a clear identity problem, observed in several of our managers, which gives us a reason to return to this theme.

The role of professional expert, and operating outside the core business

Another problem experienced in exercising management based on a leadership role is that managers often have difficulty liberating themselves from their role as professional expert. When managers are appointed, they frequently act in much the same way as they did previously. Manager C, for example, points out:

> Many former professionals continue to act in their old roles, even when they become managers, by intervening in questions of detail, and this is a problem. My project leaders are scientists, and they also want to get too involved in the details.

As we pointed out earlier, there are many organizations where it is considered essential for managers to have a professional background but to stay away from their co-workers' actual work as such and instead concentrate on overall managerial activities. The role of leader in particular is considered significant in this context. One of our secondary actors, Manager P, for example, answers the question of whether his subordinate manager should stay outside the lab:

> Yes, that's exactly it. We want them to decide long-term directions and strategies.

Many feel that managers who meddle by asking intrusive questions about a project are practising micromanagement, which is seen as a bad thing. Yet it is not always easy to maintain this distance, since, in their job, many adhere to a view of themselves as professional co-workers. And it is far from certain that "meddling" is a fair description. Some managers describe themselves first and foremost as professional experts such as scientists or engineers, and say that they would not have been able to lead the business if they did not have that professional experience:

> I'm still first and foremost a scientist. It's important for managers to identify themselves as scientists. If we left the science behind us, that would cause problems for my work. I need to understand how a scientist thinks and understand what contributes to innovations and make the best of that. My managerial role is not just something passive. I'm here to see the opportunities and make connections

which wouldn't be made otherwise. We have a proactive role.
(Manager P)

In many cases, it is easy for managers to get too involved and thereby do what many say it is essential to avoid (see Chapter 3). Another of our secondary actors, Manager N, says that co-workers often want him to get involved in operational questions to do with the project:

> Yes, they often want to hear my opinion and discuss the project, and I often stop and discuss fairly detailed questions with the scientists. You have to have enough knowledge to be able to handle any question at all that comes from your co-workers.

Several underline that their previous work with the actual core business has left its mark. This is, of course, not always negative. For many others, however, their view of their work is somewhat contradictory. On the one hand, it is important for them to "liberate" themselves from previous working roles and routines. On the other hand, they are sought out and easily drawn into discussions and work which is more similar to what they did in their role as professional expert than they perhaps think they should do in their managerial role. For Charlie Chase this is obvious:

> I work as a project leader in a main project, so I work as their coach. I also work with questions to do with work methods and processes, but still quite a lot in the role of specialist. I'm a sounding board for the project. I'm very activity oriented. Even if I try to be a bit more of a support, I'm involved and active in the project.

Chase describes himself here as activity oriented and deeply involved in various projects. Yet we could see in Chapter 3 that he was keen to distance himself from his expert role, which he considered almost as a dead end – he talked then about the importance of being able to leave the role of "technical gnome". We could also see in Chapter 4 that he described himself as being focused primarily on exercising leadership, as a result of his MBA education and the company's encouragement for managers to work with leadership, among other things. These claims to be a leader and exercise leadership are, as is apparent, not without problems. Chase has a long and successful background as an expert. He is considered by many – although not by himself – to be the best in his field in the company, and his technical knowledge is sought after. This means that Chase spends most of his time on technical questions and that in his interaction with his co-workers it is, above all, operational details which dominate, not the type of overall leadership with which he likes to identify. As in the case of Book, we see that the work is not about simply being an authentic leader and working with overall and long-term questions. He is drawn in to the substantial business and must consequently compromise his leadership ideal to match the reality he meets in the daily life of the organization.

As in the cases above, we can also observe here how a strong identification with the expert role is considered to conflict with the ideal of a managerial approach which focuses on strategic and overall questions. This implies that presence in the business practice cancels out or weakens the managerial work. However, it is also possible to make the opposite case: it is difficult to exercise leadership if you are not present and involved in the core business. This depends to some extent on the type of managerial work concerned but it is also about emphasis and approach: do you participate in the practical (operational) business or not, do you give too much time and attention to questions of direction and looking ahead? As a counter-argument to the idea that presence in the practice obstructs leadership, it can be contended that absence from the practice does just this. We observe that the majority of managers advocate absence from the practice as something of an ideal and that too much presence is the same as inadequate (or weakened) managerial work.

This situation may appear to be particularly critical in knowledge-intensive organizations, such as scientific or technically advanced R&D organizations, but it is also found in many other organizations, including public sector organizations, which we will now look at.

Leadership within or beyond the daily business?

One of our public services managers, Nora Noble, underlined the importance of external networks for her work with development and renewal. This was her "thing", unlike leading the daily administration, which she found boring. It was one reason she left a previous managerial job, which had also included some friction in a challenging environment:

> I'd definitely had enough of management in that particular local organization. I wasn't good for the clients and it was a demanding environment. I couldn't widen my perspectives any longer and I was tired of people. It was just a load of everyday hard work and I didn't feel I had the chance to widen my perspective and see the overall, long-term view.

The tough environment was one reason why she turned to other environments and organizations in the hope of working with what was closest to her heart: development and renewal. She also stresses the problem of working with uninitiated part-time politicians who barge into various matters with desires and demands which frequently turn most of what has been agreed upside down.

It is with regard to this that Noble says that the daily business is not something with which she feels comfortable. She derives no energy from it, and it does not fit her view of herself and her capacities. Instead, she tries to do things which are in line with her development and change-oriented identity.

Yet, at the same time, she must balance the development and networking roles with the routine demands of the business for documentation and managerial responsibility. As we mentioned earlier, these demands are an increasingly dominant element in the daily life of many managers. As one manager put it:

> You spend one half of the day working and the other half documenting what you've done.

Noble talks about administration and demands for documentation as a necessary evil and, unlike many others, can delegate the job to other people:

> But just writing the reports takes time. It doesn't bother me too much. I use other people to help me with most of it. I'm very aware of what I'm good at and what I'm not so good at. Actually, I'm pretty good at that too, but to be honest, I find it boring.

In other words, it is difficult to identify wholeheartedly with routine administration such as reporting and documentation, as opposed to development and renewal. Yet even if the latter sounds better than administration, development does involve a fair amount of administration. Development work is often at least as much about this as it is about pure creativity and new thinking. It often involves following and implementing new standards and routines. The content may not match the attractive ideals implied by words such as renewal and development. Noble may have stressed earlier that she can do most things when it comes to development, but in reality there are still many pitfalls:

> We're in a development phase with a new organizational structure, but I can see that it's not the best alternative for the citizens. I look over at my colleagues and think, "This isn't good at all", and can see we're being counterproductive with this structure. So we try to discuss it and find a solution, and it all goes well until we get to the question of resources. Then it's not so easy to find a solution any longer. And you can't tell other managers how they should allocate their resources. I think that's a bit harsh. It's difficult and inhibiting and gives rise to the odd swear word.

Limited resources and structural conditions limit the opportunities to make a difference as a manager, and inhibit leadership. This is no great surprise, but may well be something people do not take into account when they talk optimistically about the opportunities to exercise leadership through development and change. Noble, after all, describes her leadership as a question of gaining influence and says that people listen to her because she is a natural leader, in particular in the question of development and renewal. But when it comes to the opportunity for leadership, there is perhaps not such a great difference between the daily business and the work with development. We could perhaps say that the distinction between the activities in terms of opportunities to influence and make a difference is partly an illusion, which is not altogether unusual among many managers/leaders, as we will see (see also Grint 2005a). It may be more fun to work with development matters, and it is possible that people think they are better suited to that, in particular if the business itself is arduous, but the differences are perhaps not so great in terms of leadership. "Development projects" do, in fact, provide a certain platform for satisfaction, self-esteem and self-confidence, since the frame is more appealing, and when much of the work involves planning and other symbolic matters, you have a little more freedom, unlike when, as in Noble's case, you work directly with clients in public services, who can be difficult to deal with at times.

Strategist or janitor?

Many managers appear to be able to move reasonably freely between the ideas of working with strategic questions and leadership and then working mainly with administrative managerial work. But in some cases there is friction. We observed, in the case of Benjamin Book in particular, but also of Nora Noble, that having experience of different managerial roles can give rise to a feeling of tension between work situation and identity. There are also examples of slightly stronger clashes between ideals, based on who you see yourself to be, and reality. In Chapter 4, one of our central actors, Carol Courage, described the necessity of creating a common culture and overall approach in the managerial forums for which she was responsible. She also stressed this as an expression of her own style and personality. But the managerial work soon proved to be considerably more complicated, and Courage quickly found herself being forced into activities which forced out the overall questions, which she thought were the most important. After having been in her managerial position for some time, she says:

> I'm struggling with my role. I actually have three roles which I'm
> struggling with, and I can't see how they go together. One is as local
> site manager for infrastructure support to the research organization.
> That means the building, security questions, post office,
> telephones, paper, and so on. Then I'm also the internal and external
> representative for the local business. I'm also chair of the senior
> management team. And I'm struggling with these roles – I can't find
> a way to balance them. I think these roles will go down different
> paths in the future. I can't understand why the person who discusses
> business strategies also has to be the office cleaning manager.
> They're quite different roles. They have nothing in common.

Here, there are three aspects of management which Courage describes as three roles. First, she describes the managerial work involved in a specific job – site manager – in the organization, taking care of the infrastructure. This is a role which causes frustration and which leads to questions about what her position really is and what she herself stands for in all this. Second, she describes herself as a representative for her organization. This means having a representative and mediatory role *vis-à-vis* different stakeholders, a role which is given particular expression in the external relations, where Courage appears as the most senior manager. Third, she describes the role as chair of the senior management team – which Courage often calls the "strategic management team" – which she formed when she took up her managerial appointment. In this role, Courage wants to act as culture generator and change agent. This is the role she finds most meaningful. These three roles bring more than expectations of how she should act in different situations. They also mean different ways of seeing herself as a person and as a manager: as administrator, symbolic figure and cultural change agent, respectively. Since the roles pull her in different directions – high fragmentation – this also leads to different definitions of management and what it means to be a manager, and these are not fully compatible either with each other or with the aims which Courage, in this case, had for her work situation.

It is, perhaps, not surprising that Courage finds the role of operational manager, "site manager" – a managerial role which involves dealing with technical infrastructure such as IT support and maintenance of physical plants – the least appealing. It also involves the local implementation of shared group financial control and coordination systems, and regularly giving information about these at local level. This includes reporting the outcome of the local business and following up the control system to more senior managers in the organization. According to Courage, this is a role of manager as "janitor":

> If janitorial questions continue to take up most of my time then I won't stay in this position for long. I have twenty people who report to me, and that's too many, because they often send small problems up to me instead of dealing with them themselves. I have to deal with questions like where we should put up coat racks, and things like that.

The reader may feel no surprise that Courage finds this unsatisfactory, particularly given that the importance of managers exercising overall and visionary leadership is often stressed at group level in organizations. At the same time, these questions are typical managerial tasks. It is also in these questions that it is perhaps most evident that it is, in fact, possible to exercise leadership in the sense of influencing coworkers so that they see themselves and their tasks in a new light and act in a more well-considered way.

Leadership is not something which happens primarily– even though this is sometimes the case – on prearranged and much hyped ceremonial occasions, such as when some manager attempts to fire up the masses with an inspiring motivational speech or makes plans for a large-scale cultural change, but rather something which is accomplished in the daily work and as an integrated part of other managerial activities. In Courage's case, it is possible that attempting to influence the views the "coat rack co-workers" have of themselves and the job, and to make them more mature and independent, might help them improve their skills, which would allow Courage to release time for what she herself sees as more important tasks. It is, perhaps, strange that Courage sees the fact that small problems are sent up to her as a barrier rather than an opportunity to exercise leadership. As we saw earlier in the case of Benjamin Book, the latter is seen only with regard to the bigger questions, such as working with the whole, creating shared values throughout, and so on, not delegating and making people rethink in questions of initiative and taking responsibility. In many cases, leadership is turned into a clearly defined and grandiose activity, separated from the daily organizational processes.

We can also observe this phenomenon in Noble, who describes working with the big, overall questions as a way of "living leadership". She says, for example, that she wants to work with development questions and that the daily business is not her thing, because she does not feel that it matches her motivation and drive:

> I can't make it dynamic. As far as I'm concerned, there's no energy. I need to be where the action is. So something has to happen.
> Working with administration is too slow for me.

This illustrates how strongly many managers (and in some cases their subordinates too) are characterized by a view that leadership means working with very big, important questions: developing the organization, creating overall unity, working with "strategic issues", and so on. We can talk here about "grandiosity", an inclination to make leadership something really grand and exclusive, where unimportant little things such as ensuring that the work itself goes smoothly do not really count (Alvesson 2013a). Leadership which is about making people who work with administrative questions – "janitorial questions" – do their job properly becomes no more than a disturbance factor. But leading managers who are responsible for reception, cleaning services and other such tasks is just as much a question of leadership as is focusing on questions like company culture and long-term direction in meetings with more senior managers. When Noble talks about "where the action is", she is thus referring not to the actual core business but to some efforts to change. These rarely lead, however, to much in the form of practical activity (Alvesson & Sveningsson 2015). Yet the feeling that this – which is often fairly abstract and, for the business, peripheral – is "real leadership" appears to be fairly common.

We find a contrast to these individuals' view of leadership as something outside the everyday and actual core business in Henry Harding, who specifically emphasizes active participation and a strong presence in the work. He speaks out sharply against attempts to exercise leadership far from practice via talk about things which need to be changed. The meanings of "real" diverge.

*

To sum up, so far in this chapter we have described two problems. The first is that managers find it difficult to work as strategists and leaders; most of their work is operational and administrative, which they say does not match who they are and their values. They are forced into working with questions that are more fact oriented than they consider is appropriate given that they want to work more "strategically". This operational managerial work provides little or no identity confirmation. Second, managers find it difficult to liberate themselves from the professional role and are drawn in to details which many would prefer to stay away from. This, too, leads to problems in confirming the managerial identity and uncertainty about the importance and relevance of the managerial role. The expert role often dominates and undermines the managerial identity. Both these problems are about being forced into – or finding themselves in for other reasons – activities which are closer to the practice than they think matches their view of themselves and their actual skills. The managerial ideal clashes with the organizational reality, which leads to frustration and identity problems. What they do (are forced to do) is not in line with who they are (think they are). But the role as an understander of human nature and someone who likes people is also problematic.

UNDERSTANDER OF HUMAN NATURE – IDENTITY
REINFORCEMENT OR IDENTITY PROBLEM?

In Chapter 5, we showed that the majority of managers stress that they communicate with, listen to and build good relationships with their co-workers, at times beyond what is required for the business processes in a substantial sense. With regard to the managers' self-understanding, we can talk about managers as understanders of human nature, paragons of virtue and quasi-therapists. Much of that sounds good, and there is nothing to say you should not form your management based on this ideal, but in practice it is more complex and far less straightforward than it might sound. Many of our managers face constant dilemmas and challenges in their efforts to exercise the human-centred, good management.

One such circumstance concerns the dilemma between being forceful and decisive on the one hand, and cautious and confirming on the other. This is, of course, a balance which everyone has to find in their interaction with others. It is about getting your own way and having an influence over the direction and development, but at the same time accepting other people – a balance which involves negotiations, adjustments and compromises and which many managers feel requires them to go too far in adapting and constraining their own identity. In Chapter 3, we saw that our managers see themselves as natural leaders because they feel that they have a natural drive and ability to convince and influence people. Many of the traits and characteristics mentioned frequently appear as typical qualities in popular lists of what characterizes a leader; we referred to this in Chapter 2 as a variant of the trait theory. When asked why he wants to become a manager, Matt Mooney, for example, answered that he naturally enjoys being in charge – acting firmly and with integrity, as it might be described – and having control over what is happening. This is his managerial identity, and he says he feels good when he acts in this way, quite simply "taking command": "And being in charge makes me feel damn good." Nora Noble is another who has pointed out that she is someone who influences:

> When I talk, people listen. I have a natural ability to make other people listen and to influence them.

Stuart Smart also describes himself as a natural motivator, even when his own managers are present. When it comes to the management team meetings, for example, he points out:

> I take up a lot of space in these situations, I know I do. There are seven of us, but I take up more than a seventh.

Gerald Goodman and Steven Stone have also described themselves as communicative driving forces, one of the reasons they have found themselves with no alternative but to manage.

In this respect, it is a question of being the person who decides, leads, manages and controls by being oneself. As we have seen earlier, the managers talk about being themselves in strongly moral tones – they are true to themselves or, as they often put it, authentic. In contrast, we can, however, see that a big part of being someone who understands human nature is about trying to give others the opportunity to speak, listening, accepting and confirming other people's views and ideas. The last-mentioned means not being too forceful and enthusiastic, since this can make it harder for co-workers to voice their opinions and feel involved in decisions. There is then also a risk that your co-workers will not see you as a paragon of virtue (which can also mean that the confirmation of your identity as a good manager will not be forthcoming). Our main actor Stuart Smart describes himself as being not just strategy oriented but also someone who can listen and be sympathetic; the reader will perhaps remember that he described himself as someone who likes people in Chapter 5. However, it is not always easy to combine a natural role of driver with being a strong pro-people person:

> Sometimes I feel I need to rein in my motivational role there, because I really want to move things forward in discussions, to control discussions. But I rein it in. I don't always succeed. Some people might feel a bit left out.

Gerald Goodman from International Construction Ltd. repeatedly says that despite his nature and his managerial role, he is an altruist and tries to care about his co-workers, even though the roles appear to be difficult to reconcile:

> I can get really excited, but I've changed. Nowadays I say to myself: "You don't need to win every battle. Look at it from a long-term perspective, otherwise you might destroy this person, you might be wrong." I try to hold back. I have a problem with this, but I don't need to talk all the time. I'm active, but I can't be anything else. But maybe I don't need to talk all the time. But I'm competitive, and I have to remind myself to give other people time. I don't need to preach for ten minutes, even if I'm sure about something. I must let other people have time.

Goodman articulates the dilemma between expressing himself and being able to influence on the one hand, and allowing others to speak on the other, as a struggle. He manages to achieve this by reining in his natural self, by trying to set limits for his innate ability to influence, even though it means having to restrain himself. Here, consideration for other people sets the limits for how authentic he can be. The ideal of authenticity comes into conflict with other – at times superior – ideals, such as respect and consideration for others. The restraint in the interaction on Goodman's part coincides, of course, with a desire to appear as a good manager who listens, so that his co-workers will confirm his managerial identity and thereby reinforce his self-esteem.

Our main actor Steven Stone from Global Industrial Products Ltd. also points out the dilemma of combining the natural role of leader with seeing other people's needs for acknowledgement and recognition:

> I try to take it easy, but I can't. It's a question of what you do with your leadership so that you don't use it to dominate and take time from other people, because that's not good. I have to find a balance between taking up time myself and allowing others to do that – take up time when necessary and let it go when necessary. I end discussions to keep to time, and it feels terrible. Once I told myself not to say anything, not to be visible, not to exist and to let other people take centre stage. It was really tough, but I don't want to be the one who dominates and is the centre of attention.

Yet again we see the dilemma Goodman and Stone face in acting as understanders of human nature who like people by giving co-workers scope when they themselves are natural leaders. This ideal decrees that as manager you acknowledge others, but if you believe you are a natural and authentic leader, it is reasonable to take centre stage and receive a lot of attention. Acknowledging and listening to your co-workers is a fairly widespread leadership ideal today (Barbuto & Wheeler 2006). If you deviate from a leadership ideal which is seen as progressive and humanistic, you may be seen as a dominating manager and even, perhaps, as something of a loud-mouth, rather than as a modern leader. The confirmation of your ability and popularity may not be forthcoming, undermining your managerial identity and, of course, your base for having influence.

Another of our main actors, Matt Mooney, also says it is often difficult to combine what he calls the coaching role – in this case, listening and acknowledging – with his natural style as the forceful and more controlling manager:

I've coached previously and tried to listen to people but it's ridiculously easy to give people solutions when you're sitting talking to them. But one reflection is, of course, that you shouldn't give them the solutions; instead, you should coach each person based on their individual learning style.

Mooney says he finds it difficult to listen patiently to other people's opinions because he sees himself as someone who is impatient and wants to reach a quick decision – traits which risk rebounding on his possibility of accepting other people and improving his understanding of human nature and people skills:

> The biggest insight I got from the leadership development programme was that I'm impatient. And that I shouldn't in fact keep a check on my impatience but that I should express it. But I need to think about how I express it, how it appears to other people. Because when I lose patience, I start agitating. I repeat myself, I push hard and many people over the years – and I've had feedback about this – switch off. People stop listening when I talk too much and when I repeat myself.

Instead, Mooney points out that he needs to work on his communication skills:

> I need to reflect and listen. But I've got better at this by asking myself this question: "What were you thinking now?" Instead of questioning what other people say, I try to use other methods.

At the same time, it is difficult not to be sceptical and question other people, or be the one who is responsible for different questions. Mooney points out, among other things, that there are people in his organization who frequently blame all the problems on other people, which can make it difficult to be affirmative and take a positive approach to these people:

> Of course it's a challenge when you've got co-workers who are negative and always see problems and who always throw things

back at you and feel sorry for themselves. People who think that everything bad happens to them. And it's a challenge to deal with people like that. Some people have a limited arena and express a kind of integrity which makes it difficult to get inside them and win their confidence. In other words, there are people who feel sorry for themselves and say all the problems are dumped on them. The trouble is that I often fall into the trap of trying to help them instead of being straight with them and saying, "This is what it's actually about." But it's a trap which makes you feel incredibly bad. You're trying to do something positive, but somehow you're being cheated.

We can observe that it is often difficult to put the humanistic under-stander of human nature ideal (with a positive view of humanity) into practice in an imperfect reality – the ideal clashes yet again with the reality. It can even become a managerial trap in which it is easy to get caught and from which you can escape only if you abandon the ideal and instead practise its direct opposite: take full command, according to how you yourself see things as a manager and want things to be done.

According to Mooney, there are also a number of rather common organizational situations where you cannot simply show acceptance and give co-workers unconditional attention and sympathy. These concern first and foremost circumstances which disturb both the ongoing production of services and also major plans. They might involve points in time which are particularly difficult:

When we work with the budget and different kinds of planning, there are often clashes because people are involved in a lot of projects. And it can be a hassle, because people don't think they have time to do everything, and that in turn leads to a lot of people going off sick. These cases of sick leave are difficult because you don't really know if it's genuine. So then you get to the question of whether you need to bring in someone to cover for them, and that depends on whether people really are sick or not. That's the kind of circumstance which disturbs the production and upsets the plans.

Here, a certain scepticism towards the co-workers' ability, reliability and morals is expressed. It is not exactly the sympathetic and listening (quasi-)therapist who appears, but Mooney expresses a clear distance to the ideal of the people-loving understander of human nature. This is at least true of the popular and proper variant where positive action leads to positive response and the good, humanistic manager receives a response in the form of co-workers who do a good job. It can be a good idea to be the positive understander of human nature on occasion, as a kind of *impression management*, but it is perhaps not something which must always be taken in deadly earnest. People who are negative, who complain and cheat, do not perhaps deserve or attract the understanding humanistic leader. Authenticity here may instead mean KITA – kick in the ass – managerial supervision is an honest reaction. The understander of human nature ideal is certainly not unimportant for how you see yourself and may well contribute to reflection and consideration about how you act in different situations. At the same time, it is important to make sure that plans are followed and the daily business moves along as usual, which means that it is not always possible to spend time trying to get under people's skin in order to give them confirmation or develop them, or to be governed by considerations of what makes people feel good.

As we have seen, Mooney is not the only person who is struggling to build a coherent picture of himself as an authentic, naturally forceful manager and genuine friend of the co-workers. Gerald Goodman finds that his Mother Teresa ideal (which was mentioned in Chapter 5) clashes with some of what he practises:

> Seeing myself as Mother Teresa almost destroyed me because I didn't want anyone to feel bad. I'm sure some people see me as always being hard but they may have realized I've got other sides too. This has been useful in my contacts with other people.

We can observe that the clashes between being strong and forceful, on the one hand, and considerate and helpful, on the other, make it difficult to maintain a coherent picture of what you stand for as manager, which has negative consequences for self-view and self-esteem. Being a manager who sees yourself as a self-sacrificing nun is not without complications.

Steven Stone also describes the difficulties of handling different managerial ideals as a struggle:

> It's difficult for me to take a step back. I want to be active, but make an effort not to talk all the time. But at the same time, I was chosen for this job because of who I am, so I don't think I should change too much. It's idiotic for someone who wants to talk a lot to be quiet. You're expected to act in line with who you really are. I'm far too articulate and really try to hold myself back and not talk too much in all situations. But I was chosen because of who I am, and I'll never change completely. It wouldn't work.

Here it is more evident that the different ideals pull in different directions. On the one hand, managers are expected to act according to how controlling and motivating they see themselves to be in different situations. We can observe here a local expression of the heroic ideal of the grand leader who only acts in line with his natural traits. This is seen as reasonable and sensible, in line with an idea that some people are naturally suited to be leaders, so why should they hold back these natural leadership traits? On the other hand, as we have also been able to observe, they should also hold back much of the controlling and forceful behaviour in order to allow others, their co-workers, to be heard. The post-heroic ideal of the progressive manager who has a more listening and moderate style which allows the co-workers to be seen and heard speaks for the latter.

There is a tension between these two ideals – the forceful, authentic manager versus the post-heroic humanist. This varies somewhat depending on the significance the different ideals have for the managers. In one case, the contrast might be weak, or it might be possible to manoeuvre round it, for example if you are authentically non-forceful and find it natural to give your co-workers a lot of scope. It might also be the case that you have efficient, skilled co-workers who are in harmony with a good, humanistic manager. In other cases, this might be more difficult, for example if you think that co-workers who complain do not always have much to contribute, but deep down think that it would be good if you yourself were most visible, communicating effectively, did not have to listen so much and went on getting things done. But some managers might feel that behaving in this way (natural and authentic) is not good enough, and be forced to restrain or even fake their behaviour in order to appear as a good manager in the eyes of others, in particular their subordinates. Here, the conflict is a struggle which involves not just being torn between different general ideals, but also about how these ideals are expressed as behaviour and interpreted by co-workers in the manager's near environment, and how this complicates the work with one's own identity.

As we mentioned in our theory discussion in Chapter 2, there is much talk today about what is termed the personal leadership. The idea here is that managers should attempt to personify their management and allow their personal self to be directly expressed in their work. Instead of acting a role and pretending to be something you are fundamentally not, you should be true to yourself, or "be yourself", as it is so often called in popular contexts. This is also echoed by our managers, but proves to be anything but simple to express when reality creeps in. It is difficult to know which leg to stand on and which of these represents one's "true self". Attempting to craft a coherent idea of who you are – as a clear and stable self-view – and allow the authentic to form your work appears to be far from obvious or possible. The personalization of managerial work is, instead, something vague and complex which is constantly being developed, adjusted and compromised, depending on the situation in which you find yourself. The forming of practice and managerial identity is characterized by conflict, struggle and frustration. There is even a risk you will be destroyed, as Goodman puts it, with reference to his conflicting identification with Mother Teresa.

The double-edged blessing of ignorance – the manager as village idiot

A related form of identity problem is the difficulty of sustaining strong self-esteem as manager when you do not understand the core business. You might believe you understand people, yet find it difficult to make a correct assessment of what they do and achieve. We discussed earlier that managers distance themselves from the substantial work and instead spend time on more relations-oriented matters, possibly because of a greater disinterest in the business (when they make the transition from professional career to managerial career), but also because they do not understand the particulars of what they actually produce. Our main actor Bert Bacon described himself earlier as a facilitator and a kind of spokesperson between those formally in a subordinate position and superior managers. He stated that the managerial job is, paradoxically, not about knowing the particulars of the business but about focusing on co-workers' emotional difficulties. From an identity perspective, however, this is not without risk, even if – or perhaps even because – it happens to be the latest management trend. Bacon explains that he is sometimes seen as

> the village idiot – yes, I'm the village idiot in the sense that I don't understand the details of everything I talk about, but no one expects me to.

Bacon further points out that as the village idiot, or uninitiated manager, you always risk being taken advantage of by both superiors and subordinates in a way which weakens a stable and coherent self-esteem. Calling yourself a manager is generally seen as a privilege, but if it means that you are seen as being plain ignorant about the business, it can backfire:

> As manager, I'm not expected to know so much about the details in the technical work as people here do. Of course I trust them, but there are many situations where you feel that some people may be taking advantage of your lack of knowledge. Situations where I

think it's difficult to say I don't understand the situation or that it's difficult for me to assess whether they're right in certain questions. It makes me feel unsure, and this is reinforced by the fact that I don't get any feedback that I'm actually doing the right things.

Seeing yourself and being seen by those closest to you as the village idiot is a double-edged sword. It is possible that none of those closest to you expect you to be anything else in a technically specialist organization, but it can also be difficult to maintain status and self-esteem if you do not – at least sometimes – receive any confirmation that "village idiot" actually has a positive meaning, and that everyone agrees with that view. This problem is compounded by the lack of factual knowledge. A manager who does not understand the business he or she is responsible for is more dependent on clear confirmation of the leadership itself. The managerial work then becomes more diverse and less clearly defined than for a manager who has a good understanding of the technical and operational work. The knowledge authority is in itself a strong source of respect and can compensate for shortcomings in *people skills*. It should also be pointed out that a lack of insight into what people do can lead to co-workers taking advantage of this ignorance. Bacon experiences a serious lack of confirmation that what he is doing is right, and this contributes to his doubts about his work. This is developed further in the next chapter, where we focus more on the importance of feedback for identity and self-esteem.

Understanding human nature – genuine caring or management trick?

A dilemma for many managers is how far they can push the positive understander of human nature ideal. Benjamin Book says it is essential to be friendly and decent, acknowledging co-workers through various small gestures such as remembering names and special days and being a good listener. However, there are limits – you cannot listen to everything:

> You have to find the balance. When you've drilled through to the bottom of an organization, you see the problems. From having talked to editors and other people who sit and gossip behind each other's backs. So I tell them, "Now I'm getting out, because I can't listen to this anymore", but when I started as CEO I wanted to take full control over the organization and I've since realized that there's so much to do. And then you feel, when people come to you from lower levels and they're very open, they want to get things off their chest, but now ... I can't do it any more, I can't give them the time any more, and of course it doesn't feel right that I can't do that.

Here it is the view of the self as a person who listens and is accessible which is difficult to sustain. This is an identity which Book has painstakingly built up over a number of years and which has been confirmed by countless co-workers, in particular at the newspaper publishers where he used to work. However, carrying the picture of himself as a good friend over to the publishing firm where he is now the CEO has proved difficult:

> At first the employees didn't know what to make of me. Now things are more open and they dare to say what they think and make jokes. Now people feel they can joke with each other and give each other *nicknames* without any unpleasant consequences. They joke, and that's good as long as it's done in the right way. I'm comfortable with the fact that they can make jokes and be the object of jokes, in a positive way. The jokes shouldn't all be about the same person, because there's nothing positive in that, but I don't see that today, and we're closer now. But you always need to keep a certain distance, which can be difficult. Sometimes you're having fun, but then the situation suddenly changes when some people have to make more of an effort, and then you can't be a friend. This is obvious in salary negotiations, for example: they're on one side and we're on the other. I can't do something I don't agree with.

Here there is a dilemma between closeness and distance. The understanding human nature ideal is largely about building close personal relationships. It is important to get to know "the person" in the co-worker. This should contribute to the reciprocity and identity reinforcement in both directions: the manager gives attention and identity reinforcement and receives positive feedback and proof of his or her good management. Sometimes, however, the manager must be a manager, not a friend, as Book puts it, which can potentially undermine the relationship as friends and complicate the identity. This aspect of management, too, is presented by Book as being honest and direct, even though it is not in line with being a good listener and flexible and willing to take part in a kind of friendly relationship. We see here that being "authentic" can thus cover a great deal. It means being authentic, making jokes (but not too often!), being a friend, but also a manager who keeps your distance, demands more effort and negotiates salaries.

Treading the fine line between being a friend and being the manager is not easy. Even if Book has frequently pointed out that his behaviour normally leads to a respectful reciprocity between himself and his co-workers, the picture is at times less straightforward. Seeing yourself as a friend, and acting through simple everyday gestures, does not always produce the intended result and can even undermine credibility. One of Book's co-workers, whom we met earlier, says:

> He goes in and gets too involved. He runs round to all the co-workers and discusses everything and I think that's a bit dangerous both for him and for the company. He loses sight of the whole when he gets involved in everything. You have to have faith in your co-workers, as it were, and let them get on with it.

Another co-worker, whom we also met earlier, is critical of Book's behaviour:

> Benjamin is enthusiastic and progressive. But sometimes he goes too far. You hear him at meetings saying, "That's good, good, good",

and overdoing everything. It's become too routine. It's not him, it's just a way of expressing himself, there's no thought involved, it's over the top. The other day, he [Benjamin] lost his temper when a co-worker spoke out and said, "I'm not signing these papers with all these spelling mistakes again", and he went crazy because she'd marked lots of spelling mistakes. But the day after, he can go past her desk and say, "Hi, how are you doing?" and carry on like that. I don't think he's being sincere, when he told her she was stupid the day before.

Book's behaviour here is interpreted as being inconsistent, which leads to his co-workers questioning his intentions and the authenticity of his behaviour. We also remember from earlier in this chapter that Book was seen as having had his wings clipped in relation to the owners, something which contributed to undermining the picture of him as a CEO with a high degree of authority and authenticity. It is easy to talk about being authentic, but difficult to express it consistently in practice. Book himself is rather vague when he describes his behaviour in terms of management tricks to engage and motivate people in a number of more difficult questions, such as changes in the organization or even winding down the business.

Another of our main actors, David Dean, has had the same reactions from his co-workers. Dean is passionate about the coaching style of leadership but, unfortunately, his co-workers have come to view this style as false and manipulative since they realized that they do not have a say in questions to do with the core business, such as the school's expansion, the number of pupils, resources and other similar questions. Dean's insistence that his style is anti-authoritarian has been seen as something of a camouflage for the corporate management's strong demands for extensive adaption to fixed principles and frameworks and the reluctance to conduct discussions with lower levels within the organization. One of the teachers says:

You don't get an answer to your questions, either. We had endless discussions with Dean, and he always stressed our participation in the decision-making. But then, when Dean had burned himself out, we discovered that we hadn't been involved at all in the decisions about the number of students and other important questions. That makes you feel really betrayed.

As in the case of Book, we note that the manager's ideal and self-view are not confirmed by co-workers. Dean himself is in a tight spot here, since he understands that the teachers want to have the responsibility for a number of smaller resource matters to do with their specific needs. His co-workers, however, feel that they do not have any real power in important matters and instead want Dean to pursue these questions with senior management. The teachers appear to be less in need of an understander-of-human-nature-*cum*-therapist – which they see as a management trick, since Dean still does not seem very interested in what they have to say– and more in need of a spokesperson upwards. Paradoxically, Dean's strong identification with the coaching style of leadership makes it more difficult for him to be a coach, since this approach is unlikely to be successful if coaching is to be used as the solution to all the problems. If the manager's coaching efforts are to be credible, they must be combined with other forms of management. A certain critical distance to the preferred leadership ideals is therefore recommended. More about this follows in the next chapter.

CONCLUDING DISCUSSION

While our main interest in earlier chapters has been in how managers see themselves, what they stand for and how they act and achieve, in this chapter we have moved closer to what managers do in practice. We have sought to draw attention to discrepancies between managers' views of themselves and their ideals on the one hand, and what they actually do and what happens in an imperfect reality on the other. The interpretations, identity and values held by individuals are often believed to frame and form their practice, something which is particularly evident in popular talk about authentic and personal leadership (Avolio & Gardner 2005). Yet the reality is seldom so clear.

Self-view, values and ideals do not necessarily characterize behaviour. The latter may be mainly a response to expectations, demands and rewards, more than one's own identity and convictions. In our study, it is clear that the often idealized view that managers have of themselves and their efforts is in contrast to a reality – or their own shortcomings and confusions – which does not allow itself to be shaped by their expectations and aspirations.

The relationship between views and practice in management is often complicated and imprecise, and sometimes plain contradictory. In this chapter, we have addressed a number of topics based on this.

One such topic is the contrast between streamlined and almost textbook views of the leadership ideal associated with overall strategic and cultural questions and/or the exercising of positive influence on co-workers with the help of emotional intelligence, an understanding of human nature and noble values on the one hand, and the administrative and operational organizational reality on the other. Much of the managerial work involves administrative matters and establishing practical conditions in order for the business to work: questions which have an impact on recruitment, premises, budgets, form-filling, labour laws and IT. In the range of meetings they participate in, much is about subordination to organizational systems and their own managers, as well as coordination with colleagues, and it is not easy to exercise leadership in such a situation (even though it is, of course, sometimes possible to exercise leadership across formal hierarchies). A great deal of time in meetings is spent on activities where someone else, or perhaps no one, controls the agenda. Sometimes it may even be meetings' rituals which control – they get stuck on the details of conventions regarding things such as social intercourse. Some managers appear to move smoothly between conflicting views of what they work with: they advocate leadership ideals, but work with technical and administrative questions. Others see conflicts and frictions in the work: they see the administrative and the technical specialist work as frustrating deviations from, and barriers to, what they think they are naturally good at, and want to do. For some, like Stuart Smart, there is a clear discrepancy between talk and reality which contributes to a certain identity friction. For others, like Carol Courage, the question of whether the work is about being a cultural change agent or head janitor is distinctly painful.

Another theme is how other actors prevent our managers from living out their leadership. Benjamin Book, for example, is often outmanoeuvred and instructed by the company's owners, sometimes in direct conflict with his intentions and communication with his co-workers. Public services manager Nora Noble feels she is being controlled by ignorant politicians and the limitations of other units. David Dean finds himself caught in the crossfire between the corporate management's demand to implement set policies and the specified model for working methods, on the one hand, and co-worker demands for this model to be revised and for Dean to be their spokesperson rather than just senior management's lackey, on the other. Managers are often severely limited by both systems and actors, and in such a situation it can be difficult for them to express their own ideals and views. Managers often want to appear as leaders with followers, but closer inspection shows that this not infrequently gives a misleading picture – a picture which is unfortunately passed on in many studies, a large portion of the literature and many management training contexts.

A third theme is whether the manager – as exerciser of leadership – should be present in the practical work or remain at a distance from the core business. One ideal which is articulated by many managers is what we call absence from the practice: that is to say, you should maintain your managerial identity and not go back and be too much of the engineer or scientist, or whatever your professional background. Neither should you interfere in the work of individuals – this is interpreted as a lack of respect. The ideal becomes instead an interest in overall, long-term questions or in the well-being of co-workers. In this way you pad around on the outskirts of the productive work which (you hope) is being done. One alternative is to try, like Noble, to work only with development questions, which means you see less of the actual organizational practice. On the other hand, distancing yourself from the practice may be a virtue of necessity, at least if you are a manager who, like, say, Bert Bacon, does not fully understand what people do, which is common not least in organizations which are knowledge-intensive and technically/scientifically specialized. It could thus be claimed that absence from the practice has its disadvantages. Henry Harding illustrates presence as a leadership ideal. Showing an interest in and taking part in the core business, knowing what is happening and exercising leadership which has a significant bearing on productive behaviour and result may not be wrong. At the same time, the idea that the manager should represent something other than engineer, researcher, case handler, and so on, in the division of labour, and the problem of meddling, should not be overlooked. We do not take a stance on this, but believe that both extreme absence from the practice and extreme presence in the practice can be problematic. Many of the managers we studied appear to have a distinct preference for the former rather than the latter. At times this may be taken too far.

Throughout this chapter, we have also observed that many managers experience their environment's perception, encouragement, support and view of how they act as manager as central. We observed this earlier, in particular in Chapters 4 and 5. Even managers appear to find the need and desire for some kind of confirmation central. In the following chapter, we will examine this problem with the help of the concept of identity.

7 Feedback, ignorance and self-esteem

The ironic elements of managerial life

In the first chapter of the book, we talked about the diversity of managerial life. It is seen as attractive and influential, but also as complex, hard work, difficult to interpret and at times boring. The complexity and diversity have often been attributed to the large number of activities with often tenuous links, which generally creates a fairly fragmented managerial existence (see, for example, Carlson 1951; Mintzberg 1973; Tengblad 2012a). In contrast to this focus on the "exterior" aspects of the managerial work (functions, tasks), in this book we have taken an identity perspective and focused on the managers' "inner world": experiences, interpretations and creation of meaning. Above all, our aim has been to understand how managers in a changing, complex and diverse world attempt to shape a coherent self-view – identity – which can act as a relatively stable platform for their management and managerial work. Much of this has centred on two overall themes: on the one hand, strategy, cultural influence and other "big" questions, and on the other, relations-oriented questions to do with encouragement, confirmation and support.

Both these themes are potential points of departure in the creation of a managerial identity, but in the book we have shown that these sources are unreliable and unstable. It is difficult to create and sustain a stable, well-functioning managerial identity. The discrepancy between the ideal and the reality is, as has been shown, often striking.

Managers' relationships with co-workers are frequently complicated. Simple, clear-cut ideals and solutions rarely have the expected effect. On countless occasions in this book, we have pointed out that managers' identities are strongly relational. Traits, competence and performance mean relatively little in comparison with the ability to relate to other people. One important question is how important the relationships and the strong sensitivity are in making it possible to sustain a coherent managerial identity. What part do other people and conditions in their near environment really play in how people see themselves as managers? What importance do they attach to feedback from other people about what they say and do as managers, and what role does this feedback play in identity confirmation? What is the significance for the individual's managerial identity of leading complex businesses without fully understanding them?

In this chapter, one of the things we focus on is the importance of feedback in a broad sense: that is to say, how managers understand and reason about feedback from others. We point out, among other things, how an intense need for confirmation creates different dependency relationships between managers and co-workers on several levels. Cherished forms of leadership contribute to raising expectations and demands for confirmation. We begin the chapter by presenting different forms of feedback and thereafter critically discuss the importance of these for managers' identity and self-esteem. The feedback is then analysed with a touch of irony, against the background of the authenticity ideal cherished by our managers. Although they see themselves as natural leaders, their self-esteem is often strongly dependent on positive feedback. This is followed by a section showing how ignorance of the organization's core business can reinforce identity uncertainty, which is not always compensated by the ideal of absence from the practice. We end with a short concluding discussion. But first we address feedback and confirmation.

THE IMPORTANCE OF FEEDBACK AND CONFIRMATION

There is no question that human beings need feedback in order to function. Sometimes this is largely automatic: the woodcutter sees an instant result and the bus driver who avoids accidents and keeps to the timetable when conditions are normal has good reason to feel satisfaction. In "human interactive" contexts, the need for instant feedback is more varied: managers who see co-workers eagerly and admiringly awaiting their utterances can feel secure (unless appraisal interviews and salary reviews are due). Managers who see co-workers sigh, fall asleep or roll their eyes when they present the new vision probably understand that their leadership efforts have not met with approval. Yet co-workers may often sit and listen politely, and it is not easy to read the response behind a poker face. There is also often no form of instant, clear feedback. The response is often faked: they nod in agreement with the manager's words, but may not attach much importance to them, or may make jokes when the manager is not present. Our impression after many studies – including some of those reported in this book – is that managers and management are not always particularly knowledgeable about what is actually going on in their organizations (see, for example, Alvesson & Sveningsson 2015; Schaefer 2014). Studies of relations between leaders and co-workers have often shown that managers and subordinates do not evaluate the leadership relations in the same way (Cogliser et al. 2009). The manager's understanding of him or herself and the relationship is thus not always confirmed by others.[1]

Managerial work has no precise definition, and it can be difficult to determine whether or not you are doing a good job and what importance other people attach to your work. In particular, it has often been difficult to clearly discern the effects of the manager's actions, which contributes to a general uncertainty about the importance and actual status of the managerial work, not least leadership (Meindl et al. 1985; Pfeffer 1977). Although many people stress the central position and influence of the manager, this may be an

[1]   Organizations often use questionnaires where co-workers mark statements about the manager's leadership. Co-worker questionnaires are often less reliable as a basis for knowledge than research is, even though much research is too superficial and uncritical to provide much knowledge. Subordinates may suspect that what they write will have consequences and be careful to keep on the right side of the manager and therefore give positive evaluations. Sometimes they may want to "get their own back", for example after a conflict or an unsatisfactory salary conversation, and exaggerate the negative aspects. It is not easy to be seen as a good manager by a co-worker who is dissatisfied for some reason. Moreover, questionnaires are generally blunt instruments, and even when co-workers try to give good answers, there is significant doubt about the value of the description.

expression of a strong inclination to ascribe importance and causal effect to the manager, rather than a result of reliable observations and analyses of practical actions and the actual course of events within the organization.

We have seen in a number of cases how our managers have tried to reinforce the managerial work and managerial identity by forming special managerial and management teams comprising a carefully selected group of managers. Carol Courage formed a strategic management team made up of a selected group of managers with, as she put it, the aim of making them "feel like managers". The very use of the term strategic and the selection of a small group of people indicates to them (and to others) that they belong to a small group of particularly important people in the organization. Similarly, Benjamin Book formed a management team with a small number of managers when he joined the company, with the aim of reinforcing their managerial identity. Book talked about "giving them a bit of a boost": in other words, making them feel important. These are attempts to establish stronger ties among the managers as a group and between the managers and the company, and to raise the levels of motivation and commitment in the managerial work by confirming the managerial identity. Management training, too, is in many respects about this.

In this chapter, the main focus is on the type of feedback used to talk about oneself, for example formal or informal, and the importance of the feedback for the managerial work and identity. The latter normally varies from manager to manager, and they often use several different types of feedback which can, moreover, sometimes lead to conflicting and ambiguous results.

Based on our material, we believe four typical situations regarding feedback are worth noting:

(a) absence of feedback
  – from subordinates
  – from superiors

(b) negative feedback
(c) positive feedback
   – managerial dependence
   – mutual feedback and confirmation

(d) ambiguous or inconsistent feedback.

There are relatively few managers who find themselves unreservedly in any one of categories (a), (b) or (c). Everyone receives some feedback, however unclear: no one receives feedback which is entirely negative or positive, and no one can escape a certain degree of ambiguity or inconsistency. Nonetheless, in the majority of our cases, the over-riding impression is that one of these variants dominates. We stress central elements of non-forthcoming, negative, positive and inconsistent feedback in our managers' existence rather than place all the people we studied in one category.

ABSENCE OF FEEDBACK

The lack of (positive) feedback appears to be a big problem for many managers, in relation to both subordinates and superiors. In both cases, we see frustration and doubt. We begin with the relation to subordinates.

Absence of feedback from subordinates

In the previous chapter, we observed that Benjamin Book has problems with feedback in terms of confirmation in his new organization, Big Publishers Ltd. His approach as the decent, observant and present manager is not just a simple managerial recipe which can be repeated in any organizational environment; the confirmation of what he sees as his natural managerial identity is disappointing and inconsistent: decent, but not particularly genuine, and rather weak. The identity and image he built up at the newspaper publisher proved not to be something he could pack into his briefcase and take with him to his new workplace. It is easy to view identities and images as a result of personal character and traits, but it would be truer to say they are the result of situation-specific processes in which relations and interactions between people play a major role. Identity and image are thus a question of local constructions which are intimately interwoven with specific environments and actors (Watson 2008) rather than standardized and objective traits which have a similar influence and result independent of the environment. Let us listen to how Book experienced the situation when he arrived at the publishing firm:

> You get here and there's a computer, a chair, a desk. No secretary. They'd sent over the code [for the locks in the building]. Everyone was very pleasant. I get here and start asking people questions, but you don't really know them. Time passed, and I went down and spoke to some people, but the time passed slowly. At twelve I went down to the others, but they'd gone to lunch without me. So I stood there on my own and thought: "Is this how it's going to be?" I didn't even know what the routines for lunch were, where it was or how to pay for it. But then I went back, and sat there, and it was four thirty and then I drove home. I was fumbling around in the dark, and I didn't really know where to start. At first, when I went home, I'd think: "What the hell is this?" It really got to me. I was mentally exhausted when I got home, completely finished, but not because I'd been working too hard – on the contrary, I was working less than I ever had. I went from a world where I was king and could do as I pleased and had people to back me up, to a world where I had trouble finding someone to have lunch with me. If I could have stopped the world and gone back as if nothing had happened, I would have done.

This is a special situation, since it is at the beginning of his employment, but its severity gives a picture of the need for confirmation and the drastic effect when this is not satisfied. Many of us – and perhaps a surprising number of managers – are heavily dependent on confirmation from other people. Book expresses despair over its absence. From an existence as a central figure with constant positive feedback, he comes to a (temporarily) rather anonymous existence. Book indicates that he lost his way in this. When we meet him just after his arrival at the publishing firm, he talks a lot about his time at the newspaper publishers and how the people there saw him as a manager. He tells stories about how much he was appreciated and also gives an abundance of illustrations of the high esteem in which he was held by his co-workers. The narration itself is, of course, partly a therapeutic attempt to restore a portion of his self-esteem, but the stories illustrate the enormous significance of positive feedback from subordinates. Even though this is still partially absent when Book has been manager at the firm for some time, he stays in the organization and tries to re-establish his previous identity slowly but surely. However, this is difficult, and he receives a mixed reception among his co-workers; several are, as we saw earlier, somewhat sceptical. Book's attempt to be truly popular and persuade others of his personal qualities sometimes backfires, partly because he tries too hard.

Carol Courage also points out the problem of feedback from subordinates. She says that much of what she does is confidential and so people who complain that she does not do very much generally do not know very much about it:

> I try to persuade the senior management not to take decisions which will have a negative impact on our local unit. I put up a fight and put an incredible amount of working time into that. I have confidential discussions with the senior management which I can't talk about. Personally, it feels hard when people question what I do, it's heartbreaking. One of my colleagues says it's like working with HR questions – you do so much for people, but you can't talk about it. You can't say that someone is having a breakdown or that a manager had a drink problem, and I dealt with all that, and then some idiot goes and gossips. There are lots of things which take my time that I can't talk about. So when I get questions about dirt on the roof or what I really do, that really irritates me.

There is no gratitude in this world, as they say, and here we see an illustration of how hard work which receives no appreciation or recognition can lead to frustration and doubts about the value of what you are doing. The main problem here is that other people do not understand, but this rubs off on self-view. Doing the right things behind the scenes does not count for much if you do not receive recognition for your efforts.

In Book's case, confirmation is not forthcoming because people do not know who he is or what he stands for (that is, if he stands for anything at all). Even though some appreciate his social interest, many do not buy his claim to authenticity and humanity. This is not just an initial reaction, but one which persists (at least during the year or so in which we followed him). In Courage's case, confirmation is not forthcoming because no one really knows what she does (if, in fact, she does anything at all). In all these cases, we are looking at managers who have taken up their appointments relatively recently, which is why confirmation from co-workers is more important for them than for old dogs in their posts. Yet, our other managers also indicate a strong need for confirmation, although this is not aimed solely or primarily at subordinates. In general, the importance of confirmation from subordinates should not be underestimated; modern working and business life places great emphasis on being liked and receiving various forms of recognition from those around you. This is true not least for managers. It makes them feel better and more comfortable. In the long run, it also often means that their social and political position within the organization becomes stronger. The subordinates are therefore an important group, not only for senior managers, who can build a stronger power base vis-à-vis the board of directors and owners, but also for middle managers, who can strengthen their position vis-à-vis more senior managers and other colleagues. If subordinates speak well about you, if they are happy to fill in surveys about the atmosphere at work and their manager's leadership skills, and so on, with positive comments, you can easily build a reputation as a good manager and maybe a coming man (or woman), or at least increase the chances of keeping your job.

Absence of feedback from managers

Relations with superior managers are, of course, also significant. Bert Bacon points out that he does not receive the feedback which would give him a boost. In answer to our question of whether there is anything in his work that frustrates him, he says:

> The lack of feedback. It's killing me. It's absolute torture, I could scream. My previous work was seen as very successful, and I got a lot of positive feedback. The thing that gives me a kick is positive feedback from above and below, from customers and from superiors. Feedback from my team too. And I'm going through something of a drought in that respect. I get some good feedback from my co-workers, but there's no result from further up in the chain, no positive feedback. No one says: "Well done, Bacon, things seem to be going well, you're on top of things." But that's when you can see people getting excited – that's when I get my kick.

Bacon appears here to be almost desperate. The strong desire for feedback can also be linked to uncertainty about and diversity of the meaning of the managerial work – without external confirmation, it is difficult to know if what you are doing is right. It is not so much the respect and admiration of followers that is central in Bacon's case, but rather confirmation from his managers that he is doing the right thing and actually is a manager. It is almost as if the self dissolves because of the absence of strong, positive feedback. It is rather like an addict in strong and urgent need of a fix. But here it is praise and confirmation which eliminate the pain and give the "high" or even euphoria (kick).

Yet another of our main actors, Stuart Smart, wishes he had feedback in the form of recognition:

> If you make a suggestion here and the work you do ... I mean, you don't get any feedback about this from the managers above you, you don't get any recognition for what you're doing.

The absence of feedback here is a source of doubt and frustration. Smart says:

> I've had really strong doubts about myself. I have doubts because I often think that I don't get any recognition for the job I do. No one ever tells me I'm doing a good job. There's no feedback. No one says I'm doing anything particularly bad either, but you can tell by the atmosphere.

As with Bacon, we observe the absence of positive feedback – confirmation – which has repercussions for the view of the self as a person and a manager. In Chapter 3, we mentioned that one of our main actors, William White, felt he was "invisible" and not appreciated, which was the reason he wanted to try to become a manager. In his case, what he wanted was the confirmation that he was someone and something. Being seen and appreciated are the driving forces. Fundamentally, it is perhaps about the feeling of reconciling yourself and your existence. The environment's lack of generosity, lack of interest or inability to understand cause problems for a number of the people we studied, not only before but also after acquiring the managerial job.

The ironies of managerial life I – natural managers who need self-confirmation

The need for confirmation varies somewhat among the managers above, but it is evident in all cases. Benjamin Book has been experiencing an anonymous existence at the publishing firm for some time, David Dean, as we will see, feels after some time that he no longer has any legitimacy as a leader and Carol Courage feels dissatisfied because she receives no recognition for her toil with challenging personnel questions. In these cases, what they lack is the understanding, respect and admiration of their followers. For others, the problem lies with more senior levels. Bert Bacon says that the lack of feedback "is killing" him, and Stuart Smart is extremely frustrated by the fact that managers at higher levels are not confirming his good ideas and initiatives. As a result, they doubt themselves as managers and their self-esteem is shaky.

The need and search for confirmation illustrates that management is played out in a complexity of mutual relationships where self-view and self-esteem are at stake, perhaps more often than we think. Many of our managers see themselves as natural managers. They see managerial work – and in particular leadership – as a central part of their identity. Their ambition is to personify their position and form it according to their own self-view. When this is not confirmed by the environment, their identity and self-view as manager (leader) is rocked. This is one of the many ironies of managerial life: seeing yourself as an undisputed, natural leader – unable, in fact, to be anything but a manager (leader), if we are to believe several of those we studied – yet at the same time being strongly dependent on those around you for confirmation of this obvious, natural state of affairs. This points to a strong need for interpersonal reciprocity – you are something in relation to others. Yet, at the same time, this need for self-confirmation undermines the very idea of the naturally authentic leader, the strong leader who is governed by his or her inner traits and abilities. The relations and confirmation, the interaction with others in the organizational environment, are seen here to mean much more than the personal qualities of individuals. The claims to have strong, natural leadership traits do not appear to be entirely credible. It is ironic that so many of the managers who stress their distinct traits and that they are cut out for leadership are still, in the end, so sensitive to what co-workers – and sometimes superiors – think.

This overemphasis on the fundamental traits is perhaps not so strange given the dominance of the trait theory in business journals and pop-management literature, among leadership consultants and leadership developers – and even in western culture as a whole (Collins 2001). There is an overemphasis on the purely individual, yet we human beings are rarely so self-sufficient or strong. Our need for others to like and confirm us is strong. It may even be stronger than ever in a culture where it is essential to be flexible, to get on with

210 MANAGEMENT: IRONIES, LABYRINTHS AND PITFALLS

people and adapt in order to meet customer wishes, fashions and changing circumstances (Sennett 1998). Jan Wallander (2003), former CEO and chairman of the board at one of Sweden's largest and most successful banks and many other large companies, observed that executives are rarely as independent and strong as many would like to think, but are sensitive to trends and inclined to imitate others. The general inclination to imitate other organizations has been confirmed by a large amount of research (DiMaggio & Powell 1991). This culture, however, also encompasses the idea that people are unique, independent individuals with fixed personality traits and identities. Things are thus shaping up for a number of contradictions and confusions – and our managers show clear indications of this.

NEGATIVE FEEDBACK

Sometimes there is a clear dominance of negative feedback. The results can be noticeably negative, even if it is seldom obvious to what extent this is due to a particular manager. Parts of the environment may, however, make it clear that they see shortcomings.

David Dean at The School Ltd. receives strong negative feedback from his subordinates, the teachers at the school. We know from earlier that Dean sees himself as a coach or facilitator; he also describes himself as a consultative leader rather than a manager: "I'm less of a manager and decision-maker." In his view, the hallmark of management should be supporting and encouraging the staff, whom, Dean expects from, to take the initiative and make decisions. This form of coaching leadership is a style of management which, according to Dean, has been successful in other businesses he has led, for example as former manager for a service unit in a large financial services company. At The School Ltd., however, the coaching leadership style does not work as well. The teachers see little value in Dean's leadership style. As we mentioned in Chapter 6, they expect Dean instead to support them in their demands to senior management for more resources and to give them answers more often than coaching.

The teachers see Dean as a weak manager who fails (lacks the mandate) to give his co-workers any influence in major decisions. He finds himself on a collision course with the teachers, several of whom left The School Ltd. after a while (as did Dean himself, but more about that in the following chapter). One of the teachers, John, says of Dean's coaching style of leadership that "the coaching style didn't work at all". Another says:

> He didn't dare to make any decisions, partly because he was strictly controlled by the senior management. He had no chance to say or do what he wanted. He always said he would sleep on it, even in small questions.

Plain speaking indeed. The coaching style of leadership is rejected by his subordinates, thereby undermining his self-esteem – the good coach is, after all, what characterizes Dean's genuine nature. He talks about a leadership style which "crashed", and one might say that the leader crashes here too. It is also difficult to replace the coaching style with something else, and Dean does not want to try to pretend – to exercise impression management – to be someone he is not. His self-esteem is undermined to such an extent that Dean stops going to work and suffers a severe identity crisis (which we will develop in the next chapter).

Carol Courage is another who, in addition to the lack of feedback mentioned above, also received some negative confirmation of her managerial behaviour. The formal role as site manager at a research unit differs from her previous role as CEO, but in some ways Courage sees the job as site manager as an extension of the work of the previous CEO. She forms a strategic management team with the other senior (co-)managers with the explicit purpose of working with strategy and culture. She is determined to leave her old role as a project manager behind her and instead shape the unit's overall direction. She has the expressed support of the company management.

So far so good. Unfortunately, however, all these strategic and culture-oriented ambitions and activities do not come to much. Instead – as we saw in the previous chapter – she is frustrated by the fact that her superior managers constantly seek her out and check details of infrastructure issues (including the location of "coat hangers"). This takes time and energy from the strategic and culture-generating activities which she claims form the core of her true managerial work and identity. New forms of control with demands for increased reporting upwards are a further reason why Courage is forced to use various managerial forums to discuss administrative questions rather than strategies and organizational culture. The ambition to make managers feel like managers – in the sense of consummate leaders – is consequently somewhat diluted (as we saw in Chapter 4). Even though many in the so-called senior management team appear to regard IT, reporting systems, premises and other matters which affect much of the technical and physical coordination as important, Courage says that more comprehensive, central questions are marginalized. Thus, the feeling of being engaged in something big and meaningful is also absent.

The demand for details from superiors and subordinates provides negative confirmation of Courage as manager because she interprets it as meaning that she is being used for questions with which she does not identify. Other people's expectations of her role and her own identity diverge. At the same time, she receives no positive confirmation of the things she does identify with: strategy and culture. Neither do her immediate (co-)managers – who can be considered as equals since they do not have a responsibility to report to Courage (who is site manager) – confirm Courage as anything other than the person who is in charge of the infrastructure questions. One of these managers says:

> She doesn't actually have a mandate to lead anything. She is supposed to lead the buildings, the finances and the flower beds in the company grounds. She is supposed to lead the resources and the

buildings and salaries in general, but she is not supposed to lead any projects or work with performance management.

The situation is reminiscent of that of many middle managers, including those we met in Chapters 4 and 6, who are keen to describe their jobs in terms of strategy, but in practice work with operational matters.

Gerald Goodman and Steven Stone are two more managers who find it difficult to maintain self-esteem as a result of negative feedback. In Chapter 6, Goodman described the struggle to uphold self-esteem when co-workers see you as tough and loud rather than respectful and listening:

> I know that many people think I push too hard and get worked up in many meetings. It's no fun, and doesn't actually match who I am. Of course it's hard when people don't see who I am, and there are misunderstandings, of course, and that makes me doubt my role, because I don't want to be a bad manager.

We also find negative feedback in the case of Stuart Smart. Smart describes himself as a leader who wants to work with strategy and at the same time be an understanding friend. He also wants to combine this with the role of expert he often has as project leader. He stresses that he knows himself and knows what his special capabilities are, although this is not confirmed by his manager. Smart tells us:

> I know my strengths and weaknesses as a manager [the leadership roles of being strategically oriented and a good listener], but the funny thing was when I told my manager, whom I speak to in confidence. I said, "I've got a very good self-view, I can see myself objectively", and he said, "No one can do that, especially not you". And it was totally spontaneous, and he knows me well, so it made me think: "Have I got it completely wrong, am I so totally wrong?" He thinks I don't see where I fit into all this, that my self-view is wrong. I just don't understand it.

We can observe here that the negative feedback contributes to a strong feeling of doubt in his own ability and the feeling of having misunderstood the view of his own management.

The ironies of managerial life II – the ideal as a problem

We see a couple of ironies in the negative confirmations above. A strong conviction of having found their true place and direction in (the work) existence – the right leadership identity – is not confirmed by their environment. The strong belief in themselves as natural leaders expecting to do leadership appears almost as a trap.

This is most noticeable in the case of David Dean. "Coaching is the solution, what's the problem?" sums up his basic outlook, an approach which he says has been proven to work. Yet this is in brutal contrast to the views of those around him, who see coaching as irrelevant for dealing with major problems in the workplace. Sticking to this kind of leadership is devastating.

Carol Courage is another who has problems as a result of her leadership ideal, since it collides with her environment's expectations and demands. As we have mentioned earlier, Courage was picked out for leadership training in strategy and leadership early in her career. The job as site manager finally gave her the opportunity to start putting into practice much of what she had learned and to live up to the management team's expectations – or at least talk – of strategic leadership. That is her interpretation. At the same time, however, the organization is introducing changes towards greater micromanagement, transparency, standardization and centralization, increasingly common elements in conjunction with a major breakthrough in the desire to measure – balanced scorecards, documentation systems, and the like – at the end of the 1990s. In practice, this means that the site managers at Global Pharmaceuticals Ltd. are reduced to executors – who implement and follow up – of financial control systems and other administrative and operational processes which are outside the substantial research business. In her own eyes, Courage may be a strategist and culture creator, but these labels do not give a true picture of what she works with in practice, and some parts of her environment are irritated by too much talk of these. What is more, those around her are more interested in salary systems which work, premises which are clean and tidy and flower beds which are well maintained.

The managerial platform which Courage has acquired after a long career turns out to be an illusion – it looks good from a distance, but on closer inspection all the nice details disappear. The strategic cultural change agent finds that the demands and expectations of her environment are more in line with those of head janitor. It is flower beds rather than culture which are to be cultivated, say others who constantly come to Carol with what she sees as petty questions.

Many of our middle managers are in a similar situation. Cherished ideals which they have learned and which are praised in principle by those around them are not particularly sought after in practice. The delivery of things other than coaching, strategy and culture is seen as more important.

Leadership styles which have been carefully cultivated generate identity claims which the imperfect reality undermines. Sticking to ideals rather than bartering them by being flexible and opportunistic does not appear to be a winner in terms of identity – despite all the talk of the importance of integrity, consistency and clear values.

In the case of Stuart Smart, too, we see how his belief in the kind of person he is is punctured by his manager, who maintains that Smart's self-view is, despite tough competition, more inaccurate than most people's. Based on our study, we are inclined to agree with Smart's manager – our impression is that many managers' self-view is a little haphazard. We will return to how we can understand this.

POSITIVE FEEDBACK

We observe two variants of positive feedback: one which concerns each manager's dependence on their own managers for identity confirmation, and another which describes the mutual identity confirmation which can occur in the interaction between manager and co-worker.

The manager's symbolic significance for identity

The significance of positive feedback and confirmation is strongly expressed by Manager A from Global Pharmaceuticals Ltd. when he describes the relationship he had with his managers when he was promoted to a senior managerial post:

> You don't get to the higher positions in an organization by chance, and I have every confidence in my managers, Michael [immediate manager] and Daniel [senior manager of A's unit]. They give a lot of positive feedback and are less focused on finding fault and complaining. I appreciate that. I hadn't seen my most senior manager until quite recently. Then we had a meeting with all the newly appointed managers from all over the world. I saw Michael standing chatting with Daniel at the other end of the room, and suddenly I see the guy, Daniel, striding across the floor towards me and I just kind of freeze. Then he comes up to me and says: "I'm Daniel, and I understand you're A, and I've been talking to your manager, Michael", and then he said, "The job you've been given is one of the most important in my organization, and I've been talking to your manager, and I know you're the right person for the job". It only took him five seconds to say that, and I was weak at the knees – think how great it is to say that; instead of saying the competition was stiff and I'm glad you got it, saying the opposite: "I'm glad you want it."

Positive feedback gives a strong identity confirmation among senior managers too, as in this case. In the case above, the direct physical meeting between the most senior manager of the unit and the newly appointed manager, Manager A, is an almost euphoric experience for the latter. In less than five seconds he is transformed from stiff and exalted to soft and gratified. The senior manager's determined steps and focused gaze may have reinforced Manager A's willingness to adopt an admiring follower position (possibly a general tendency when we are approached by someone who has managerial pondus and in addition covers us with flattery), and it is difficult to ignore formal positions in contexts such as this. It is perhaps not so much *what* is said but *who* (in formal terms) says it which causes Manager A's reaction. We can add that managers in higher positions often acquire a certain charisma by virtue of the fact that they are at a considerable distance from the majority of co-workers, at least in larger organizations. A large, well-situated office, a high standard of dress, a secretary to control access, frequent business trips, meetings with even more senior managers, a certain skill in handling formal situations (addressing large groups), perceptions that people on higher levels must be really clever and special, among other things, mean that they are surrounded by a certain mysticism (Wolvén 2012). This helps to explain Manager A's reaction. The willingness to elevate his superior manager to the skies contributes to reinforcing the latter's position. And the more elevated his superior becomes, the more significant his confirmation of Manager A becomes for himself. The same is also true in reverse. Managers are apparently admired even more when they "give a lot of positive feedback and are less focused on finding fault and complaining". It becomes something of a society for mutual admiration.

From the example above, the first thing we can see is that managers can, sometimes with simple means, control the self-esteem and emotional satisfaction of lower managers. (Benjamin Book, however, appears to be less successful in this matter, not least as he is seen as being rather unsubtle and thereby not credible in his praise. We can compare him with Bert Bacon, who talked above about the absence of confirmation from his superiors as painful ("torture")). Second, we can see the strong emotions involved as an expression for a personal commitment to management. It is the whole person who is involved in this. The identity – and the feeling of coherent, strong self-esteem – are at stake in the interaction with the manager. Based on this we can, third, see a marked managerial dependence. A wrong move by the manager – even an apparently trivial one, such as the lack of a morning greeting – can make people feel uncomfortable for the entire working day and perhaps spend most of their time wondering what is wrong and what will happen next. Have I done something wrong? Am I about to lose my job? At the same time, this type of comment expresses a kind of managerial dependence which is often a little surprising, especially when there is no reason to be worried about keeping your position. In the example of Manager A, we see a fairly senior manager with many years of experience of independently leading different types of research activities. Yet the confirmation from a more senior manager is still experienced as almost euphoric and exhilarating.

One of our secondary actors, Manager Q at Financial Services Ltd., described how she usually asks her own manager to put in an appearance among the co-workers – both those with and without managerial status – at some point during the day, with the aim of boosting self-esteem, including that of her own manager. Visibility here does not mean getting involved in factual working matters but

> making an appearance and signalling presence just by saying hello and expressing general friendliness. I think this kind of thing is terribly important, and I know it means an awful lot to my co-workers, especially those who have managerial positions themselves. There have been times when people haven't been able to do any work for several hours because the manager hasn't acknowledged their presence and they don't feel they've been confirmed in any way.

This is about activities consisting of mainly professional co-workers – sometimes with slightly more managerial responsibility – with independent work and managerial tasks. More senior managers are, in other words, extremely important for the confirmation of many, even when this is not about purely factual questions. When William White first started at Advanced Technology Ltd., he made a presentation of his co-workers' work for his managers; he describes it as his first delivery:

My first delivery to my manager was to explain what my group works with. What the group is supposed to work with and what roles we need. The day I was going to make my presentation felt really good, because I knew that my group had prepared this presentation really thoroughly, they had seen it and they'd helped to write it. It felt really good to give an overall presentation of each group's area of responsibility. And it was great that I nailed it, because there I was, the manager, and I'd only been here for two months. I'm not sure you expect so much of a manager who's been with the company for two months.

Making a successful presentation for your manager is here a source of joy and confirmation. When Global Pharmaceuticals Ltd. hired a major consulting company to implement cost savings in connection with a change, they failed, according to several of those centrally involved, to implement the savings. One of the project leaders from a pharmaceutical company, however, Manager R, said that good presentations of the project to top managers were one reason they received confirmation of a job well done:

We'd done our part when we suggested what should be done, but our suggestions didn't turn out the way we expected. Things were watered down and there was a lot of discussion with the research units. Some things have been done, but not at all as much as we expected. You have to remember that the project was part of Global Pharmaceuticals Ltd.'s promise to their shareholders, to save money by making the organization more effective. But then it was all watered down, and I don't know what happened to all the billions that were going to be saved. But what has come out of it is, despite everything, the presentations we made for the company management in London. After we'd done that everyone thought it was an amazingly good project and well implemented, that much is clear.

Seen against the background of the project's ambitions, it would be easy to talk about a failed change project. Yet in taking their point of reference in the formal presentation to managers, the focus is moved from the actual outcome to the symbolic outcome and its importance for some key individuals involved. The project is deemed successful based on the quality of the presentations to top management and the importance the presentations had for the self-esteem of the managers involved. The top managers thought that it was a good project, and confirm the job and identity of the managers involved, and the actual weak result then becomes less important than the managers' praise (Alvesson & Sveningsson 2011). In this case, it is more important to receive praise from the superiors than to do a job you are satisfied with.

Feeling "damn good" – mutual identity confirmation

In the cases above, the focus is on the followers' (that is to say subordinate managers') feelings of satisfaction in interaction with their respective managers, but we also find something similar among our managers in relation to their respective subordinates. The therapeutic attention to the co-workers' well-being repays our managers with an identity reinforcement. The managers talk warmly about receiving positive feedback on their empathetic style and know that their co-workers like to be acknowledged. They say that their co-workers like them, which is particularly important since this is not about efficiency but is also a moral question: you should treat your co-workers well, which they confirm by liking you. Matt Mooney says his best managerial traits are empathy and an interest in people. He stresses that he knows that his co-workers appreciate this, and in Chapter 5 it emerged that the confirmation from his co-workers makes him "feel damn good". He also describes how this has helped him to develop:

> I know they like and appreciate it. It comes up in the co-worker surveys we carry out regularly to test the atmosphere in the organization. It's important for me and makes me a stronger person. It confirms that I work well with them.

The emotional dimension in the confirmation – that the relationship with co-workers should feel right – is also central for Benjamin Book, who had problems at the publishing firm because his immediate co-workers felt his wings had been clipped. As part of his attempt to strengthen his position in the company, he engages his co-workers in various activities, including a development day:

> It felt incredibly good on Thursday, we had a nice evening together. Developing the staff, an amazing day, that makes you feel strong. It's days like this that make it worthwhile. You get confirmation from the staff: "We've got a CEO we can trust, he knows what he's doing and it's good to have that kind of CEO. He's strong and gets things done, so we've got him to fall back on." It feels great to know that they've got confidence in you deep down. They know that I'm there for them – that's what I want to be known for. The most important thing for me is not to be a celebrity CEO, the most important thing is to feel this positive attitude from the staff. When it comes down to it, you want them to say: "He's someone you can respect, because he's honest, direct and you know where you are with him", that kind of feedback.

What is emphasized here is the reciprocity of the confirmation. The development day proved to be a strong source of identity reinforcement and improved self-esteem. The personal and, perhaps particularly, the emotional aspects of the relationships with co-workers were strengthened, which is said to benefit those involved. Managers who actively seek this identity reinforcement can, with apparently small means, enable their self-fulfilment. As we have seen earlier, however, several co-workers see Book in a different way to what he himself believes, which makes it all slightly tragicomic.

Another of our main actors, Nora Noble, feels that she has positive feedback from her co-workers in the sense that she feels she has their confidence and thereby the mandate to be their leader. She says in Chapter 3 that people do not question her when she speaks and that her co-workers have confidence in her ability as a manager and leader. This is partly a result of the fact that she is herself and is honest with her co-workers. She points out that she makes a point of "avoiding political games and secrecy", which helps to increase the confidence of her co-workers. Here there is reciprocity. What she gives her co-workers, she gets back through their confirmation of her leadership.

The ironies of managerial life III – everyday magic and therapeutic managerial cultures

The illustrations of Managers A and Q show the importance of positive feedback and confirmation even for supposedly independent and senior managers. With the help of everyday magic such as making yourself visible, greeting, exchanging glances and making small talk, managers can control and influence the self-esteem and well-being of managers and co-workers. We noted above all in Chapter 5 how they increasingly develop pictures of themselves as paragons of virtue and (quasi-)therapists and that social and emotional skills are given an increasingly central place. Against the background of the emergence of what is sometimes called the knowledge society, with its concept of increasingly qualified co-workers who demand independence and individualism, we might think it a little ironic that self-esteem and well-being appear, at least to some extent, to depend on acceptance and confirmation by senior managers in what might be considered rather petty ways.

The significance of this everyday magic has grown at a pace with the emergence of a therapeutic managerial culture in which emotional elements such as coaching are becoming increasingly stronger (Western 2008). This therapeutic managerial culture, which, moreover, also finds expression within a number of areas of society, is seen in our studies to have a crucial influence on how management is formed. We also see this in the case of the project leader – Manager R – and his presentation of the consulting project to his managers. It is not what is actually achieved that is important – it is more important to receive confirmation from your managers. A poor result seems to be less important than satisfying your managers. This is not just a question of the manager's approval being good for your career, salary or other typical material reward factors. Manager R retired soon after the project in question, so his managers' positive attitude to the project has a place in his psychological rather than his career account. Competence and tangible results are assigned less value than the fact that other, and in particular senior, managers are impressed and like you.

One important aspect of these everyday magical activities of managers is their reciprocal nature, in particular in relation to co-workers. The everyday magic is expected to contribute to reinforcing the manager's identity as the obvious authority in organizations (Sveningsson et al. 2009). The manager acknowledges co-workers and in return receives appreciation and approval. Matt Mooney experiences that his managerial identity is reinforced when his staff like the fact that he acknowledges them. Benjamin Book talks about how he actively works to make the staff confirm him as their trusted CEO, something which contributes to his identity reinforcement. The approval of the staff here represents a kind of tangible result of the managerial work. Even though it may not be clear what is in fact contributed, there is at least something tangible which you can point to and emphasize as being important: people's approval. Charlie Chase receives indications from co-workers that he is managerial material and wants to have this confirmed in turn by even more senior managers. (They do this to some extent through providing education and positions, etc., but this is undermined slightly by the way in which Henry Harding in particular turns to him in the daily work, where he is viewed as a technical expert.) Nora Noble offers confidence and honesty and in return is given the mandate to be a leader (and consequently manager) by her co-workers: at least this is how she sees it.

The irony in the spread of what we call *the therapeutic managerial culture* (which is said to contribute to renewal and development) is that in practice it risks leading to unfavourable dependencies – both emotional and, more, symbolic – which in the worst case lead to undermining the autonomy of both managers and other co-workers.

"The therapeutic manager" sounds progressive, and there may well be times when it is good to have social and emotional confirmation which contributes to people's well-being, but mutual confirmation also risks treating co-workers like children or turning everyone into pleasure addicts (Sveningsson & Blom 2011). This hardly helps to provide all-round feedback, including negative such, learning, development and renewal, which everyone today talks about as central competitive advantages for the majority of organizations – and also as a task for our managers. In these mutual confirmations, it is important for managers (and others) to remember that it is also about confirming someone who holds a position of power and resources which is formally superior. One might think that co-worker confirmation is, ironically, not at all about a particular *person* but about a particular *position*, which is often uncritically glorified. Even those managers who make an effort to personify their position often have strong support from the formal management. Meeting and receiving praise from the CEO is seen as something special – receiving it from someone else, even if it is someone who used to be the CEO or is very clever, does not count for quite as much. Co-workers accept people for the reason that they hold a managerial position on which they are dependent in various ways, not just for their income but also, and just as much, for confirmation and well-being in general terms. There is a certain charisma attached to the managerial post, in particular at higher levels. There is thus, as we could see above, a certain "laying on of hands effect" in managers' attempts to confirm co-workers: at least in the case of the managers studied.

AMBIGUOUS OR INCONSISTENT FEEDBACK

It is inevitable there will be some level of ambiguity in feedback and confirmation, except perhaps in the case of major stars and people who are completely inadequate. But sometimes the ambiguities are conspicuous as a result of strong inconsistencies and imprecision.

Several of our managers experience doubts and ambiguities as far as feedback is concerned. William White believes that he is the perfect example when it comes to being open and honest, but is unsure about whether his people see, understand, take in and value this. A work seminar where our main actor Charlie Chase's co-workers are to discuss his leadership begins with him leaving the room so they can discuss freely amongst themselves. The co-workers say that he is always very busy and they should perhaps suggest that he put a little time aside to be available to speak to people. When Chase comes back, he says that he is curious to hear what they have agreed and adds, perhaps to increase the likelihood of hearing something positive, that it is important for him to be present in his relations with his co-workers.

Ambiguities in the views of co-workers are perhaps even more evident in the case of Benjamin Book. Like the other managers in this study, Book feels managerial life is unclear, and this also applies to feedback. In general, he believes that confirmation, in particular that of his co-workers, is important, but at the same time he says it must feel right:

> The worst thing I can hear about me is "He's very nice". That's not a compliment, and it's not something that helps you develop. You might say to someone, "Great job, you've got the right idea, very good, great to hear". And if it's something you yourself also feel you did well, then that's OK, and that's the same for everyone. People need to be given confirmation.

And Book also receives some positive confirmation which reaffirms his self-esteem:

> My colleagues speak positively about me. Some of our customers talked to another company who'd said good things about me. They said that they wanted to develop their cooperation with us when I was appointed CEO. I met another company last week, and they didn't want to work for us before, but now they're interested and think we've got a good CEO. That's positive, this confirmation is not the same as sucking up to someone. In my opinion, the worst

thing is when they say you're good but don't mean it, when it's not genuine. I want to be seen as someone who is candid, reliable, honest.

Book emphasizes, perhaps most strongly of all those in our study, how important it is that feedback is sincere. Yet this is contradictory and even paradoxical, since Book is in some cases seen as not being genuine. His co-workers feel that he gives praise when it is not deserved, and see him as inconsistent and exaggerated in the way he acknowledges co-workers. Ironically, the manager who declares the importance of authenticity more than others is also the one who, more than many others, is seen as being false. At the same time, this is not a clash in the same way as the negative feedback which Dean in particular, but also Courage and Smart, encounter. Book and Chase say they receive good, positive feedback, but at the same time this cannot be said to be particularly clear or consistent.

The ironies of managerial life IV – managers dependent on authenticity

The discussion about confirmation is about the managers' person with regard to relations with, and sensitivity to, the views of others, even though the material work situation in itself also has a certain significance as a source of feedback. The strong subjective nature of the managerial work is essential for understanding the huge importance of confirmation. Instead of seeing management merely as a work role with more or less explicit expectations and mandates, you invest yourself and your identity in it. Management as a position in a hierarchical division of labour, on the basis of which you have to perform a number of activities instrumentally, is only a small part of what it is all about. To some extent it has always been this way – how the managerial role is interpreted depends on one's own interests, ambitions, background and identity – but in our modern society and its working life, it appears to be more common for managers to strive to form their work in a way which is more personal and charged with emotional meaning. Roles have become less something which stands between the self and the environment and more something which has fused the self and self-esteem (Sennett 1977). This is perhaps not true so much of routine work, jobs to which there is a certain distance, but more of jobs which involve career and status, where you can claim to do the job in line with your own self – and do not have to simply follow instructions or do role-playing.

In all our cases, this means that people attempt to breathe life into the managerial life with the help of leadership. This deviates from an earlier ideal of the manager who controls and leads through a high level of professional competence and where managers perhaps assigned less subjective, emotional meaning to all their actions or worried less about what people thought of them. Respect for the formal status went a long way. Today we are more sensitive to what other people think. Being disliked and unpopular can exact a heavy price. Within the management field there is a move away from the formal towards the intimate, from competence and respect towards approval and friendship.

Some of the ambition to personify management is both made easier and the result of a growing interest in what is sometimes summarized as *authentic leadership* (Avolio & Gardner 2005; Yammarino et al. 2008). Authentic in this context usually refers to (a) knowing yourself and your strengths, weaknesses, preferences, etc.; (b) acting and interacting with others in a way that corresponds to your true self and does not fake that self or pretend to be someone you are not; (c) having a balanced view of how others view you and valuing feedback from others objectively; and (d) following morally decent basic values in controlling your own self (Caza & Jackson 2011; Nyberg & Sveningsson 2014). Authentic here is a happy mixture of different ideals; self-knowledge does not necessarily mean acting in a genuine way, caring about how others see you or being essentially good. We do not, however, further examine the criticism of the concept here (see Alvesson & Sveningsson 2013), but note that the idea of authenticity is widely spread and is cherished by many managers.

What is important is to have personal core values which should not be compromised. Adapting to social and political conventions and norms is a deviation from the genuinely personal (Shamir & Eilam 2005). It means that you are playing a role rather than being yourself. Being authentic means constantly striving to be yourself, which we can see is expressed in the efforts to personify the managerial work. The opposite of these circumstances is often regarded as an expression of bad – false and non-authentic – management and leadership (Fairhurst 2007). Yet being oneself is rarely unambiguous, partly because the contemporary self is seldom unitary or consistent (Shotter & Gergen 1989). Managers' attempts to exercise authentic leadership are filled with conflict since it involves contradictory identity ideals (Nyberg & Sveningsson 2014).

The genuinely personal frequently proves to be ambiguous and is inadequate in stabilizing self-esteem. Despite describing themselves as natural managers, with the right managerial traits, many managers are unsure of whether they really are of the right calibre, and consequently seek approval from different people around them. More senior managers are important in this respect as they grant security and self-confidence, but the admiration and appreciation of other co-workers is also important for stabilizing the managerial identity. Here it is important that people see your authenticity so that it makes an impression. William White is unsure about whether his co-workers have in fact observed how open and honest he is. It is one thing to try to be so, another for your co-workers to see it and be influenced. It is possible that you may have to try even harder, but too much openness and honesty can be embarrassing.

There is a fair amount of irony in this. On the one hand, managers stress that they are natural leaders; they say they have the right qualities for the job and that it is these authentic traits which in effect guide them to the managerial job. They are people who have always got things done and set the agenda for others, which in itself indicates that they are not followers. On the other hand, these inner qualities they claim to possess do not work particularly well as a guide. They do not give enough security and stability in the managerial work, leading our managers to seek confirmation elsewhere. Yet this confirmation is frequently inadequate – it is not always sufficiently clear and strong for others to see you as a good manager or respond in the way expected. Self-esteem and managerial identity sometimes have more to gain from knowing that someone appreciates your decency or excellent PowerPoint presentations than your actual work results. The former is easier to assess and have an opinion on. This superficial and unreliable aspect of confirmation indicates uncertainty and fragility in the question of managerial identity. The ambiguities in the feedback indicate there are difficulties in preserving credibility in the aim for authenticity – it is not enough to (merely) be yourself and be good at what you do.

The overall impression from the managers' reasoning about different forms of feedback is that they are more dependent on other people for their self-esteem and self-view than was apparent in the idea of the personal and natural managerial work and in the authenticity formula for good leadership. Instead of being a naturally autonomous manager who gets things done relatively independently of local circumstances, they are strongly dependent on the confirmation from others for their identity stability and self-esteem. Identity is, in other words, something you must work on and struggle with in order to establish and sustain it, rather than something which comes naturally and which can be handled with small means. This is in contrast to the widespread belief that a natural ability for leadership brings unproblematic relations and automatic confirmation.

Understanding the importance of the natural traits for management and leadership – the trait theory, which we addressed in Chapter 2 – is a view of leadership which dominates today. This approach also has great impact in the media, among leadership consultants and in various leadership development contexts. However, the trait theory, and not least authentic leadership, are leading to the social and organizational cultural contexts becoming less relevant, and can be seen as a relatively naïve way of viewing leadership

(Alvesson & Sveningsson 2013; Ladkin & Taylor 2010). Managerial work and leadership is developed in interpersonal interaction where relations, interpretation, processes and situation-specific contexts are central. This is evident among all our managers, although Book and Dean are particularly illustrative. Both ignored the specific aspects of their new place of work when they assumed that previous recipes for success would work there too. Their personal convictions and approaches are not particularly successful – the outcome has more to do with the interpretations and response of those around them than their own traits. It is also ironic that both Book and Dean, who stress the aspect of having a good understanding of human nature, appear to have difficulty understanding how their co-workers think and respond. The ideals frequently take over and they are controlled by the map (such as praise and coaching as the means) rather than by the reality (local conditions and their co-workers' perceptions and frameworks for interpretation). When their co-workers want clear direction and managers who can act to meet their demands, this clashes with Book's and Dean's ideas that establishing a pleasant atmosphere and coaching respectively are the formulae for successful leadership.

Uncertain results as a part of the feedback problem

Feedback and confirmation have primarily been about the managers' aims to personify their management, and the overall approach and understanding human nature aspects in particular have been central. The emphasis when talking about the importance of feedback for self-esteem and self-view is primarily on the activities that are more distant from the practice. The reader may wonder if this is not also important when the manager works with activities which are both closer to the practice and more operational and administrative, and has a strong focus on the result. We know that people's self-esteem and identity are often linked to the outcome of their work. We mentioned the woodcutter and the bus driver at the beginning of this chapter; they see a tangible result of their work, which undoubtedly contributes to a certain self-esteem.

Yet, with an occasional exception – such as Henry Harding, as we will see later – self-esteem and self-view do not appear to be particularly strongly linked to the result. Put differently, the results of the work – deliveries, budget targets, productivity, quality metrics or other economic indicators – do not appear to represent such strong sources of a positive and coherent identity as do everyday magic and symbolic confirmations (even if the results influence the managers' identity work, as we will see above all in the next chapter). One reason for this is that results of units – which are highly dependent on complex networks of other units – are often difficult to determine and can seldom be linked directly to the manager. Many managers, ours included, belong to complex organizational contexts where what they do is intimately linked to the actions of others, making it difficult to establish their own contribution to a company's total result. Furthermore, in R&D and other development activities – where many of our managers are active – it often takes several years before it is possible to determine the success of a particular development project. There are so many units and individuals who are involved in different phases and who exercise mutual influence that it is not clear, to say the least, who should receive the credit or the blame for a particular outcome (Jackall 1988). What is more, things change all the time; people leave or change jobs, units are reorganized, competitors do something unexpected, economies rise and fall, and so on. Chance plays a big part. Only rarely do the results speak for themselves.

Yet what also emerges as important for the managers' identity work, alongside the everyday magic and symbolic confirmation, is the question of knowledge (or lack of knowledge) about the company's core business. Sometimes this becomes a problem which causes identity uncertainty, but sometimes it can also be seen as a useful background against which they can be confirmed as a good manager.

ABSENCE FROM THE PRACTICE AND IGNORANCE –
IDENTITY ANXIETY OR IDENTITY CONFIRMATION?

The difficulty of creating a coherent self-view with self-esteem is also partly associated with how you feel you understand the organization's core activities and the confirmation which can come from being directly and visibly involved in them. Many of our managers certainly emphasize absence from the practice as a moral ideal, but in some cases it is also a result of not having a clear understanding of the core business. This accentuates the feeling of uncertainty and complicates the question of gaining acceptance, legitimacy and confirmation of their management. The need for feedback, and the level of sensitivity, is undoubtedly greater and more complicated if you do not have a deep understanding of the business area for which you are responsible. Some of the acute need for confirmation we observed above can thus be related to the managers' lack of knowledge about the business. They fumble around, and become more dependent on other people telling them they are good enough. There are two aspects here. First, you cannot be sure whether or not you are doing a good job, which is why feedback is important. Second, you are more dependent on the goodwill of your co-workers – in theory, they can pull the wool over your eyes when you do not know what they are doing or cannot assess the result of the work particularly well – which is why their appreciation of you is important, since the inclination to cheat you will then probably decline.

Bert Bacon at International Foods Ltd. initially believed that the managerial role was synonymous with the person who knows most and best. Early in his career he watched "the smart people in suits and ties" and has wanted to become a manager ever since. But at the start of his managerial career, he felt he was only able to ask silly questions and play the role of village idiot – which was in stark contrast to his initial view. As a result, he felt vulnerable:

> This managerial role in logistics is really hard for me. I've read about
> cross-functional teams on the MBA, and that's what you want: a

new pair of eyes – or a hand grenade to wake people up, someone who asks the silly questions to make people think. But I find that really hard, because I feel I really am asking the silly questions. I really do feel stupid, that's hard for me. For me it's like rolling a big stone up a hill. If I let go, it will crush me. In my job, and with my lack of knowledge, I lack credibility. One of the people who works for me here has worked here for twenty-five years and is an expert. I came in as his boss to a job he thought he would get. Where's my credibility? They could easily pull the wool over my eyes. I trust them not to be dishonest, but it's not that easy, because I don't know anything and I accept that. It's one thing for the managers to put me in this position and say, "You're the hand grenade – it's your job to ask silly questions", but it's quite different for me, as the village idiot. I'm in charge, and people expect me to make decisions about things I know nothing about, so I'm anxious.

I think they know that I don't know much about the work. I ask really basic questions about what they're working with. And I'll go on doing so, certainly. In the past, I've done my job knowing that I had a very good understanding of the technical matters. And I've realized that it's incredibly difficult here, for two reasons. One is that I've come to a new product segment, new tools. The other is that the people in my group are the most knowledgeable you can work with as a software developer. It's extremely difficult to understand.

(William White)

White does not understand the experts' work and must therefore develop his "capacity to talk relationships", or else he will lose "legitimacy", as he puts it. Here the managers are looking for new grounds for authority and legitimacy bases – it is about seeking confirmation that you are actually doing the right things as a manager and thereby attempting to re-establish or preserve self-esteem in a managerial job which is vague and hard to understand. Modern approaches to management and leadership can contribute here with some edifying material, such as that the manager should avoid detail and instead be the person who makes the decisions in broader organizational and strategy questions. It is the more overall and indirect circumstances and people which are increasingly the focus in management literature. Much of this is, moreover, made a moral obligation: it is seen as a good thing if the manager stays away from the core business as much as possible and instead concentrates on the indirect coordination of visions, values and other things, and makes sure that people generally feel good, through coaching and so on. Lack of knowledge and absence from the practice need not, in other words, be a problem, but are morally correct. It keeps the inclination to micromanage in check.

Gary Gardener, who also works at Advanced Technology Ltd., is one of the managers who express a strong conviction that it is morally right to avoid focusing on detail:

> I'm a very proactive person with a strong personal integrity, which means I get irritated when my managers start poking around in details. I don't poke around in the details in what my co-workers do. I usually tell people not to send things to me to check, it's a waste of time. I don't look at the details, but more at the overall picture.

Many of our managers have expressed scepticism about the way their own managers at times get involved in details and the fact that they themselves are sometimes urged to spend time on details in a way which is similar to micromanagement. For the majority, this is, as we said in Chapter 4, a question of a moral stance which partly coincides with the kind of person they view themselves as. A good person (that is to say, oneself) does not poke around in details and get too involved, which is what the less good people tend to do – the latter lack respect and understanding for other people. Here we see an attempt to achieve a coherent managerial identity based on a moral conviction about the correct way to approach the work of co-workers. Ignorance regarding details of the business is acceptable. A number of modern views on management encourage and give support to this "ignorance" approach.

In order to reinforce the feeling that ignorance is the right way, Bert Bacon even stresses that it can be seen as an advantage if you are not an expert, since you do not then need to make the effort to appear to be substantially in command or pretentious:

> I try not to be presumptuous and pretend to know something I don't know. They accept me for that. Nobody thinks I'm the expert, which is fine.

Bacon is trying here to reduce ignorance as a source of uncertainty and instead make it a resource for building identity. Many of those in our study appear to be saying that a morally good manager is a (factually) ignorant manager. Bacon stresses, for example, his lack of technical expertise as something which clears the way for a style which is accepting and encouraging, rather than controlling:

> I see management as a discipline in itself. You don't need to be a technical expert to lead, you only need to be a good manager. That means you don't have to know about all the nuts and bolts – it's about making sure these nuts and bolts are well oiled. One of my strengths is that I'm not good at some parts of my work, and accept it. The business here is driven by teams, not individuals. I accept that and encourage people to get involved and perform better. If that's what my job is about, then I think I'm good at it. If my job is about being an expert then I'm terrible at my job. I do the things that match my strengths. They're the experts, and I'm there to coordinate them and give them the resources they need to do their job. I'm there because of my management skills.

Feedback and confirmation of ignorance in factual matters is here turned into something morally good, since demands and expectations concern other matters. This does not, however, prevent ignorance contributing to uncertainty and nervousness for many managers. As is indicated above, some talk about the importance of coaching and being a sounding board for their co-workers, while others talk about being open and supporting them more indirectly so that they can take

care of their tasks efficiently. They also say that a part of the managerial work is about daring to accept their ignorance in some areas. Yet
again, we can see how the therapeutic aspects of the managerial role
are being given increasing prominence among the majority of our
managers. But since this is so vague in terms of work performance
and, moreover, only works via individuals – not via work or results –
the feedback becomes extremely important for managers. They thus
become extremely sensitive to what other people think of them. The
therapeutic element is not only directed at the co-workers but also has
an effect on the managers themselves, who also need to be seen and
confirmed by co-workers and others for the sake of well-being and
identity.

One of our managers, Henry Harding, however, deviates from
this approach in that he sees presence in the practice as central for his
management. Like other managers, Harding is, of course, keen to
receive positive feedback, but in his case it is feedback regarding what
he has achieved in terms of results and outcomes, rather than how
much of a humanist he is. He appears rather insensitive to the views of
others (in which some find him authoritarian and self-centred). People
do not need to like you and think you are good at what you do for you to
have self-esteem and identity. This is clear in, among other things,
Harding's portrayal of his managerial career, which is, without exception, about the extremely difficult challenges he faces when he comes
to a new organization and how, thanks to his focus on action, he
overcomes most of them. More about this in the next chapter.

CONCLUDING DISCUSSION

Many managers in modern organizations often stress that they are
natural managers – they make their management something personal,
which they claim is a genuine expression of who they really are.
Leading, allocating and controlling the work is no longer enough.
The result is that the managerial work is charged with identity and
emotional content, which means that many managers are occupied
with what are almost quasi-therapeutic activities intended to

reinforce both their own self-esteem and also that of others. A central element in this is feedback and confirmation. Although the managers describe themselves as natural managers, this does not appear to be enough to create a stable and secure managerial identity. External confirmation is also required. Their own managers are particularly significant in this respect, but co-workers too are important for confirming that managers are good enough and are doing the right thing in terms of relationships. The managers themselves further stress that they are good at confirming others, and this makes them appear as decent and good managers. It is interesting to note that those around them are not at all as outstanding in this respect. Other managers are said to do micromanagement, to be asocial or pretend that they know things.

The significance of confirmation suggests that interaction, relationships and processes are more significant for how the management develops than is apparent in Chapter 3, where the managers instead stress their largely context-independent personal qualities. The latter are certainly not insignificant, but appear to be subordinate to the situation-bound circumstances. It is the confirmation of others that is a crucial basis for identity, rather than their own natural authenticity and the obviousness of their management/leadership ability which is associated with personality. It is, of course, ironic that managers who emphasize their person in terms of traits (and give the impression of heroic leadership, of making other people listen and follow) are so strongly dependent on others for their managerial identity.

Much of today's leadership literature is characterized by a quasi-therapeutic approach; there is a lot of talk about authentic leadership and daring to be yourself, about influencing other people's emotions, identification, self-confidence and well-being. We see in our cases above a strong personification of management in which it is precisely the emotional and personal aspects which have a prominent role. At the same time, the question of confirmation of their managerial work and thereby their own person becomes central.

This development is not without problems. Above all, there is a strong risk that different forms of managerial dependence are established or reinforced when the general message is that individuals are strongly dependent on being seen and confirmed by their manager, in much the same way as children are dependent on their parents. Since we talk here about personal and emotional relations, one might assume that co-workers' self-esteem and self-view are formed, in part, according to their manager's "everyday magic". A manager who does not say good morning, does not seem to listen or does not remember someone's name, consequently, risks sabotaging or undermining the self-esteem of co-workers, and this is unlikely to benefit either co-workers or organizations. Yet, if our self-esteem depends on the manager's ability to nod in our direction at the right time and to remember our birthday, we are perhaps making ourselves more vulnerable than necessary, in particular if we work with independent tasks. It can, in any case, not be discounted that all this care and confirmation which the "good" managers offer make it easy for people to develop a dependence. They may even suffer withdrawal symptoms if the manager does not massage their ego. At the same time, this does of course vary. It is also true that credible confirmation can take a long time to accomplish. A friendly greeting and a spontaneous pat on the back are not the same as feedback which is directed more specifically to what the person is or has accomplished. "Authenticity" may here include also critical feedback and can be rather demanding.

The managerial dependence reinforces managers' positions in a way that also makes managers, and in particular, perhaps, middle managers, vulnerable. They are almost forced into a quasi-therapeutic role (in part encouraged by management training). These, too, require some sort of identity confirmation. The manager gives of him or herself and acts as a therapist, but also wants confirmation of what he or she does, in particular since this is so uncertain and dependent on the right response. The unreliability of feedback should not be underestimated. People sometimes give the impression that something is good when they do not mean it. If people are friendly, they are friendly in return, yet this need not mean that they have been positively influenced, but may merely be a question of a superficial social game. In the worst case, a friendly and positive manager indicating genuine liking and positive feedback of a subordinate's performance may make it difficult for the latter to accept less positive feedback.

The quasi-therapeutic leadership ideal leads to strong mutual identity confirmation, in which both the manager and co-worker focus on how self-esteem can be upheld and reinforced by means of the relationship. The self and the identity become central in this context, since the emphasis on oneself must be made with authenticity and emotion. Many experts and practitioners in the field of leadership stress the importance of not playing a role or acting falsely and pretending to know more than you actually do. Ideals within learning and modern management involve opening up and becoming responsive, cognitively, emotionally and in your behaviour, to new ideas and suggestions, all to make yourself more flexible and useful and thereby able to keep up with the developments. The managers we have studied have taken this message on board. The authenticity ideal means there is a lot at stake.

For some people, the therapeutic aspect is no doubt something of a role-play to which they maintain some distance rather than take it seriously. They make sympathetic noises, but allow their thoughts to wander away from rather than towards the complaining co-worker in front of them. Yet many are undoubtedly more convinced of the importance of taking care of their people and find it more difficult to maintain a distance. Several of our managers appear to hold this view. If managers do not then receive confirmation of what they do, then it is possible that their own self-esteem and self-confidence will be damaged. They expect others to see that they are open, honest and being themselves, and this should be reflected in the form of obvious approval. This seeking out of positive feedback complicates the managerial work considerably. It is not at all certain that co-workers are as easily influenced as many managers and the majority of leadership literature would like to believe. For this reason it is often not easy to receive a strong response and confirmation. Most of us no doubt meet many people in our daily lives who seem to be open, honest and pleasant, and the question is whether these qualities are enough for a manager to achieve a clear leadership effect. For example, David Dean has opted for the listening (coaching) style, but fairly passive listening does not lead to anything, and his co-workers are infuriated. Less listening would probably have led to lower expectations and to Dean not being so strongly rejected.

In the following chapter we will continue with a close study of managers' experiences and work as they have been formulated in the last two chapters. A deeper and somewhat more critical study shows that it is definitely easier to talk about a leadership focused on strategy, humanism and moral authority than to make it work in practice in an often untidy organizational world, where operational and administrative tasks dominate and in which co-workers are not always so easy to please.

8 Managerial life and forms of identity work

We have so far addressed managers' views of themselves and what they do as managers – exercise leadership with some distinction – and shown that in practice they frequently deviate from this to some extent. The clarity of what they stand for and do, ideal as opposed to practice, is, as has been shown, not always the best. We will now intensify the discussion of the implications of this for identity. In the previous chapter, we dwelled on the importance of identity confirmation. Our managers' strong dependence on this means, ironically, that they do not at all appear as the authentic natural leaders they often present themselves as, and which often receive strong support in leadership literature, in particular popular such. In this chapter we continue the critical scrutiny of the consequences when the world does not always fit together in the way we think it does. One might say that in the best of worlds, ideal and reality go hand in hand: our self-view and our actions are in harmony. But as we can see, this is far from always being the case – and the managers we have studied are by no means exceptions. Contradictions, inconsistencies and confusion characterize the work situation and experiences of many of our managers. Managerial work is controlled by many different, contradictory and to some extent fragmented forces such as, for example, different ideals and role expectations, the demands of the environment and their own interests and ambitions (Clarke et al. 2009; Jackall 1988; Watson 2001). Managerial work is not about a number of clearly defined tasks to be performed in good order (Mintzberg 2009; Tengblad 2012b). The more precise significance of being a manager thereby becomes uncertain and varies greatly according to the context in which it is to be exercised. But what happens to the managerial identity (self-view) and self-esteem in such contexts?

Managerial life is not just about leading others; managers them-selves are subject to other people's attempts to control and regulate both managerial work and managerial identity (Sinclair 2011). This control is frequently experienced as frustrating, in the sense that it makes it more difficult to be a manager in the way desired. The personification of the managerial job and thereby the self-realization as a "natural" manager and leader is undermined.

The chapter begins with a brief reminder of the complex and challenging situation in which many of our managers live and which makes it difficult to maintain a stable self-view. This is followed by a section in which we describe five outcomes of attempts to maintain a positive and coherent managerial identity: identity adjustment, identity expression, identity juggling, identity wrestling and identity crash. We then discuss how managers deal with conflicts of identity using various mechanisms such as decoupling, fantasies and hopes for the future. In the closing summary, we present a critical résumé of these outcomes and mechanisms. We begin here with an in-depth discussion of what can cause problems in the managerial life.

CHALLENGES AND THREATS TO A POSITIVE SELF-VIEW

Many of the managers studied have a complex work context and difficulty obtaining an overview and feeling that they have control over both the organization's and their own situation or that they have good and reliable interaction with their co-workers. Many have a multitude of things to be done, not least when they are in a context of change.

Carol Courage's company, Global Pharmaceuticals Ltd., is in an intensive period of change, which is making her feel overwhelmed:

> There's an awful lot of information at the moment. There are balls flying in from all directions, and it's up to the individual to duck the small balls and catch the big ones and make something good out of them, but as an individual you're vulnerable at the moment.

Many people are trying to get her attention for things whose relevance is difficult to judge, and it is hard to juggle so many uncertain balls. Courage continues:

> Today anyone can throw a ball in. People without authority can suggest an initiative, and there's always someone who'll pick it up. But you have to be selective: What comes from the senior research manager and from my immediate manager? What's important and what's not important? As an individual you have to be very focused so you don't get lost, you have to know who you should listen to. I listen to my manager, I listen to the research manager, but not to anyone else.

Many managers have clear ideas about what they can do, what they believe in and what they value. They frequently fill this with a strong personal meaning – they are genuinely faithful to a managerial style that accurately expresses who they are. We have previously referred to this as attempting to personify management, in particular according to their understanding of what modern leadership is about. David Dean, Carol Courage and Benjamin Book, for example, have very clear ideas of who they are and what they want to do. However, the demands and views of their environments are not quite in line with these ideas, leading to major difficulties. Stuart Smart and William White share this experience, but to a lesser degree. We have also seen how Gerald Goodman does not believe that he can live up to the idea of the natural manager because it clashes with his environment's demands for a humanistic style of management. Gary Gardener points out that the low levels of integrity among his immediate managers play a part in his own irritation and frustration. For Matt Mooney, the friendly understander of human nature ideal clashes with the demands from senior management to follow plans and manage the daily machinery of the business. Steven Stone, too, experiences clashes between different ideals. In his case, the dilemma is whether he should give his co-workers the opportunity to speak or whether he himself – as the manager – should be the one to take command for the most part. Nora Noble is struggling with some friction between her managerial ideal and operational demands from the daily business activities. Bert Bacon is uncertain whether the positive understander of human nature ideal matches with what the organization actually needs and if he can trust his co-workers. William White is suffering from identity insecurity because of his own managers' inability to recognize his innate managerial potential. Both Henry Harding and Charlie Chase appear to be allowing the leadership ideal – the forceful role model in Harding's case and the good leader of people in Chase's – to take over the view of what happens in the interaction with co-workers in a way which makes communication with them more difficult. This type of friction between reality and ideal and/or between different ideals is not unusual, and their importance is accentuated considerably when the managers involved also identify strongly with one of the ideals in question – or even with the different ideals.

It is important here to point out that identities as "anchors in the existence" are not just about clarifying and stabilizing a self-understanding which then secures stability, clarity, security and direction once and for all (that is to say, within a period of time). Identities are not created in a vacuum but appear in social contexts, in relations and interaction with other people. Identity is a result of social processes, which work more or less without friction. An identity which has been developed and which then generates an inner security and direction in one particular work context can be a source of friction, conflict, confusion and even personal crisis and breakdown in another. Dean, Courage and Book all have previously confirmed identities to go on, but these have been developed in other contexts and they cannot simply be carried around like portable software programs which can be installed anywhere with the same result. Sometimes even individuals who have developed a strong, clear feeling of what kind of manager they are and what they believe in can find themselves in particular trouble, compared to individuals who are less convinced about their leadership identity. This is particularly pronounced in the cases of Courage, Dean and Book, who find that the changes in their work situation have resulted in previous harmony between their self-view and the expectations of those around them disappearing and being replaced by collisions and conflicts. Their sensitivity and flexibility appear to be limited. But what happens when a particular self-view does not lead to adjustment and harmony between the individual and the social situation? How is this experienced, and how does one deal with it? We will now attempt to answer these questions.

FIVE FORMS OF IDENTITY WORK

In this section we will intensify the discussion on friction and conflict by pointing to five typical situations or variants of identity work, of which two are characterized by some degree of harmony or moderate friction, while three are characterized by varying degrees of difficulty, which we describe as identity struggles. We then present three ways of dealing with the conflict and friction.

We should stress that we address here different types or variants of identity work and friction, and we use different people to illustrate our thoughts. This does not mean that the individuals in our study perfectly match a certain type. On the contrary, the majority display, at different times or in different respects, elements of several variants, not least over time, but they serve nonetheless as illustrations of the different types, which is why the main actors we have studied who appear below are used mainly to illustrate one particular type.

Today, it seems as though a manager who enjoys working with administration is required to justify this in some way. As has been shown, self-view – the identity – is challenged in almost all our cases, to varying degrees. Sometimes this is a question of minor discrepancies between self-understanding and the work situation and/or the signals from those around. But the identity often finds itself at odds in some way with the organizational situation, demands, expectations and other managerial ideals. The identity work which arises from a serious clash takes the form of an identity struggle. The managers must struggle to build a self-view which does not deviate or (in the long term) differ too much from the demands of the organizational machinery, other popular ideals or co-workers' interpretations of what a manager should be like. Alternatively, they can maintain a self-view which deviates, but in that case they must work hard to protect themselves from the disapproval of those around them. We do not address the cases where complete harmony prevails, which are, in all likelihood, rare. All the managers we studied in depth were characterized by tensions. In some cases, the friction is limited to minor elements, and we refer to this as identity adjustment. In other cases, the identity work is characterized more by reinforcing identity than by friction and conflict; we call this identity expression. We thus have two "positive" and three problematic forms of identity work:

- identity adjustment
- identity expression
- identity juggling
- identity wrestling
- identity crashing

The first two imply a certain degree of harmony, with a moderate adaption and active expression of identity, respectively. The third is not unproblematic but means that the individual just about manages to get by. The last two contain elements of struggle and friction: in the final variant the problems are insurmountable.

These identified (!) variants of different identity projects/ identity states are hardly mutually exclusive, but overlap or appear in (overlapping) sequence. In terms of process, for example, crashing and wrestling can supersede each other – unsuccessful wrestling leads to a crash, but the individual may be able to fight his or her way back or on to some new, different situation, for example from humanist to "cynical realist" or from manager to engineer (with previous managerial experience, rather like "scarred veteran" or "informal leader"). Juggling can become wrestling, and even crashing, if you are suddenly forced to do tasks which move you further away from the ideal identity. You might find yourself in a situation where, instead of having experienced a lengthy period of harmony, much of your time has to be spent working on cutbacks and redundancies, which raises doubts about who you are and what you can do without tying yourself up in knots and being forced to reassess your self-view. Below, we look at our cases, taking our starting point in their main forms of identity work.

Identity adjustment

Our modern existence is characterized by a multitude of relationships, demands for flexibility and a considerable degree of uncertainty (Knights & Willmott 1989; Sennett 1998). With the emergence of new kinds of work tasks, demands, relationships, situations and new ideals, there are only a lucky few who are not at times faced with challenges regarding how they see themselves, and forced to reassess. Not even when everything is constant over the years can we avoid the need to revise who we are: if you have had the same job for twenty years, there is the additional identity theme of ageing, or the lack of dynamics and change.

Managerial work contains a number of tasks which managers do not always like and which they might not work with, or be exposed to, in a perfect world, but they do them without it causing difficult identity problems. They might find some activities boring or even stupid, find it difficult to be subordinate to a particular manager, think that the organization feels too narrow, disagree with some policies or values. Some of this is "identity-neutral", which is to say that they do it without thinking about questions of self-view and personal meaning, while others are more "identity involving". The latter require a certain revision of self-view – or that they actively persuade themselves that "that's not me". They feel that they "must" assume a role, they see it as something temporary, and so on. Identity adjustment continues during a long period of working life, even for reasonably well-adjusted people. It can be frustrating and hard work, but goes relatively smoothly.

Matt Mooney illustrates this. We see here that the understander of human nature ideal contributes to the identity adjustment because he has to rein in – adjust – his natural leadership and not be the driving force who has solutions to all the problems, even though he sees that too as a part of his natural managerial identity. His managerial work is characterized by a desire to be the person who is in charge of what takes place in the business; it makes him feel good as a manager, and his managerial identity and self-esteem can be maintained and reinforced. However, this is a style of management which is to some extent challenged by the understander of human nature ideal, since he interprets it as meaning that he must rein in his naturalness. This leads to a certain tension regarding how he should see himself and his actions, and to some extent undermines an unequivocally positive managerial identity. The self-view of the leader as a driving force – the hero – is adjusted slightly to meet the understander of human nature ideal, which, as our managers see it, means also treating people well. Here the co-workers are a particular problem since they are, in Mooney's view, not capable of shouldering the responsibility that comes with the more "interactive" or care-oriented leadership, and instead throw questions back and assume a more marked position as followers. This complicates matters further and makes it difficult to stick rigidly to the ideals. As a result, Mooney at times sees the positive understander of human nature ideal as a problem, as something one finds oneself in, even though he knows he ought to have acted in a way which corresponds to his natural managerial style and leadership. In this case, the ideal guides the way he acts in the wrong direction – it is an ideal which sounds right and proper, but which at times reinforces problems and frustration.

It can also be difficult to express the positive understander of human nature ideal in a credible way if people do not demonstrate commitment and presence at times when the workload is high. Mooney wants to be a good humanistic manager, but if people go on sick leave to avoid working when things get a bit tough, this naturally makes it more difficult to practise effective management based on high ideals and a positive view of humanity. Self-view and a humanistic ideal must sometimes be revised. In general, however, this is a minor problem.

Identity expression

One of the main points we make in this book is that, in the majority of cases, identity work means some form of struggle to maintain a coherent and positive self-view. The desired managerial identity is experienced as being unattainable or undermined, which necessitates various forms of compromise. This is probably the most common scenario in modern-day organizations with their varying and contradictory demands and unreasonable ideals about the meaning of management.

Sometimes, however, it means allowing the identity to have a powerful impact on the organizational environment and making the workplace environment adapt to the identity, rather than, for the most part, the other way round. It is consequently not primarily about trying to revise, modify or adjust the identity (in an attempt to hold together an increasingly fragile self-view when the reality "demands" compliance with and adjustment to organizational and social norms), but rather about building and reinforcing the identity in an organizational context by allowing it to be expressed openly. There may be obvious sources of conflict with a high level of friction between self-view and organizational environment, but a strong and largely successful identity expression makes it possible to achieve a certain measure of harmony between self-view and reality. It goes without saying that everyone tries to express themselves in their work to some extent, but, in most cases, they end up in a fairly well-adjusted and predictable managerial ideal – such as the humanistic ideal and "working with overall questions" ideal, which we described in earlier chapters. Identity is then adapted to suit established managerial ideals and cautious forms of identity expression. "This is who

I am, but 'I' am like managers in general." The identity expression is then adapted to the situation. Some managers with a lot of self-confidence and clear ideas attempt to express themselves and their ideals more proactively. A charismatic person may sometimes tame their environment. (Steve Jobs at Apple is an example. See Isaacson (2012).) In these cases, it is not so much about adapting to the situation, but more about allowing one's own self-view to colour it.

Of our thirteen carefully studied managers this is most evident in the case of Henry Harding. Like many of the other managers, he sees himself as a natural, authentic manager, in terms of autonomy and independence. In his case, this means that he has the opportunity to make his mark on the organizational environment – through his work and interaction with colleagues – in a way which largely corresponds with his self-view. Rather than finding himself in an ongoing identity struggle, Harding believes that he can realize and express his identity in his work and in his relations with others. These feel that their opinions do not always count, but conflicts and opposition do not rock Harding's identity. It remains intact, at least during the time of our study, and is possibly even reinforced by difficult challenges, since Harding believes that the organization's ability to deal with these successfully is the result of his own efforts. Conflicts with people who in his opinion talk too much can reinforce his identity as a man of action. Here it is not a question of compromising the self-view, but rather of working for its impact and realization in order to achieve a result.

Unlike, for example, Courage and Book, Harding sees presence in the practice as the managerial ideal. Taking an active part and being engaged in the core business, finding out how projects are progressing and what is actually being achieved in what he sees as explicit results are central elements for Harding. He fulfils this through his close commitment to the practice and his active involvement in this.

> I support my co-workers by doing things. I don't go running around talking to the engineers but show them the way by actually doing

things which lead to market acceptance and us doing the right things. If you're going to change things you really have to do it, live it.

Harding acts as a substantial, engaged role model, rather than a strategist or therapist who is remote from the practice. We see here an attempt to reproduce the managerial identity based on a conviction that one's own actions are superior and can inspire others (see Chapters 4 and 5). Confirmation comes when you see that others act in a similar way and that you can then make an impact. In this respect, Harding differs from many of the other managers. In his case, it is the absence of active participation – distancing oneself from the practice – which can create identity crises and anxiety.

The challenges form the backdrop for his own heroic efforts. This is how he describes the situation when he arrived at Big Technology Ltd.:

> I was recruited by the CEO and found a disaster here. Big
> Technology Ltd. was a company without a strategy, without any
> planning, without a clear direction. A few vague desires for us to be
> a supplier, but we were nowhere near that. Development was in
> complete internal chaos. Our service was poor, we had no
> discipline, and we didn't have any real spirit in the company either.

The stories always end well, since Harding came to the rescue and saved the situation using unexpected and innovative behaviour. This is not uncommon in stories of authentic leadership (Sparrowe 2005). Harding has this to say about the development at Big Technology Ltd.:

> I've initiated a change process now which has led to a completely
> new way of working with developing systems and developing
> solutions. I've built a project organization that works well, and on
> my very first day here I started to get us on the right track and try to
> define how we're going to work. We're beginning to see the result of
> this now, and we're going to continue to work hard with this so we

have an even better project organization. That's what leads to a positive atmosphere.

The story gives Harding convincing (for himself) feedback on his contribution and confirms him as a successful manager. He does not feel that he is expected to act as an overall strategist or sophisticated understander of human nature, at least not in a way which gives rise to any great identity friction or identity struggle.

In summary, we see here identity work which takes the form of allowing the self-view and narrative of achievements to take centre stage. The idea is that by expressing his identity – in a clear and, for others, visible form – he shapes his environment. In terms of process, the friction between self-view and organizational environment may be significant – he meets a fair amount of hostility, since others see him as authoritarian, insensitive and inconsistent – yet this does not give rise to doubt and compromise, and his identity remains intact. This is supported by noticeable organizational results which are a consequence of Harding's identity expression and role model behaviour, according to his portrayal and self-understanding. This may not always be entirely accurate, but Harding's self-view appears to come out of it well, at least in the short term, despite the fact that that he is disliked by some of those in his environment. Since the core of the identity is practical activity and result, he differs from many of the other cases, who associate managerial identity more with talking and relationships. This latter group are strongly dependent on what others think, which leads to a certain vulnerability.

Identity juggling

Identity juggling is a mild form of identity struggle which is the result of a slight friction between self-view and the expectations and demands of the environment. There is a gap between what one does in the job, the work content, and how one sees oneself as a manager, the identity, but this does not always give rise to strong doubt, suffering or other experiences which lead to profuse identity work. Identity juggling can potentially lead to wrestling and crashing – it is difficult to keep your balance when you have a lot of balls in the air and feel you are making too many compromises in your view of yourself – but it can also be a question of something you live with and piece together for long periods of your working life. The working life often brings periods of time when you only just get by. You may feel that what you are doing is not what you want to do, you may brood over a difficult relationship with a co-worker, but it does not threaten the self-view in any radical sense. Even when the gap is (occasionally) bigger, it still does not cause any major identity crisis since it is dealt with in a way which ensures that wrestling and crashing are avoided. The friction is generally manageable, and it is possible to avoid a more serious identity struggle.

Some of our managers say that they only partially find expression or confirmation in the managerial role and its expectations and demands. Here there is a certain friction between the identity and the organizational demands and expectations, which gives rise to weaker forms of compromise which do not challenge the self-view too much. Nora Noble is interesting in this respect. She is responsible for, and works mainly with, the daily administration, but there are a number of reasons why she does not find this easy and at times sees it as a necessary evil. She is more interested in development projects and therefore finds it difficult to identify wholeheartedly with the daily administration – work which conflicts with her view of herself as a leader. It is not an extreme friction, and Noble does not formulate any drastic anti-identities (like Courage) or appear to be close to an identity-hostile situation, but there are elements of frustration associated with what she calls the role of official. A certain amount of compromise is inevitable but if the difficulties are reinforced there is a risk that the identity juggling will develop into more of a wrestling match.

Stuart Smart is another manager who experiences some friction between self-view – in this case associated with the view that he is the overall coordinator in the work context – and the expectations and perceptions of the organizational environment. He feels that his personality finds some expression in his work role – as the person who often takes overall charge and coordinates the work groups when it comes to what is to be done and why – but that he could take a much greater responsibility for the whole since he is more of a natural leader than his superior managers realize. There is little scope for this in his work. Now he must compromise somewhat with his identity – and operate on what is, in his opinion, too junior a level in the organization. When his manager challenges his self-view he finds himself doubting it.

We can also observe some identity juggling in Gardener's case. Gardener describes himself as an emotional person who can easily take over in meetings and control the discussion. He does not like this since there is a risk that he will be unable to live up to his integrity ideal of not micromanaging co-workers. Since he is very upset about the fact that his own managers micromanage and are unable to keep their moral integrity, it is important that he himself tries to be clear about this. But this is not always easy, since it is not only his own managers who are not entirely honest about what they do or want to do, but also some co-workers. This means that he is forced to compromise his integrity ideal and control to a greater extent than he would like. Gardener juggles a desire for clarity – he describes himself as a structural fascist – and the desire to demonstrate flexibility and be seen as a good human being.

To sum up, identity juggling is the mildest form of identity struggle. There is friction between self-view and environment, but it is, on the whole, manageable. This may be because much of what managers do corresponds well with the person they claim to be (Noble) – here there are elements of partial identity expression, even if the adjustment to various demands and restraints are part of the picture – or that they do not experience the difference between ideal and reality as particularly provocative (Smart, Noble). They may not do only what they would do in the best of worlds, but they still have a decent work situation. The self-view is not too challenged by doing things that do not fully match how they see themselves.

We can see a more dramatic struggle between ideal and practice in some of the managers who struggle to sustain the managerial ideal. We describe this as identity wrestling.

Identity wrestling

By identity wrestling, we mean the way in which the individual's self-view is only mildly confirmed by others or by their own achievements and is therefore in danger of being undermined. The individual is forced to engage in intensive identity work to maintain, repair, reinforce or revise the self-view in the light of what is, for them, an unfavourable social situation. The outcome of this can vary from the identity being maintained and reinforced – perhaps through sensible behaviour, the influence of others or a revised self-view – to the battle being lost and the identity crashing (which we address below), at least temporarily. But ongoing identity wrestling, with occasional victories, highs and lows, is perhaps most common, in a given work situation and for many people during large periods of their working lives. One major reason why identity wrestling endures in our time is the strong message sent out by changing pictures of ideals with regard to careers, titles, leadership ideas and other status indicators. We are living in a time in which different ideals of what is attractive are communicated, and there is a clear discrepancy between ideal and reality, which burdens many people's identity projects and self-esteem (Alvesson 2013a; Foley 2010).

Many of our managers can be understood in terms of identity wrestling. With regard to process, this is a medium-intensive struggle, at times characterized by strong doubt and uncertainty of the ideals and their significance for a positive managerial identity.

Charlie Chase is one of our identity wrestlers, albeit at the slightly milder end of the scale compared with those mentioned below, who have harder battles to fight. Chase aspires to be a leader who works with strategic planning and group dynamics, instead of being confined to the technical. However, his environment – co-workers, but above all managers – call on him as a technical specialist and force him back into the professional role. The situation gives rise to friction and subsequent frustration and identity wrestling. Chase feels that his professional freedom is hampered by having to compromise his self-view and frequently work on technical tasks, which weakens his picture of himself as a more personally engaged leader. In the long run, it is difficult to preserve a self-view which is not clearly confirmed by others. Chase finds himself in something of a straitjacket.

Wanting to be a friend may be commendable, but it frequently causes problems for our managers. Seeing yourself as someone who understands human nature, as a quasi-therapist and humanist, is not always compatible with some of the daily demands for productivity and delivery that go with management. The former is about making people feel good, but the normal demands the business makes on managers are more varied and not always focused solely on the satisfaction of employees. Management also, of course, involves making difficult decisions, controlling and monitoring business outcomes, setting priorities which sometimes disadvantage individuals or groups and at times winding down businesses. There are not many managers who have much to say about these circumstances or include them as a central part of how they see themselves as managers. They seem to deny or marginalize the subject. Instead, stressing that your heart is in the right place and you can help your co-workers to feel good offers more of a boost (for self-esteem). Yet sometimes less enjoyable tasks come up, as we will see below.

Something which poses an identity dilemma for some of our managers is the balance between being the driving force who takes command and being the person who holds back and allows others to speak – the latter being in line with the understander of human nature ideal.

For our managers Goodman and Stone, this appears to be a source of identity conflict. Both see themselves as strongly natural leaders in terms of drive, communication and the ability to persuade and motivate others. Both identify to some extent with a classic heroic leadership ideal. They are active and influence others, who take the position of followers. Yet Goodman and Stone also position themselves as listening and restrained, and allowing others to speak – the understander of human nature ideal, where you keep a lower profile. Combining these ideals – being a driving and a restraining force – is difficult for our managers. Some are able to juggle the positions and manoeuvre their way past problems relatively smoothly. This is common, but in the cases of Goodman and Stone, this conflict is strongly accentuated.

Gerald Goodman emphasizes how he fluctuates between conflicting ideals and demands regarding how he should act as a manager. On the one hand, he must live out himself and be the natural driving force in the interaction with others. On the other, he has a streak of Mother Teresa in him (as he himself puts it) and wants the morally good to find expression by allowing others some attention and the opportunity to speak. However, the latter means that Goodman is not able to express his proper and true self; he talks about how he almost destroyed himself when he tried to curb his authenticity. Here we see a moral struggle between ideals with completely different sides: to put it drastically – destroy or be destroyed. Both ideals – getting things done and paying attention to others – attract, but are mutual identity traps.

In Steven Stone's case, there is also a battle between these ideals – between being the person who naturally takes command, and being more reserved and less dominant. Stone suggests that his behaviour may be immoral because he feels terrible when he is too dominant. On the other hand it would not be right – indeed, it would be plain "idiotic" – if he did not act according to his personality – in his view he has, after all, been made a manager because of his personal traits. He must quite simply attempt to play the role of listener and understander of human nature on occasion, but not too often, since that is not the kind of person he is. Here the struggle is between what Stone understands to be a people-friendly managerial role and his natural self, between being "terrible" (not listening) or "idiotic" (not pushing), as he puts it.

We can thus note that managers who engage in interpersonal activity such as chatting with and listening to people find themselves wrestling with identity. It is not easy to separate identities, since they are at times experienced as being difficult to combine or mutually incompatible. Here the identity dilemma develops into an identity struggle in line with different ideals and values which are in part the result of how the managers see themselves as human beings, but also of incompatible external expectations and demands.

We find another form of this slightly milder wrestling in William White. White is, above all, wrestling with the fact that more senior managers do not realize his managerial potential. He works well with his immediate co-workers but feels ready for bigger and more strategic managerial questions. In White's words, he has an unused identity potential which is not being confirmed by his closest environment. Dissatisfaction with his managers' inability to actually see White's greatness – lack of confirmation in the form of, say, promotion – contributes to a certain identity uncertainty and the fact that he has so far been forced to compromise in his opportunities to influence the company's strategic efforts.

While the four individuals mentioned find themselves in light or middleweight variants of the wrestling, Bacon in particular – but perhaps also Book – are in the heavyweight class. The absence of feedback means that Bert Bacon is wrestling with severe doubts and uncertainty about the managerial existence, which he experiences at times as almost unbearable. Bacon stresses a leadership ideal based on ignorance, but this is a double-edged sword, since he does not feel that he can express it without at the same time losing credibility. In other words, he feels that he cannot form his leadership ideal (technically ignorant, managerially competent) since this would, somewhat paradoxically, risk weakening him as a manager. It becomes a struggle between the value of being open and having a general managerial knowledge, on the one hand, and the value of knowing what your co-workers are doing and being able to assess them correctly, on the other. The absence of feedback reinforces the feeling of compromise and of not really knowing which position to take.

We also see Benjamin Book significantly compromise his ideals when he moves into a new job. His style as both a strategist and an understander of human nature, which was previously appreciated, is met with mixed reactions in the new organizational environment. The identity as strategic leader and direct, honest person is undermined by the organizational circumstances which make Book look like a follower whose wings have been clipped. In his relationship with the owners, he is all too often forced to lie down and surrender, which undermines both his feeling of control over the organization and the respect of his co-workers. His identity as an understander of human nature is not confirmed by his new environment, and the chances of a positive managerial identity are rocked. From having been a much-loved leader, he is now forced to act in a way which paints a picture of him as a follower whose leadership is being called into question. With his co-workers, he must compromise his ideal of closeness and instead give in to the new job's demand for greater distance. There is a great deal of going backwards and forwards – where joking and informality and maintaining authority as CEO do not sit happily together. This results in strong contradictions and a lot of compromising, which in the long run risks weakening the (previously confirmed) managerial identity he has built up during his managerial career.

In conclusion, identity wrestling is a moderately serious form of the ongoing identity struggle. It is characterized by finding it more difficult to combine self-view with the demands, expectations and ideals of the organizations on occasion or for a longer period of time. This situation gives rise to dilemmas and identity conflicts. The compromising leads to self-views and ideals not always being sufficiently strong identity anchors in the working life. In terms of process, this is about a struggle characterized by doubt and uncertainty – it is not always obvious where to stand – and about separate ideals, but in consequence also, to a great extent, about the willingness to

compromise and (often enforced) flexibility in the identity positioning. The manager is more pragmatic, and more often seeks temporary
solutions to sources of conflict, although this makes identity stability
more difficult.

Identity crashing

In some cases, it is impossible to reconcile individuals' understanding
of themselves, their ideals and ambitions, on the one hand, and external demands, on the other, and the relationship between identity and
reality is filled with conflict. Sometimes the imperfect environment is
experienced as frustrating, yet self-view and self-esteem can be held
together reasonably successfully, perhaps by taking a strong cynical
position or seeing yourself as acting out a role. However, a strong
contrast between self-view and an environment which undermines
this often results in the identity being threatened with collapse. We
refer to this as crashing. It need not mean a finality, such as suicide or
early retirement, but it can be a sign that the identity creation failed
for a period of time, with the result that the sense of well-being is very
low. There is no positive link between the individual's self-view and
the content of the work.

Identity crashing may not be particularly common, but two of
our thirteen main cases are clear examples: Courage and Dean. When
we began the studies, they were very optimistic regarding their new
jobs, and both referred to previous positive careers which gave good
cause for confidence. In other words, we have not come into contact
with them via occupational health services or therapists. Our selection comprised managers who believed that they were successful in
their work, at least initially.

As we saw in the previous chapter, Carol Courage regards many
of her duties as having been forced upon her, dubious and alien to her
person and her abilities:

> Let me give you a really silly example. If someone asks me: "How
> many strands of hair do the people at Global Pharmaceuticals Ltd.

have?" I have to understand that the question is being asked out of pure madness. I can put an immense amount of time into discussing the task, but it doesn't give anything. I can also send the question out to the entire organization and cause chaos – or ignore it.

The example above is, of course, fictitious, illustrating Courage's experience of some aspects of her work and the business as rather surreal. She is presented with demands for detail which she does not see as meaningful in any way. She interprets these demands as an element of the job as janitor, which she describes as a strong anti-identity, that is to say something which is in sharp contrast to what she feels she ought to be working with in her managerial work. The job is, thus, essentially the complete antithesis of the person in question. At the same time, it is a high-level position, with several hundred subordinates, in which the holder is expected to be active, and Courage has had high expectations of self-fulfilment. (Routine jobs are often identity-neutral – feelings such as "I'm only working here to make some money" make the job less highly charged.) What is particularly interesting in this context is Courage's emotionally charged description of what she does *not* want to be as a manager, namely a janitor. It is thus not the case that it is easy to keep the self-view separate from what one is forced to do – which is often possible up to a point – but rather that work content and the expectations of others have direct and brutal repercussions for the identity. You could say that Courage to some extent defines what she is and wants to be by actively and emotionally saying what she is *not* or does *not* want to be. In other words, she constructs the situation as identity-hostile. There are many things we human beings are not, or do not want to be, but there are only a few of these which we actively use when we position ourselves (Dukerich et al. 1998). Even if we do not enjoy doing the washing up, we probably do it without making a fuss about it not being our job. By describing elements of the managerial job as janitorial, Courage indirectly creates a strongly value-charged and contrasting position which is intended to reinforce the picture of who she really is and what the managerial job should actually involve, namely the cultural and strategic questions.

The role of manager as janitor makes it more difficult for Courage to act as culture generator and strategist, which creates immense tension and frustration. Courage's role as representative for the organization in a number of external situations also causes frustration. Her external environment ascribes her a position as the most senior manager of the local organization (site manager), rather than a kind of head janitor. Here, too, expectations and work content clash. In this respect, the representative role contributes to increased fragmentation of the managerial job and further tension and frustration. The roles are not compatible, and the self-view is pulled in different directions: the external environment's expectations of Courage as top manager are in contrast to her experience of the job as (chief) janitor, and internal expectations which also incline towards the latter, if less clearly. She does not take the opportunity to influence culture on a small scale or to define operational questions as strategic – something which other managers often do (see, for example, Harding in Chapter 4). Rather, she herself actively generates antagonism, unlike almost all the others who evade, make excuses for or minimize contradictions in their work. The crash becomes at the same time a consequence of the inadequacies of the environment and of her own unwillingness to compromise in the way she acts and what she sees as natural managerial work.

We wrote earlier that Courage wanted to become a manager because she was eager to liberate herself from her previous professional role, which was seen as too narrow and not really "her". The previous professional role can here be seen as an identity trap. A trap means being forced or expected to identify with something which you feel you are not. By being forced into a role as janitor, however, Courage appears to have been caught in a new and more difficult identity trap, that of administration. In this trap, the identity is strongly marked but at the expense of not being confirmed by the reality. The existence becomes almost surreal – as suggested by

Courage's example of counting hairs. In this crazy world, the self-view is threatened by collapse.

Courage is not unique. School manager Dean also describes how he was trapped in a locked position where he was no longer able to communicate with his co-workers and the most important thing was to get by and deal with things administratively:

> Some time ago, when things were really bad, I wasn't getting anywhere and I couldn't find a way out. That was how it felt at work, and for the first time in my life I didn't want to get out of bed in the mornings. I couldn't get through to people any more, I wasn't communicating. The days at work didn't produce anything. My relationship with my colleagues was non-existent.

The feeling of being locked in a trap or labyrinth (not getting anywhere and having difficulty getting out) is obvious in this case.

The problem with the feeling of being locked in, or caught in an identity trap, which has been put forward by numerous managers, should be seen against the background of what appears to motivate many to make the leap into management, namely the opportunities to be a leader and exercise leadership, in other words to exert a positive influence on people.

Many of our managers describe themselves as natural managers who equate the personified management with self-fulfilment. When this does not produce the anticipated outcome, they become frustrated and lose interest. One problem for some of them is that their expectations are too high and their image of managerial work unrealistic, and that they are unable and/or unwilling to compromise and adapt to the work situations which lie far from the pictures of the ideal of attractive leadership presented in pop-management literature and leadership development programmes.

Dean is one example of the problems popular ideals and perceptions about management and leadership can cause. As we showed in the previous chapter, his strongly cherished coaching style was met with resistance among his subordinates, who instead made other demands on Dean, in particular that he should be their voice upwards in the organization. Like Courage, Dean found it difficult to change his expectations and way of working. His leadership had, after all, been successful in other contexts, so why would the coaching style, which had moreover been lauded in much of the literature on leadership and given a lot of attention by the majority of leadership developers, not work in a context such as a school? We can here note how a strong identification with coaching as a leadership style is an identity trap rather than a productive identity resource; the managers mentioned become stuck in a locked view of themselves and what they stand for, which makes it impossible for them to do the job in a way which satisfies their environment. We can note that many of the managers' strong faith in some of the ideas they advocate does little to help them exercise management sensibly. If anything, it makes it more difficult to understand the local circumstances and to develop management which is based on a greater understanding of the specific social context in which they operate.

In the cases of Courage and Dean, we note that they clearly have difficulty reconciling the demands for administrative management with the role of cultural change agent or leader. The contradictory demands can lead to identity conflicts, with devastating consequences.

Both cases accentuate the question of how much say you really have as the manager (Watson 2001). It is hard to tame your environment so they will follow the view of leadership you present. Courage gives an illustrative description of her managerial work in three distinct roles – janitor, representative and leader – where the first takes a different direction from the other two. In this case, the fragmentation helps to undermine the establishment of a more coherent interpretation of what managerial work involves. Mintzberg's (1973) ten managerial roles can be seen as a platform for an interesting and stimulating breadth and variation in the managerial work, but sometimes, as we have said, it all goes in completely different directions, and since less positive roles carry more weight, the fragmentation becomes a problem. In Dean's case, it is more a question of an inability to take on more than a single role – the role of coach – which causes problems for him.

In conclusion, identity crashing is the most serious form of struggle – or clash – between identity and the environment's demands, expectations and alternative managerial ideals. The identity crash is characterized by extreme friction – direct conflict – between self-view on the one hand and demands made by the organizational machinery and others on the other. In terms of process, the crashing is preceded by a high-intensive identity struggle which is characterized by a marked unwillingness to compromise and rigid identity positioning. The intensity of the struggle is partly a result of the managerial work and leadership being formed in deeply personal terms – such as authenticity – where compromises or revisions of self-view are seen as a personal betrayal of the ideals to which you hold fast. The situation constitutes an extreme source of conflict, from which exit (of some kind) appears to be the only way out.

*

To sum up, we have five forms of identity work with regard to the seriousness in the degree of identity outcome (see Table 8.1).

HANDLING MECHANISMS

Up to this point, we have described a number of identity positions and processes where the majority of our managers have had difficulty reconciling their self-view or their actions with their environment's response and interpretations in a well-integrated and consistent way. It is only in the case of Harding, and to some extent Mooney, that we can see any great degree of harmony, integration and relatively clear support for a particular course of action.[1] In other cases, the self-view is more uncertain and problematic, and it is rarely a question of acting explicitly in line with one's own identity in such a way as to draw applause from the outside world. The cases described show clearly that a great deal of

---

[1] In Harding's case, the harmony, as we have said, applies to his identity. With regard to his relations to others, there are certain signs of conflict, as some people think he is too authoritarian and ruthless.

Table 8.1 *Identity outcome in identity work*

Identity outcome	Identity element	Identity process
Identity adjustment	*Adaption*	*Minor compromise*
	Harmony	*Marginal friction*
		Manageable conflict
Identity expression	*Self-sufficiency*	*Unwillingness to*
	Making explicit	*compromise*
	Integration	*Low friction but*
		potential social
		conflict
Identity juggling	*Doubt/uncertainty*	*High willingness to*
	Low-intensive struggle	*compromise*
	Identity tension	*Pragmatism*
		Low-intensive friction
Identity wrestling	*Contradictory demands*	*Willingness to*
	Medium-intensive	*compromise*
	struggle	*Medium-intensive*
	Identity traps	*conflict*
	Some fragmentation	*Cracks*
Identity crash	*Anti-identity/strong*	*Unwillingness or*
	identity trap	*inability to*
	High-intensive struggle	*compromise*
	Disintegration	*High-intensive conflict*
		Extreme tension

identity work is often required in order to avoid cracks in the managerial identity project becoming all too noticeable. Three overlapping mechanisms to deal with this are worth pointing out (in addition to more drastic measures such as exiting, like Courage and Dean, by changing jobs or attempting to change your essential identity, for example with the help of new leadership concepts). These three are as follows:

- decoupling
- fantasies
- hopes for the future

As in the question of the five variants of identity processes and situations above, this is not a question of obviously separable or mutually exclusive possibilities. But this does not mean that demonstrating the different distinct elements is not justified.

Decoupling

Several of our managers try to separate their talk of themselves as leaders who exercise leadership from what they actually do as managers, the administrative and operational work, in an attempt to reduce identity conflicts and tensions. Leadership sounds attractive, but in reality is hard to realize. The attractiveness is one reason why people describe themselves as leaders in certain situations where this leadership can be confirmed and potentially appreciated by those around them and where they are not directly exposed to critical scrutiny. But they might not make such strong claims to be a leader in the workplace if they felt it would not be so strongly confirmed by co-workers and colleagues. So even if the positioning is determined and articulated, it appears to be controlled to a large degree by the context in which these claims are made. It is not uncommon for people to talk about their management as leadership with more senior managers, HR professionals and educators, and maybe with friends and acquaintances (and with researchers, journalists and others who do not always take the trouble to examine the circumstances more closely), but to focus largely on traditional work tasks when talking about their job with colleagues and immediate subordinates.

We often hear that companies and organizations want managers who are leaders, yet, at the same time, the administrative and operational demands are significant. All organizations, and large ones in particular, depend heavily on the smooth administration and implementation of the management team's decisions, and this is not exactly something which happens by itself, but rather which makes up a considerable portion of the managerial work. There are often clear demands to work with practical questions that concern setting salaries, furnishing rooms, budgets, IT systems and other more routine administrative questions. Carol Courage is far from unique. Managers frequently say they have little time over for other things, such as leadership in a more precise sense (Alvesson & Sveningsson 2003b; Kairos Futures/Tidningen Chef 2006). There is, of course, the occasional manager who claims to enjoy working with administration, but this is often expressed as something surprising and not a little odd. Not being a "bureaucrat" apparently makes you a leader with other qualities. Administration is, thus, a source of dis-identification for many people, and the administrator becomes an anti-identity. The problem is, of course, that so much of the behaviour matches this anti-identity, and, in Courage's case, she appears to feel, almost all of it.

Emphasizing that you are a leader who works with leadership undoubtedly appears to be a breach of style when you are toiling over budgets, sales figures or a new IT system, or discussing expenses with co-workers and superiors, in various interactions. At more senior levels in the company, these tasks are presented, at least sometimes, as matters managers should not spend too much time on since they mean you are getting involved in details – "micromanaging" – which you ought to let someone else take care of, although it is often not clear who. In practice, however, it is often central for the managerial work. Despite this, the managerial identity is fused with, even controlled by, ideas of leadership. Managers talk their way to a positive picture of themselves as leaders exercising leadership. They thus zigzag between sitting in meetings and working with budgets, IT, approving travelling expense claims, and so on, and occasionally doing some form of leadership activity – such as preaching values, lifting spirits or dealing with conflict – and see the latter as an essential part of the managerial work. Much of the practical managerial work is decoupled from the managerial identity as leader which they are trying to keep intact.

We noted earlier that Stuart Smart spends most of his time on practical managerial tasks to do with meetings. There are a number of overall questions to be dealt with, but his managerial work is dominated by questions of work schedules, detailed time management, mapping and planning project resources and other administrative activities which are directly linked to the execution of specific assignments and projects. His managerial identity, however, is strongly characterized by the leadership ideal; Smart frequently says that he works with more strategic questions, even though these form only a small part of his managerial work. Here there is a decoupling, or separation, of identities: saying you do something attractive – leadership – with which you identify strongly although you in fact work with something else – operational control – which is considered less attractive. This is common among our managers, and it was also expressed by, for example, Managers E and G in Chapter 4. Nora Noble is another of our managers who appears to decouple her identification with development questions from her main work with the daily business. It is the latter which takes up most of her time, but this is not something she wants to point out or identify with. Instead, she stresses leadership and development, even though they constitute a smaller part of her managerial work. Noble is handling the elements of friction in a way that means she will avoid the kind of crashing we saw in the cases of Courage and Dean. The administrative activities are kept at a certain distance from her identity; she says that they are something she conscientiously ticks off without getting too involved.

It can, however, be difficult to sustain a picture of yourself which is at odds with what you do in practice for a longer period of time. Such decoupling can eat away at identity and undermine self-esteem. It may not be easy to see yourself as a leader in your own eyes if you do not do something in line with your claims and receive some confirmation from co-workers. Yet, on the whole, the element of friction is handled by the flexible and well-adjusted managers above in a somewhat vague and problematic way. Managers move between claims to leadership with a capital L and working with operational and administrative questions. They stress that by being open and honest, acknowledging people and spreading a pleasant atmosphere, they have a positive influence on people and thereby work with leadership. This type of behaviour gives the impression of bridging the contradiction and managing the decoupling.

While the decoupling managers succeed in keeping different themes separate, Courage does the opposite. She brings them together, with something of a bang. The administrative main tasks become a destructive main act – possibly mobilized as an expression for an authenticity, clear-sightedness and unwillingness to compromise which is not commonly found among managers. Courage is definitively not the type of person to be a janitor.

Fantasy-filled claims to the leader identity

A second handling mechanism in identity work is to deny any contradictions, inconsistencies and fragmentation and allow a fantasy-filled emphasis on leadership to form the core of your self-view, thereby allowing fantasy to dominate your view of what you do as a manager. The job and situations are constructed as leadership, despite the absence of clear leadership actions. This leadership construction controls your world view, although there is little evidence that it is anchored in reality. This may sound worrying, but it is an aspect of today's social culture, where everything is given grandiose overtones – we choose consistently positive and "reality-enhancing" connotations. If, as a manager, you believe that you are naturally endowed with the right leadership qualities (such as listening and making people feel good), it is easy to read leadership into much of what you do. When you believe that what you are dong is leadership, then that is what you see: managerial work becomes leadership, talking to someone becomes coaching, listening becomes developing people, all manner of tasks are described as strategic (we have, for example, strategic planning, strategic HRM, strategic communication and strategic competence development) (Alvesson 2013a).

We saw above how some of the managers have difficulty decoupling from the professional role. They wrestle and juggle in their effort to exercise leadership and work with overall questions, but are often thrown in to tasks in which they act as professional co-workers rather than managers and leaders. If, for example, you observe, as we have done, Charlie Chase and his interaction with his subordinates, it is hard to find any clear expressions of leadership in the way he says it is exercised. The interaction is characterized by a focus on practical work tasks and questions to do with the division of labour and project tasks. It is hard to see any sign of a leadership in which stimulating utterances take co-workers to new mental and emotional heights. Chase's understanding of his leadership contains certain elements of fantasy.

In the case of Stuart Smart, too, we can see some differences between the way in which he describes himself and how his immediate environment sees him. The negative feedback from his immediate manager contributes to a strong feeling of doubt, and Smart wonders if he is living with an erroneous self-view; the latter is something which can be likened to a fantasy product. Like Chase, he identifies with attractive leadership, but there is little evidence of this in his interaction with other co-workers, and the absence of confirmation reinforces the feeling that Smart perhaps does not work as much with leadership as he claims, or have such accurate self-insight about his strengths as he believes.

Based on the response and interpretations of co-workers, we can also note a number of fantasy elements in the way Henry Harding forms his management. In Harding's case, these are not related to the popular views of leadership – strategies, visions and an empathetic approach to people – which are embraced by many of the other managers, but rather to the claim to be a (good) role model. He associates himself with classical rather than present-day heroic myths. Harding sees himself as action oriented, and makes a big deal of the fact that, for him, leadership is not a matter of talking about it but of embodying it. Harding sees himself as a good role model, and even as a hero. But what do others think of this? Do Harding's co-workers in fact see him as a role model, someone they look up to and whose actions can serve as an example for how they themselves act in relation to others? There is no clear answer to this, since Harding's co-workers vary in their view of him and his influence. Some co-workers see Harding's behaviour in a way that suggests that his self-view has elements of wishful thinking and fantasy. One co-worker says:

> Harding is dictatorial, authoritarian, but he can't do everything himself. He's going to have problems, because he can't do everything on his own. Shaking up people the way he does only works up to a point, and then it backfires on you.

Another co-worker expresses similar view:

> He undermines and takes decisions away from people, he doesn't empower the people below him, and how long can you run an organization in that way?
>
>   I think it's sad that one person can have so much influence. He changes direction every time we meet, and he shouts and screams at people, and we'll have problems with this guy before too long.

There are other, more positive views of Harding. Some people are drawn to his ability to make decisions and get things done, which demonstrates a consistency between the way his management is formed as a role model and the environment's interpretations. Harding's picture of himself as a good role model is thus not simply a fantasy. But the result of his management – and also his attempt to personify it – does not quite match his intentions and self-view. There is an element of fantasy in his portrayal of a strong driving force and positive influence on others.

  By fantasy we do not, of course, mean completely unrealistic dreams, but rather a tendency towards a slight exaggeration of who you are and what you do, so that leadership ideals of, say, the great strategist or the efficient role model take over. Most people have this kind of fantasy, but since managers receive so much help in their fantasizing from the grand leadership industry – which is, at times, not unlike Hollywood and other dream factories – the elements of fantasy are perhaps stronger in the case of managers than of bus drivers, teachers, dentists and others who are rarely called upon in strongly idealistic forms and are more engaged in "real" or "substantive" work.

Hopes for the future

A third mechanism for handling identity friction is to cultivate hopes of a better future. Most people have had hopes and dreams of a different and better future at some time in their working lives. Seen from an identity perspective, how serious these hopes are is probably linked in part to how they feel that the work – the tasks and challenges – matches the way they see themselves and their opportunities to develop. Do they think that the work matches how they see themselves, or do they lack the opportunity to express themselves? Most often, they are probably somewhere between these extreme positions: sometimes they do something which is close to their self-view and sometimes they do something which does not match the way they see themselves. In our cases, we can see that there is a gap between managerial work and self-view, in some cases serious– with a high risk of crashing – and in others less obvious, even though things are not running smoothly.

Based on our cases, we have seen that managerial work has perhaps not proved to be quite the source of self-fulfilment it was hoped it would be at the start of the managerial life. Yet many continue to struggle on, partly in the hope that things will change in the future. It might be because they feel that they have not yet reached the right level, and therefore not been offered the tasks they feel best suited for. Once they are offered the right promotion, they will find themselves in the right position, with the chance to realize their identity claim. The problem is often that they think they are on too junior a managerial level, where they perhaps need to "bury" themselves in technology or something else unworthy (Chase, White, Smart).

The future is not only about promotion or a change of organization and time. It can also be about the hope of self-development and becoming a better manager. Perhaps they have not sufficiently developed their leadership style in line with their identity, or they may not yet be good enough at exercising what they feel is the right kind of management, in line with how they see themselves. We see this in several of the managers who appear to be saying that they want to be post-heroic understanders of human nature. They are struggling to live up to the ideal, but it is difficult to express this clearly without also feeling some frustration and holding back too much of themselves as the driving force in more heroic terms. One result of this is that they feel they do not have a sufficient understanding of human nature, but that they still hope they will be able to change this in the future, when they will try to become a better person by restraining themselves more and allowing others to speak up.

Matt Mooney is struggling to become a better manager by holding back and not being dictatorial and argumentative, something he tries to avoid identifying with. He describes this as a long-term project, along the lines of "I'm working on it", "I'm developing my style" and "It will get better". He expresses the hope of greater harmony between ideal and identity. We see a similar situation in Gerald Goodman, who emphasizes that things have already improved slightly but that there is still a lot to do. He needs to be better at allowing other people to speak up, and he is hopeful that this will happen in the future. There will be harmony at some point.

In these cases, they are dealing with what they see as an unsatisfactory situation by painting a positive picture of their future (and better) self, or a career development where their own identity will find expression. It is a question of hopes for the future which can make the present-day conflicts and friction easier to bear. It is something they must live with, but if only they can persevere a little longer, things will change for the better. The future is charged with positive expectations for self-fulfilment (Ybema 2004).

*

The three handling mechanisms can all be seen as attempts to safeguard a reasonably strong managerial identity, regardless of whether it is about separating identity from what you do, building up fantasy images or cultivating hopes for the future.

There are, of course, other ways of dealing with the question of the fragile identity in an uncertain and imperfect world. You can find a new job, lower your ambitions, search out special relationships and networks which confirm you, work in smarter ways, and so on. In our study, however, we find strong examples of these three particular forms. They are, in all probability, fairly general and have the advantage that you can manage them yourself; in other words, they are not strongly dependent on having the right employer, the scope to find particular tasks or people who will be there to confirm you.

CONCLUDING DISCUSSION

Identities can bestow a certain continuity and stability on the existence, something which can provide guidance in a complex and changeable working life. Yet identities are neither static nor given irrevocably, but change constantly in meetings with other people and contexts. In these meetings and contexts, identities are challenged and problematized. The self-view differs from, or even collides with, the way others treat you or the activities you find yourself in. This is all too often bound up with doubt, frustration and uncertainty. As a result, you are forced to adjust, modify, repair and even radically change your identity. This also applies of course – and not least – to those who work with management. Doubt and uncertainty about the managerial work make it difficult to create and maintain a coherent identity as manager.

In some cases, the effect can be dramatic, and lead to great suffering. But in more normally adjusted managers, we can clearly see struggles, frustration and tensions. Many struggle to reconcile contradictory demands and expectations with their identity. The identity claims are not always clearly supported by what actually happens. What is striking in our material is that very few of our main actors are able to reconcile their self-view with their own (main) practice or the perceptions of those around them, even in cases where the problems are manageable. The spectrum of shaky managerial identity projects stretches from adjustment, via barely adequate methods of handling, through decoupling and identity fantasizing, to a crash.

Based on our studies we have noted five versions of identity projects, that is to say the processes and circumstances which distinguish individuals in the question of inconsistency between their self-view and the ideal and view of their environment:

- *Identity adjustment* means that the way the individual sees him or herself largely corresponds to the work situation and the way they interpret how other people view them. It is a question of minor frictions in the individual/ work situation (environment) interface, which can be partially managed by revising the self-view.
- *Identity expression*, like identity crashing, is about unwillingness to compromise and rigidity in identity positioning. The individual insists that their own self is central and expresses this in no uncertain terms. The organizational environment is here adapted to the managerial ideal, rather than the ideal having to compromise with the reality. This is true at least from the horizon of the identity-expressing individual. Conflicts may arise, but do not seriously affect the identity of the individual.
- *Identity juggling* means a certain insecurity or conflict and is a milder form of identity struggle, where the ideal does not coincide with what one does, yet does not contribute to causing any great friction or conflict. The managerial work does not deviate too much from the ideals but still requires a relatively flexible self.
- *Identity wrestling* means that a number of cherished managerial ideals – often linked to various people-oriented and strategy-oriented ideals – help to create identity traps and snares which make it difficult to maintain a stable self-esteem in the managerial work. Sometimes the identity wrestling occurs between an apparently incompatible and contradictory managerial ideal, which creates frustration and doubts about identity. The manager may be wrestling with trying to express a distinct and clear identity but this comes under great pressure and it is difficult to make the existence work.
- *Identity crashing* is about strongly contradictory forces undermining the chances of maintaining a stable and coherent managerial identity. The individual is unable to handle this, and there is a risk that a particular

identity will dissolve. The actual foundation for existential security and meaning in the working environment collapses. The wrestling match has been lost or is in danger of being lost. But it is possible to recover from a crash.

These forms of identity work are managed, with varying degrees of effectiveness, through three main handling mechanisms:

- *Decoupling* means that, as manager, you create separate managerial identities which avoid collisions, in an attempt to maintain your identity by keeping conflicting forces apart. You do not allow the practical managerial work (administration) to influence how you describe yourself as a manager (leader). Decoupling leads to friction but can, if successful, ease the struggle and prevent collapse.
- *Fantasies* refers to how, as a manager, you create imaginative and attractive pictures of yourself which contribute to reinforcing the identity as leader and which make it possible to keep it separate to some degree from the practical exercising of management.
- *Hopes for the future* means dealing with the tensions and difficulties at the time, which is common in identity wrestling, by cultivating hopes for the future. It is about how you can change and become better when you reach the right (higher) level, are given time to establish yourself or have the opportunity to develop within the organization.

It is not entirely easy to exercise management by acting as strategist, change agent, coach or understander of human nature. Administration, demands for technical expertise and previous experience make it difficult to form your managerial work with your starting point in how you see yourself. People eager to work with strategy and leadership generally find themselves in a position which involves a great deal of work with bureaucracy and administration, a certain amount of micromanagement and demands to adapt. Above all, there are endless meetings, email communications, and a large number of small questions which take up a lot of time and are experienced as demanding. Such a situation does not necessarily impede leadership – it can, in effect, be conducted at any time – but it often offers rather unfavourable arenas for passionate speeches, ambitious creation of meaning, co-worker development, creation of security and emotional support – that is, what some identify as "proper" leadership. Co-workers and more senior managers are not always sources of confirmation, and may even directly reject an individual's claim of who they are and what they do. It is easy to end up in new identity traps or labyrinths from which it can be difficult to break free. The identity traps vary in degree of difficulty – some are easier and have only a small element of friction, while others are more difficult and characterized by labyrinths or direct conflicts, which sometimes results in crashing.

9 Leadership and identity in an imperfect world

Most of the knowledge about managers and leadership takes its starting point in what the manager or leader does and accomplishes. This is particularly evident in the popular literature – pop management or, as some people call it, management pornography – which puts the spotlight on formulae for success and juicy hero narratives. In academic literature, too, there are attempts to demonstrate that different types of leaders and leadership lead to different outcomes (Bass & Riggio 2006). The leader acts, others react. Countless leadership theories have been developed and dictate how the leader should be: charismatic, authentic and transformational, for example (Luthans & Avolio 2003). Or why not relational and dialogic (Cunliffe & Eriksen 2011)? Frequently, and of course above all in the popular literature, they offer clear-cut, often universal recipes for the right managerial behaviour, with the help of which all the right things can be accomplished. Another, slightly different, study tradition, which has a strong academic approach, is the study of managerial work in practice. Instead of taking its starting point in what managers should do and accomplish, it focuses on what managers actually do in the organizational everyday (Tengblad 2012a).

In this book, as we have said, we shift the focus. Unlike a great deal of other research, we penetrate the surface – styles, behaviours, tasks, functions – and attempt to gain a deeper understanding of leadership and management based on how managers attempt to create meaning and achieve a balanced existence in a world in which it is often difficult to manoeuvre. Our aim is to illustrate management and its meaning using an identity perspective. How do managers approach the managerial work, not only in terms of activities and behaviour, but also, and above all, in relation to how they see themselves, their interests, ambitions, emotions, dreams, fantasies and life experience? How do they deal with any dilemmas between self-view and imperfect reality? We attempt to capture the phenomenon of managerial life in a wider, but also deeper and richer, meaning based on managers' own horizons of experience and attempts to create meaning and coherence in their existence, which is not, as has been seen, always the easiest thing to do.

The chapter begins with a short summary of our aims and the overall theme. We then take another look at our main actors, primarily with identity elements and lessons learned. In the section which then follows, we make a critical summary of the two dominating ideals in the managerial work of our actors and many others. This is followed by a section where we discuss the problems our managers have in identifying with the ideals; here we take both a certain retrospective and a more in-depth look at earlier arguments. This leads us into a discussion of the moral theme and its relevance as a formula for managerial work. This is followed by a critical discussion of the managers' emphasis on distance to the business – we talk here about practice phobia. We then combine the moral theme and the practice phobia in an anxiety matrix and carve out five different managerial positions. We follow this up with a deeper discussion of presence in the practice and knowledge and then discuss whether many of the popular leadership ideals – the solution to every organization's problems – are not, in fact, the actual problem. We end with a list of ten points which summarize the central problems, paradoxes and the contradictory elements in modern managerial life.

THE COMPLEXITY OF THE MANAGERIAL LIFE

Our studies show that unclear demands and expectations from the environment – demands and expectations which are in contrast to, and in some cases undermine, personal ambitions and interests – contribute to making the managerial work complex, contradictory, confused and fragmented. As a result, uncertainty, anxiety and feelings of inadequacy are very common in managerial life. Previous research has shown variation and fragmentation in behaviour in managerial work. We confirm this picture, but our emphasis is on highlighting the meanings and consequences for experience, self-view, thinking and emotions. We also place great importance on relationships and look at how different leadership discourses affect and form the existence of managers.

In a changeable society and working life, full of flashy pictures of attractive leadership which are difficult to live up to, it is difficult for managers to maintain a coherent picture of what they stand for and what they accomplish. Above all, their efforts to create a more integrated and consistent idea of who they themselves are and what capacities they have, in other words the managerial identity, are undermined.

While management may be seen as a challenge, it is also seen an opportunity for self-realization. One important driving force behind the desire to become a manager is the perceived distance between who they are and what they can, and therefore should, do. Many describe themselves as natural managers – they have always had the right personal traits, and management is an opportunity to allow these qualities to flourish. They are thus guided into management on the basis of deeply personal traits. In many cases, the phasing in to management positions is described as a natural process, since they are developing as human beings and learning more about themselves and their capabilities. Yet this "naturalness" appears to be an expression for a rather naïve, romantic approach – the idea that essential, positive qualities are quite simply already in place or gradually come into flower in a clear leadership ability. This appears rather too harmonious. In reality, it is often unclear what abilities people have, and the approach to leadership is seen to have more to do with being seduced by leadership ideologies both in their education and by discourse in the media. Our observations of managers in action, like the perceptions of their environment (co-workers), frequently give a more complicated picture, where it is not so obvious what the managers are like and what they accomplish. There are often different views on this.

It is far from obvious which traits make managerial life easier. Sometimes adaptability is seen as an important asset. The complexities and limitations of the existence have a strong impact on what managers do – and also on how they are gradually formed and re-formed, for example in terms of identity. A more dynamic, situational and relational approach can be contrasted with the faith many of our managers have in their inherent characteristics. This means that managers (like others) are – in their work – more social, adaptive creatures that they appear to think. The working life forms people, and definitely managers. The views people have of themselves are also strongly social products; that is why the idea that there is such a thing as a natural leadership capability can be seen as an expression of our time's naïve love for the great leader (Burns 2003) – a positive picture which forms the ideal and self-view of many people, not always in a particularly realistic way.

Overestimating your own ability is a general tendency. The majority of people believe they are above average when it comes to understanding people, the ability to collaborate, leadership skills, and so on. Even if most managers probably are above average in a number of respects, this does not prevent an overestimation. We observe here that all our managers stress their own high moral standards – the view of the good manager as verging on the saintly, unselfish and caring, with a high degree of authenticity and honesty, is popular both in literature and among managers (Alvesson 2011b) – while, at the same time, they may make comparisons with other managers who interfere, pretend they know what to do, are political and engage in other dubious practices. It is, of course, possible that the managers we interviewed are morally superior to managers and others we did not interview, but we do not consider this to be very likely . . .

Before we move on, here is a reminder and summing up of the thirteen main characters we have followed closely in this book.

OUR MANAGERS – SUMMARIES AND LEARNINGS

While we have stressed some general results and pointed out some learnings which appear to apply to managers in general above, we will now present some insights we have gleaned from each of the thirteen managers we have studied in depth.

We take our starting point in both their main identity claim – the message of who they are and the identity version they are most taken up with and want to adhere to – and how things go for them during the period we have followed them.

Bert Bacon is in the midst of an identity struggle which contains doubt, as a result of his ignorance of the business. Bacon suspects that his co-workers are cheating him at times. He uses the metaphor of "the village idiot" to create a certain ironic distance, but the boundary between the ironic (and the value of asking silly questions) and the pathetic is not always clear. Having managerial – rather than technical – knowledge is a double-edged source of identity because it means you rely on the goodwill and intentions of others, in particular co-workers. It is one thing to ask open unbiased questions which make people think, quite another to appear ignorant. Bacon's idealizing of managerial knowledge is fragile – it does not appear to compensate for his lack of technical knowledge, and the uncertainty about what he knows, does and accomplishes cannot be dispersed by a clear view of himself as a generally competent manager with management knowledge. The struggle is compounded by the fact that he receives no feedback from his superiors, which is one reason he finds his existence painful. The basis for Bacon's identity is thus fragile. His dependency on confirmation from others is almost extreme. As with many others, management education and knowledge appear to be inadequate as a basis for the managerial identity. He has high expectations regarding how fine and important being a manager is, but when this is not backed up and given stability in the form of knowledge of the business and the articulated approval of others, it almost breaks him.

Benjamin Book says he is a person with the highest level of integrity and credibility, which, in combination with a strong humanitarian streak, results in outstanding leadership which is clearly appreciated by his co-workers. This picture appeared to be confirmed by his previous workplace, but everything changed when he moved to a new organization. Doubts about his credibility begin to spread. His case shows how dependent (at least some) managers are on context. They confuse their environment's view of them with an essential belief in how they really are, which is to say that they have a stable, inherent identity regardless of the view of those around them. It is easy to have a clear view of yourself in a positive and stable environment – in a different environment, the support for this identity can disappear and there is a risk of the identity crashing. The element of doubt in the authenticity ideal is also highlighted: this is easy to maintain in favourable circumstances, but more difficult to live up to in others, and the claims weaken rather than strengthen self-esteem and self-view. The case of Book further shows the danger of making strong claims.

Charlie Chase sees himself as both someone who has a good understanding of human nature and a strategist. What is central in both positions is the role of leader, which dominates the claim to the managerial identity. Chase frequently returns to his claim that he is particularly suited to working with both questions of coordination and wider market and development questions. In comparison with the attractive leadership, the job of engineer appears commonplace and dull and is used actively by Chase (if less powerfully than by Courage) as an anti-identity which reinforces the relevance and importance of the leader identity – his identity as a leader is, in his own words, an extension of his personality. The identity claim is, however, undermined by the fact that both his co-workers and more senior managers constantly turn to Chase in his capacity as technical expert – which he says he is not – rather than as a leader or strategist – which he says he is. The organization is sending mixed messages to Chase. In this contradictory situation, he allows the ideal, rather than the reality, of the role to control his interpretation of what is happening in the interaction with his co-workers. The ideal of the seductive leader here develops into something of a fantasy product, which is perhaps not uncommon.

Carol Courage describes herself as a cultural agent of change who contributes to strategic development. She says she has always shouldered a special leadership responsibility in the company, in different roles, partly encouraged by the company's investment in her managerial career through leadership development programmes. Spurred on by the company, and successful in her career, it was natural for her to identify with the cultural and strategic roles when she was given overall responsibility for the research unit. But changes within the group meant that her work changed from high-level company management to questions of traditional site management. She later interprets these as dominating her leadership. Courage's identification with culture and leadership is, however, uncompromising, which results in an extreme conflict between the claim to identity and the demands of the business. The understanding of leadership which Courage expresses is central for the identity conflict. Leadership is seen as something big and far from the business, something you do at given times, distinct from other managerial work, rather than as a fairly integrated part of the daily activities. Her view of leadership reinforces the source of the conflict and makes compromise and learning more difficult. Most managers decouple leadership talk from practice and "cover it up", but Courage does the opposite: she confronts her ideal of leadership head on with the imperfect organizational practice in which she finds herself. Her identity nosedives straight into the imperfect organizational world like a kamikaze pilot – neither her identity nor the organization takes evasive action, and the crash is inevitable.

David Dean is in the midst of an identity struggle which has some of the characteristics of Courage's. Here, too, we see an extreme source of conflict, unwillingness to compromise and retreat from the organization (the co-workers) in question. Dean sees himself as a people-centred manager whose task is to support the ability of his co-workers to make their own decisions and take action through a coaching style of leadership. Previous experience has convinced him of the universal excellence of the coaching style of leadership and his competence as coach-manager, but his co-workers want practical, firm and principled leadership *vis-à-vis* the company management based on their actual problems and requests. This clashes with Dean's identity anchorage in the coaching ideal, which appears here to be more of an identity trap rather than something which opens up the possibility of two-way communication and dialogue, which is what Dean says he is aiming for. The coaching ideology rules and obscures the view of the local conditions, situations and interpretations. The collision between reality and ideal is intensified by the fact that Dean not only sees coaching as the best style of leadership but also sees it as an expression of his personality. We can see here how identification with a popular leadership ideal which encourages flexibility and responsibility, in practice, develops into a strict dogma with devastating consequences for Dean, whose co-workers reject him.

Gary Gardener describes himself as a manager who leads naturally, but at the same time is morally responsible and honest. He avoids micromanaging co-workers, preferring instead to devote himself to what he calls symbolic leadership, which includes the overall and more strategic questions. This is something he has learned on countless management and leadership courses. For Gardener, this approach is a question of integrity and morals. It is about having faith in co-workers' knowledge and genuine commitment. But it is not always easy to maintain confidence and openness towards the people you work with. Gardener says that not all his managers share his level of integrity when it comes to micromanaging and that some co-workers at times behave dishonestly and thereby immorally. This makes Gardener very angry. At the same time as it angers him, his own moral stance as a good manager is reinforced because it puts him in a better light than the others. In Gardener's case, other people's low level of integrity and lack of morality act as a source of identity reinforcement.

In the case of *Gerald Goodman*, the struggle is between what he interprets as two authentic identities, which makes it a more difficult and incisive identity struggle. Goodman says that the job requires a firm hand, but that he is in reality a person who tries to "uphold the soft values of the personal meeting". The individual must feel they are seen:

> Even though I may come across as hard, I want to help everyone. But not wanting anyone to feel bad almost broke me at one time. Sometimes it's hurt and been painful, but it's also made me a stronger leader.

For Goodman, the people approach is not a role he plays at given times. We note a strong feeling of sympathy and identification with co-workers, which has consequences for their well-being. His inability to maintain distance and flexibility in the interest and empathy in relation to others causes problems for him. A manager must be able to deal with the fact that people do not feel good, which is unavoidable in working life, where it is not possible to help everyone. In Goodman's words, this is the equivalent of destroying yourself. The problem here is a mismatch between Mother Teresa – to use his own colourful analogy – and the demands to keep the organizational machinery running. The main problem here appears to be that Goodman sees himself as too moral and empathetic for management. Has he perhaps chosen the wrong road? Might the Church or social work be professions which would have suited him better?

Henry Harding, unlike many of the other managers, considers himself to be intimately bound to what he accomplishes. Performance, results and activities close to the practice are what he focuses on. He stresses his own, often mildly heroic, commitment to achieving spectacular results. Harding sees himself as a role model and has no concerns about involving himself in the details of the core activities and what his co-workers do; he sees this as a central aspect of managerial work. For Harding, as for most of the other managers, management is an expression of how he sees himself as a human being. For him, this means being hands-on and expressing himself as much as possible in order to have an impact on the business and its outcome. Here too we note a certain friction between self-view and ideals on the one hand, and organizational situations and reality on the other – many people in his environment find him trying – but he does not see this as a problem. Of all our managers, Harding is the one who expresses himself in the most tangible terms and without many of the concepts and abstractions which many of the other managers like, and have possibly got stuck in.

Matt Mooney emphasizes, like many others, his interest in people and his own high moral standing. Mooney's ideal is to think the best of his co-workers and treat them as "co-actors". The problem is that they do not always live up to the ideal. Mooney believes that they sometimes have a limited view of life and on occasion take the position of victim. There are some who cannot be fully trusted, as they may cheat in order to avoid working during difficult times. These circumstances clash with Mooney's understander of human nature ideal, which on occasion seems somewhat misplaced. Mooney also sees himself as rather dogmatic at times, particularly when he wants to get the job done and make sure other people fulfil their commitments. This too conflicts at times with the humanistic ideal. When the organization's demands for efficiency, as Mooney sees them, clash with the ideals, it can be difficult to maintain these, and there is rarely any practical guidance for how to behave in actual situations. This leads to identity doubt and frustration – what is the right way to act in acute situations where the obvious alternative is not in line with how you see yourself, and what are the consequences of such action?

Nora Noble sees herself as a leader with a high level of moral integrity, which is confirmed by her co-workers. She stresses leadership, which she says she exercises in development activities. However, these do not dominate her daily work since the routine activities, where she says she works more with management, take up most of her time. She has difficulty identifying with the latter and stresses the development projects where there is scope for leadership and where she can identify more wholeheartedly with the job. This becomes a way of attempting to reduce the friction between how she sees herself and what she does in the job. Yet, as in a number of our other cases, it appears here that leadership – what you should do if you want to be seen as a "real manager" (who is, in other words, not simply a manager but more of a leader) – cannot be exercised as long as you are working with the daily/routine business. As in the case of Courage, we see how leadership is made into something outside the daily business, something extraordinary: an activity "on the side". Like Courage, Noble also has leadership development in her baggage, which may be what is causing trouble here – she wants to emphasize that leadership is a special (especially important) activity and avoid the daily grind. Noble compromises her view of herself as leader and spends most of her time on routine matters. In this respect, identity decoupling works reasonably well for her. Her interpretation of leadership, however, leads her to hope that she will be able to spend more time working with development in the future; if this hope is not fulfilled, Noble's identity juggling may develop into identity wrestling.

Stuart Smart sees himself as someone who has the ability to lift questions to a strategic level and create overall understanding in different questions. He sees himself as being better suited to more senior managerial positions than simply working with technical questions of detail. He believes that there is a gap between his current tasks and his managerial capacities. He is trying to reduce the gap by working for a more overall perspective in the interaction with co-workers, even though this is actually a matter which lies above his position. It allows him to say that he works with strategic questions and thereby ease the friction between work and identity a little. He can thus juggle with strategic matters when he expresses himself, even if his work does not contain much of what is conventionally regarded as strategic matters, such as competitive and market strategies. Smart works more with traditional managerial supervision, where it is also important to be able to explain the purpose of what you are doing. The strategic talk should instead be seen as an attempt to raise the status of the managerial job and the managerial identity slightly – it becomes a little more attractive. One problem for Smart is that he does not feel that his capacity as managerial material is confirmed on a higher level. The attempts to create an integrated managerial identity take a knock, with the result that Smart becomes hesitant and disappointed. In this case, strategy and leadership are merely euphemisms which offer a certain (fleeting) identity reinforcement, but which also result in a mystification of his work accompanied by identity uncertainty and vulnerability.

Steven Stone is tossed between different ideals which are not always easy to unite. He strives to bring out the good in his co-workers and listen to their opinions and interests. In this respect, he wants to see himself as someone who has a good understanding of human nature. He wants to work for what is right by not dominating in his interaction with co-workers. The good manager is, in Stone's case, the one who acts without really being noticed. Yet this is a style of management which Stone himself describes as "damn difficult" since it clashes with his understanding of himself as a manager with a natural drive, and with strong skills for communicating with and motivating his co-workers. Stone finds it unnatural to hold back this innate drive that is perhaps his strength and what he himself believes underpins his career in management. The ideal of the good listener is in contrast to the driving force ideal, which is a problem for Stone because he also wants to identify with and express both ideals in the interaction with his co-workers. Yet it is often difficult to know which leg to stand on, and whichever one he chooses, he gets it wrong with regard to the way he is perceived by those around him or sees himself as manager. This is a dilemma which results in Stone being thrown into different forms of identity struggles.

William White describes himself as a natural manager with the potential to influence and control overall questions. In his previous work as an expert, he spent most of his time "buried in technology", but White says that as a manager he takes part in important discussions and meetings where things happen. This does not apply to all questions, however, but specifically those which involve some interaction with co-workers, who, White believes – he expresses some doubt at times – appreciate his listening skills and accessibility. This also gives White some identity confirmation and self-esteem; he has – to some extent at least – found his place as the good manager. This confirmation is particularly important for White, who feels that he does not fully understand the company's core competence and what the experts work with, which can lead to a feeling of not being accepted. This existence is, however, not without problems for White, who feels that his superior managers do not see him. On the contrary, he feels he has greater managerial potential, not least when it comes to overall strategic questions. In these respects, he feels anonymous and part of the large grey mass of co-workers. This is a source of uncertainty for White, who articulates the lack of managerial confirmation in moral terms. The managers do not appreciate the true value of the co-workers, something he believes he himself does very well. In the light of less competent managers, he can appear as a much better manager, which reinforces his belief in himself as a good manager, one who is, moreover, destined for even greater things.

The summaries show that the managers are caught up in a constant crossfire of ambiguous and contradictory fields of force which demand flexibility and a willingness to compromise, including on matters which are dear to their hearts. Attractive leadership ideals do not always make life easier; sometimes they make it more difficult to develop a stable identity as a base for action. We will go into this more deeply later in the chapter.

We have addressed many identity themes in previous chapters, but will analyse two distinct leadership ideals which strongly dominate our managers' understanding, or at least how they present themselves, in more depth below. Two managerial approaches are associated with these leadership ideals: moral purism and practice phobia. Both the ideals and the accompanying approaches promise solutions to the identity question, but contain traps. We start by analysing the leadership ideals, before discussing the two managerial approaches.

TWO BROAD MANAGERIAL IDEALS: GRAND LEADERSHIP AND UNDERSTANDER OF HUMAN NATURE LEADERSHIP

In our study, managers say they are distinguished first and foremost by two broad managerial approaches. One of these concerns the company's overriding, long-term activities – the strategies, organizational culture and other "big" issues. These areas of work are described as being central for organizations which exist in changeable and turbulent environments, and are often described in leadership literature as forms of transformational leadership (Bass & Riggio 2006). This is sometimes spiced with authenticity (Bass & Steidlmeier 1999). It could be referred to as grand leadership. Managers on slightly lower levels – our study is dominated by middle (or upper-middle) managers – also often claim to work with this or to be cut out for this type of more senior managerial work. The second is about the manager having a positive impact on other people. It is about making other people feel good and feel comfortable in organizations, an approach which is directed towards the more employee-oriented, therapeutic dimension of management. This employee orientation is frequently included in forms of post-heroic leadership (Badaracco 2002). This dimension too is often spiced with authenticity (Avolio & Gardner 2005). We have, a little ironically, termed this the understander of human nature version of managerial work. According to the managers themselves, it is exercised by true humanists.

The majority of our managers like to see themselves as leaders on the basis of their uniquely anchored personal traits. They describe themselves as authentic and want to appear, as managers, as deeply individual and special in relation to others. Yet the impression given is that their behaviour is rather typical, in that they adopt the same social standards – leader, strategist, humanist, etc. – when they describe themselves as managers. Rather than appearing as particularly genuine and original, they appear to have assimilated, and become skilled at articulating, virtually the same management recipe for how to be a good manager. Rather than being self-made in an authentic sense, they are formed by similar recipes in a standardized process. The media, the spirit of the age and management education produce similar managerial ideals which people buy on a large scale. What is generally accessible dominates what is individual and uniquely personal. We might talk here about a *unicity paradox* in the managerial identity: you think you are unique and genuine, but behind this lie the hidden production machinery and acclimatization to common standards of the mass society.[1]

Grand leadership

We have described how many managers position themselves as strategists, or point out in some other way that they work with long-term, overall questions. We can thus consider this as a kind of grand leadership. Gerald Goodman, for example, says that he gives his co-workers "the conditions and then look[s] ahead and see[s] what others don't see", while "the everyday" should in principle function without his involvement. This is in line with much leadership theory. Heifetz and Laurie (1997) say, for example, that the manager (leader) should stand on the balcony and be responsible for the overview and long-term matters. The message here seems to be that the spirit of the manager should hover above the daily toil. There is a kind of magnification of the manager in this contrasting of the small – details, everyday toil – with the big – the manager's overview and strategizing. Metaphorically, it is about being placed above others, moving in a greater sphere, standing for the big ideas, and so on. As with the "balcony leader", you "build yourself up" as manager, shaping yourself as the man or woman for the major contexts.

Yet for the large majority of managers this is just one aspect or function, one which is important but which takes up a small amount of the total time. In practice, as we have pointed out, administrative

---

[1]   This theme is addressed by several social scientists, for example, Meyer et al. (1987). One variant is the willingness within organizations to believe that you are unique while at the same time the evidence of unicity is similar in different organizations.

and operational matters also dominate in the case of managers who see themselves as grand leaders. Even managers on the top levels find that strategic questions take up a small amount of the working time and attention (Koot & Sabelis 2002; Tyrstrup 2002). Mintzberg (2009) points out that the importance of leadership for management is both unrealistic and unfortunate, since "leadership" acts mainly as a means for the heroization and self-glorification of managers (by both themselves and others). Wallander (2003) states that strategy discussions in a senior management context are also frequently decoupled from the business, with vague implications for tangible actions and not particularly valuable. Yet the idea, and sometimes the dream, of grand leadership is strongly cherished by many.

In our study, we can find different ways of managing the ideal of grand leadership in relation to individual practice. Here we can offer a reminder of the three variants with whose help identity is managed in the intersection between the view of the self as a person and manager on the one hand, and the imperfect organizational reality on the other. One can decouple, fantasize and take the view that grand leadership really is waiting round the corner, for when the situation improves or you receive your well-earned promotion. We can further add two rather more specific phenomena which we have observed in our study and which make it easier for managers to see themselves as grand leaders:

- describing all manner of questions as "strategic", thus inflating their importance
- an (over)emphasis on the part-time work with big questions and marginalization of the core business

Inflating importance means that some managers move relatively smoothly between ideas of grand leadership and a managerial reality which is strongly characterized by administrative and operational tasks. Some administration – work with budgets and recruitment – is seen (described) as strategic questions. There may be enough tasks that can be stretched towards the strategic aspect for the idea of grand leadership to be preserved and work as an identity base. We can describe this as concept stretching, which makes it possible for the leader to be strategic, since the word is liberated from a distinct meaning and much becomes "strategic".

The emphasis on special grand leader activities is possible when you work with something more overall which breaks with the operational activities. Nora Noble describes working with the big overall questions as a way of living leadership. She says that development questions are "her thing" and that the daily business does not suit her motivation and drive. One advantage here is that many projects to do with organizational change and development do not involve close contact with the actual business, at least during a specific period of time. This is a question of meetings, plans and PowerPoints. Interestingly, what lies outside the actual business is referred to as "where things really happen". Here there is at least scope for a sense of grand leadership.

But there are others for whom these ways of reconciling the reality experienced with grand leadership does not work. They interpret their working situation as narrow and problematic, and the aspirations to grand leadership appear primarily to bring a painful awareness of the distance between ideal and reality. Carol Courage exemplifies this. She is subjected to what she sees as stupid demands from both superior managers and subordinates. Since she has a high formal position in a large international company, it is the organizational existence and its inherent absurdities, embodied by the inability of various people to manage these, that is the main problem. Having had more junior managerial positions, she maintains that a more senior managerial position still does not offer her the right conditions to exercise real leadership.

While others often overstate what they work with, so that it appears to be "strategic", Courage understates her managerial job and presents it in opposite terms. While others "strategize" what they do, Courage "janitorizes" her work situation. Since Courage holds a more senior position than most of our "strategy managers", this is not about "objective" phenomena, but rather about discourse and construction, where over-staters and under-staters conjure up different realities.

Understander of human nature leadership

The second approach is perhaps more obviously right – understanding people and a therapeutic approach can be perceived as leading to good relations and a positive working climate. It is a question of showing openness, being compassionate and listening and generally being friendly and attentive in your interaction with co-workers. It is to a large extent about making co-workers feel good. It is, more than in the question of grand leadership, about the importance of expressing your own essence. Many of the managers stress that they are only acting in line with their authentic self – they are open, empathetic and inter-ested in people and genuinely want to develop people. Authentic here means being a good person in various ways and behaving decently towards people. The managers' authentic self coincides here to a large degree with general humanistic principles of expressing goodness towards your fellow human beings. Many of our managers appear here as something of a paragon of virtue, even though some mention weaknesses and less positive attributes.

Using psychology to manipulate or produce desirable behaviour with the help of everyday magic (listening or acting as a friend, for example, works wonders) is perhaps not wholly uncommon in work-ing life – it can even be seen as a key element in marketing and branding and a considerable amount of leadership – but it appears to be far from our managers, at least according to their own understand-ings. Their morally pure interpretations are sometimes rather idealis-tic and naïve. The ambition to protect co-workers is undoubtedly a good one – working life should, as far as possible, be a source of well-being, and managers can, of course, contribute to this – but it seems that many turn a blind eye to the complexity and contradictions. It is sometimes the case that a desire to favour the employees becomes more important than the business and the result. This is undoubtedly the case in parts of the public sector, in particular, but an increased emphasis on employees' psychology at work – possibly at the expense of other interests and priorities – seems to be an international trend (Western 2008; Zaleznik 1997).

The two ideals

The idealizing of leadership – the ideals of the grand leader and the understander of human nature – represents popular perceptions of modern managerial work (Sveningsson et al. 2009). In emphasizing the role of leader – in contrast to administrative matters, in particular, but also the technical problem-solving, operational work – the managers articulate the view dominant today that it is primarily about leadership. Devaluing other managerial tasks is popular.

At the same time as they adopt the role as leader, the managers frequently articulate a strong dislike of questions associated with micromanagement: that is to say, details, especially those of an administrative nature. This unwillingness to be "just" a manager reinforces the identification with the role of leader. Many managers are under the impression that leadership means working with very big important questions: developing the organization, establishing overall harmony, working with "strategic issues", and so on. We see here a "grandeur" which simultaneously glorifies and mystifies the existence, as well as leading to a number of failed expectations – and many of the managers we studied exemplify this.

Popular ideas in management journals and leadership education have a strong impact on managers' self-view. Most of our managers, as the material has shown, have come across modern theories of management and leadership in some way, via leadership training in the form of academic education or executive programmes. Many of the ideas have also received a great deal of attention in the media, which talks in over-idealistic – and therefore unrealistic – terms of the need for leaders who develop the business strategically rather than managers who simply look after the operations, administer and maintain the existing approach.

Leadership is often characterized by this idealization. It sounds attractive and appealing but is frequently too general and vague for managers to be able to have a reasonably informed idea of what it is, and efforts to apply it can fall flat (Alvesson & Sveningsson 2003a).

THE PROBLEM OF IDENTIFYING WITH THE MANAGERIAL IDEALS

In spite of – or perhaps thanks to – their diversity, terms such as leadership, culture, development and strategy are popular, and many managers are keen to identify with them. Yet both the grand leadership and understander of human nature variants, as well as interpretations of authenticity, give rise to a number of related problems in the managerial work, in addition to general uncertainty and confusion.

For the first thing, all the emphasis on strategy is in some contrast to what managers actually do in their work. Much of the machinery in modern organizations requires managers on different levels to spend time on what they themselves would call micromanagement. This does not necessarily mean constantly looking over people's shoulders, but rather making sure that things keep moving. In many organizations there is a move towards greater standardization, centralization and transparency, all of which require managers to work increasingly with different forms of documentation, processes and reporting, and only in rare cases work with developing, discussing or even communicating strategies. To the extent that strategies – rather than direct demands of the production, customers, legislators, authorities and other stakeholders – play any direct part, it is for most managers a question of implementing decisions and policies that come from higher levels. Much of what they do in practice has little in common with how they describe themselves and their values, which is why many experience a conflict between what they see as their true self and what the managerial job requires in practice. The consequence of this is a great deal of compromising and adapting to the organization's demands for compliance. This frequently leads to irritation and frustration among managers who feel that they are unable to live up to the ideal they associate with their own person, for example actually working with grand leadership.

Second, attempting to be employee-oriented understanders of human nature and humanists, with quasi-therapeutic elements, is far from unproblematic. Acting as a sympathetic humanist can clash with other leadership ideals, such as being a driving force, being efficient and securing results. This gives rise to situations which can make it difficult in practice to act in line with the self-view, which is why ideals also lead to people faking their behaviour in order to demonstrate humanism. There is occasionally a conflict between closeness and distance, or between being a good friend and a demanding, salary-setting manager. Giving everyone the opportunity to speak out, and listening to everyone, can be time consuming and result in long meetings and, sometimes, complaints. Effective workplaces can necessitate more limited communication. Being positive and generous with praise and recognition is a good thing, in principle, but the majority of work efforts are, by definition, average, and it is not always easy to find contributions worthy of praise. Confirming people whose performance is mediocre can be perceived as shallow and false.

What helps individuals to develop is, not least, pointing out things that are not going so well. Giving criticism is often valuable, but it is not something our managers do very often. Managers do not prioritize dealing with things such as laziness, incompetence, bad attitudes or deviations from prescribed ways of working. In our therapeutic society there is a big risk that people will take offence, and that the managerial identity as a humanist will take a knock. The understander of human nature ideal, at least, appears to be more about giving positive feedback.

There is also a general uncertainty regarding the question of being a good manager who acknowledges co-workers, where the manipulative element of leading cannot be denied. One might also ask how it is possible to determine whether this is a question of genuine concern or of management tactics aimed at improving motivation and willingness to change. It is, moreover, not definite that the latter is mainly a bad thing; a central point of organizations is that people should deliver results. Being given the best care is central for children at nursery school, but optimizing employee care and a cosy relaxed atmosphere at work is not the primary reason we have companies and public organizations. In this respect, there is frequently a conflict between being a good person who is popular among co-workers and achieving a good result. One sometimes wonders how much a good result means when it comes to employee interest and avoiding "interfering" in what people do. There are times when we avoid conflicts of ideals in order to avoid the risk of creating cognitive discord and conflicts relating to different principles and ambitions in the question of leadership.

Third, the idea of authentic managerial work and leadership, which underpins and reinforces the two variants as natural and obvious for our managers, gives a contradictory impression. In modern business life, it is popular today to be authentic – or at least to appear as such. In this, our managers are explicit. They strive to personify their positions according to their view of themselves as natural managers. Good managers ("leaders") behave in an authentic way, as opposed to pretending or acting falsely. They claim that they do not work with *staging* in the sense of playing a role, or different forms of *impression management*, but try to be themselves all the time. Here it is a question of expressing your own heart and soul and showing that, as a manager, you stand for what you say.

Strong moral overtones are attached to the role of leader. A good manager is a good person: he or she has only positive traits. That is what much of the literature on leadership and almost all our managers say. Yet, as we have seen, it is not easy to maintain a strong moral position when you are forced to compromise. In some cases, this compromising makes it impossible to safeguard your ideals or be true to your identity. One way of avoiding a moral train wreck is to do what Carol Courage did when she walked away, which is a sign of strength in the identification with the role of leader. The managerial job in question appears here to be almost a betrayal of the self-view and sense of integrity. Against this background, we could say that there is something fraudulent about the ideal of what a manager works with today – the substance does not match the promise, and the harmonious relationship between self-view and ideal, on the one hand, and the sometimes imperfect reality, on the other, causes problems. The attempts to achieve moral stability are consequently lined with traps, labyrinths and dead ends which make the managerial identity fragile and variable. One conclusion is that it is difficult to combine management with strong moral convictions (see also Alvesson 2011b; Jackall 1988).

The managerial job is diverse, and the manager's own identity and personal convictions are often not enough to clarify the meaning of the managerial job and adopt a strong autonomous position in which they can trust their own judgement based on what is right for themselves. The dependence on feedback and confirmation from others is strong, for us surprisingly strong. Of course everyone needs some confirmation, but if you are fairly sure of yourself, we might expect this need to be modest at a mature age. Somewhat ironically, we can say that a great deal of support is needed to appear – and to remain – as an independent manager. Managers therefore seek feedback not for what they do, but perhaps more for who they are. The confirmation deficit contributes to reinforcing uncertainty and anxiety about the managerial work and their own identity. It appears to be increasingly difficult for managers to sustain a coherent picture of what they stand for and what they accomplish over time (cf. Sennett 1998, who draws attention to this as a general phenomenon). This work with the (managerial) identity can, in our cases, be described as an active striving for a coherent self-view and self-esteem – we have referred to this as identity work. Sometimes this striving is so complicated and contains so many problems that it can be described as a struggle.

In the previous chapter, we identified different types of identity work. In less friction-filled cases, it is about adjustment work, or juggling. Sometimes the individual can express their identity more or less successfully and insist on the respect and compliance of their environment. This can be risky and lead to conflicts. In such cases, or when a generally complicated and diverse situation leads to a big gap between ideal/expectation and reality/experience, the individual ends up in a wrestling match and may even risk, or fall victim to, an identity crash. The latter signals an ongoing repair and reassessment job – unless the individual affected is out for the count, works with crisis management and is too far gone to think about identity questions in relation to managerial activities.

We also stressed three ways of dealing with identity in this state of high tension: decoupling, fantasy and hopes for the future (see page 268).

It is important to note here that the handling mechanisms are not only positive tools which help the individual in identity creation and management. They can also make problems worse. Decoupling can lead to a lot of attention and commitment being given to matters which do confirm identity, but are somewhat peripheral in relation to the main part of the practical work, which can have a negative effect on the latter. If the main job is not done properly, it can lead to a brutal backlash shaking one's view of the world. Even if you are a humanist who acknowledges co-workers, strong indications that you are inadequate for your main job, incapable of delivering results which satisfy customers and superiors, can be serious and prevent decoupling. Those around you may link the person with the practical managerial work to offering specific contributions, not just making co-workers satisfied. Being seen as well meaning, but inadequate for result-creating managerial work, will not get you far. The fantasies can block clarity and awareness and prevent the individual from taking command in serious problems and accepting what their environment is signalling. What is more, the discrepancy between ideal and reality can be reinforced, leading to a feeling that there is a gap. Hopes for the future may work for a while, but if the hopes are not fulfilled, this comfort mechanism will become a disappointment.

The identity is thus not always easy to handle. If you are a very clever person, with a favourable, privileged life history and a strong spirit, and if you find yourself in the right place, with good working conditions and the right (or easily influenced) people around you, your identity is normally not a problem – and nothing you have any cause to think about. But more often than not there are some frictions, doubts and difficulties. As has been seen throughout, our managers manage their managerial identity by positioning themselves strongly in the question of morals and distance to the core activities. These ways of managing identity are described next as moral purism and practice phobia.

MORAL PURISM

We have seen that the majority of our managers adopt a standpoint which we can call moral purism. This means having strong principles, a clear and uncomplicated view of doing the right thing, standing for and expressing positive values and not compromising on their leader-ship ideal. We have consistently pointed out, at times with some scepticism, managers' claims to be guided by the best intentions in relation to their co-workers. Many managers position themselves clearly as their co-workers' best friend. A considerable number emphasize not only the fact that they care about their employees, but also their genuineness and integrity. The impression they give is that they are genuinely good and want to do genuine good.

Almost everyone in our study has turned their back on micro-management and uses moral arguments to justify their focus on big questions, such as the importance of showing respect and not inter-fering in what co-workers do. Naturally there are examples of insight and admissions of deviations from a simple path. Gerald Goodman says, for example:

> There are times when you have to go into the managerial role where you have to be very assertive and make it clear you expect something to happen.

304 MANAGEMENT: IRONIES, LABYRINTHS AND PITFALLS

But this is an exception. The noble, non-authoritarian behaviour dominates the descriptions given by our managers. What is more, statements such as Goodman's are not a deviation from expressions of purism. Because it is about a "must", everything is obvious and unproblematic. Even a person of principle must be flexible when necessary.

In the chapters of this book, we have looked at the difficulty of living up to ideals such as authenticity and a strong focus on the well-being of the employees. Psychotherapists can undoubtedly focus unilaterally on their clients' best interests (within the time frame the latter or the public services pay for), but in the organizational world, the perceived needs and interests of the employees must take their place alongside all the other interests and goals of the business. The idea of a school is not to make the teachers feel as good as possible; the purpose of a hospital is not to maximize the job satisfaction and personal development of the employees. Adaptability and subordination are inevitable, and managers must work with this, both for their own part and in relation to their co-workers. The company's focus on customers and profitability is, sometimes at least, at odds with the good manager's focus on the employees, and managers who always take the side of the employees or refuse to do something they do not agree with will not last long, unless they have extreme integrity and a very strong position.

The demand for the acceptance of organizational hierarchies and company cultures, the assumption of a position as follower of the manager, ideals such as customer orientation and team spirit, career interest, sensitivity to changing times, fashions and political correctness – all these make it difficult to maintain a strong moral position (Alvesson 2011b; Jackall 1988; Sennett 1998). The interesting question is, then, why our managers – like others, and a large amount of management literature, including an abundance of academic literature – express such a clear, and in many cases naïve and unrealistic, view of ideals such as strong integrity, authenticity and general goodness (see Alvesson & Sveningsson (2013) for a critical review).

This is an expression of an unwillingness to recognize the complexity of the world and understand what managerial work and organizational existence mean. They are clearly adopting a high moral stance. This undertone is seen in almost all our managers with regard to both their essence (honest, open, Mother Teresa, good friend) and practical actions. This is an attractive form of identity support. The worthy leader receives ideological back-up from a large proportion of (naïve) leadership literature which idealizes and prescribes it. All the good things and all the interests go hand in hand: the manager's genuine personality is expressed, the co-workers feel good, the organization is effective. But our imperfect world rarely lives up to such a harmonious view.

Our study shows clearly that severe difficulties in acting wholly in line with fine ideals and identities are often marginalized, and for many people become a non-issue. The discussion is less about the practice than about what they are and what they want – essence and traits are central. Whether the spirit is then willing but the flesh is weak is something which may not be fully investigated. Decoupling, fantasizing and hopes for the future are used. These also draw attention to other people's imperfections. In those cases where it is obvious that managers cannot live up to their high ideals, the fault is often said to lie with others. David Dean explains his problems by saying that he has been the victim of people who are dependent on authority and demand authoritarian leadership. Matt Mooney's subordinates are at times unreliable and flee responsibility. Carol Courage's environment forces idiotic tasks onto her. They seldom mention their own moral ambiguity, the inevitable limitations of the organizational world, shortcomings in their own leadership ideal or their own share of the responsibility for things not always turning out so well.

The moral theme – both the explicit highlighting of their own high moral standards (they have a high level of integrity and are on the side of the employees) and the subtext (they work with strategic questions, not micromanagement and interfering) – gives the managerial work an overall positive charge. It makes the manager a force for good. As a *doer of good* you enjoy – at least in your own eyes – an acceptance and a self-view which help to build up, hold together and repair the managerial identity. Talk of morals and moral subtexts says less about behaviour and relationships than about managers' efforts to create identity. The ingredients for this are as follows:

- positive personal traits and approaches (high level of integrity, caring)
- a strong focus on the employees and what is best for them, less on what they do and accomplish, while at the same time other interests are marginalized
- ideals and forms of leadership which exclusively emphasize the positive aspects
- enhancing the importance of your own work (grand leadership, with the focus on strategy)
- clarity and consistency in the question of your own qualities
- ascribing less positive qualities and behaviour to others (managerial colleagues, co-workers) or to external circumstances

This can be seen as a formula for managerial identity work. Alternative formulae, such as stressing high levels of efficiency, outstanding performance or extraordinary qualities, structuring the business well, averting blunders, and so on, seem to be less common among Swedish managers. (This may have something to do with social norms which do not encourage boasting, but also with the difficulty of making outstanding results credible – it is rarely obvious what a middle manager – or senior management, for that matter – accomplishes in the form of making a clear impact on the company's result. This is an outcome of collectives and a multitude of forces. The industry you belong to, the state of the economy, currency exchange rates, the company's history, complex internal and network dependencies, and so on, often mean more.) The most noticeable exception in our material is Henry Harding. He believes that forceful action and strong results are the foundation of his managerial identity.

One advantage of the moral theme is that it is rather vague. It is always possible to highlight good intentions. Result and performance in various contexts are often vague, which is why it can be difficult to point out good examples, while, at the same time, it is easy to cover up less successful outcomes. Where it is easy to see the result, there is by definition only a minority who can claim a better-than-average result. It is less easy to assess the outcome of moral ideas of leadership, with its emphasis on personal being and intentions, which makes it more useful for identity work for many managers. These probably function less well in relation to the employees; as we have seen, William White, for example, is unsure if his co-workers understand and appreciate his openness and honesty, and Benjamin Book's supposed honesty is partially refuted by his co-workers' experiences of his caution and spreading of (false) praise. But as identity support, moral ideas of leadership are a great help. They offer good opportunities for constructing who you are, what you want and the meaning of your actions. It is easy to produce a fantasy image of how good you are. Most people probably believe that they have higher than average moral principles, that they are honest and reliable and that they wish their co-workers well. The popularity of literature on authenticity, for example, can be partly explained by its applicability in the identity context; it is not of any great help in the managerial practice and does not carry any obligation, but it can reinforce the managerial identity.

PRACTICE PHOBIA

Alongside the moral purism, another striking feature among the managers we studied is their desire to maintain a distance to the actual business. They do not want to interfere. Many stress that they have a clear distance to the operational work being done by co-workers. We showed this in, for example, Chapter 4, where Goodman spoke of how he gives his co-workers the preconditions but then expects them to do the job because they are proactive and reliable. One of our secondary actors, Manager J, also expressed this as delegating and having confidence in co-workers. Another of our secondary actors, Manager K, said of his management in Chapter 4 that he tries "not to meddle too much in operational matters", which "would be completely wrong, and no one would gain anything from it". His aim is to be indispensable in strategic questions but dispensable in operational questions.

Taking a close interest in what co-workers do is seen as "interfering", "meddling" and "taking the decision-making rights away from those who should be making the decisions". This sounds negative, almost a little dubious and unhygienic. People should know their place. The interpretations here seem to unite different aspects. Gerald Goodman sees things that others do not see, while these others work with the daily business – and perhaps interfere in the way that Goodman believes they should not do. Manager J is against both the miscarriage of justice that occurs when decisions are taken away from those who should be making them and people poking around in details. Manager K generally stays away from the operations and wants to monopolize (be indispensable in) strategic questions. It is possible that they mean that it is the co-workers who should be poking around, getting involved in details and meddling. The managers move in another sphere. It is all very reminiscent of the old class society – where you take care to stay within your own sphere and attempt to avoid a breach of style – "people know their role", says Goodman. The decision-making champion and the indispensable strategist make way for the role-locked, proactive fiddlers, the micro-decision-makers and the operational meddlers, that is to say, the co-workers (so might Goodman, Manager J and Manager K, respectively, with a slight touch of irony – possibly rather unkindly – be interpreted).

Here we can talk about a certain unwillingness to get too close to the operative core of the business. Rather than take part in the practical core activity with a bearing on production and result, there is a fear of contact. Goodman articulates this:

> If we don't have the right kind of leadership, then no one will go outside and bury themselves in cement and dust and dirt.

Distance must be maintained, so that the clean manager can motivate others to do the dirty work. Here we can talk about a practice phobia, that is to say a fear of contact associated with getting too involved in the work. This leads to and justifies a form of managerial work remote from practice. (It is true that managerial meetings and strategy work can also be seen as business and practice, but we are talking here about the actual core business, the operational work – as opposed to the more symbolic matters, with which many managers associate when they talk about strategy and leadership.)

This fear of contact often means that managers feel there is a risk of being drawn into tangible practice rather than maintaining the distance they believe the actual managerial work should involve. (The distance applies, as we have seen, to the co-workers' work, not their psychology. Distance to work and closeness to minds seems to be the philosophy.) But it can also mean being stuck in the practical business and not being given the opportunity to hold a position you are worthy of and suited to. In some of our cases, including Stuart Smart, but perhaps most clearly Charlie Chase, the role of technician becomes something of a straitjacket which prevents them from blossoming into real leaders. Yet for Carol Courage, too, the demands from co-workers and managers that she should take an interest in practical questions is an affliction from which she tries in vain to free herself.

Our concepts – practice phobia and fear of contact – may appear rather extreme. Some would argue that it must be a good thing, or at least acceptable for the most part, that managers do their job and assume their managerial positions in the hierarchical division of labour and do not poke around in details or request unnecessary information (see, for example, Heifetz & Laurie 1997). We have no argument with this in itself, but the language of the managers quoted suggests an approach which reflects an underlying problem. It is reasonable to believe that close contact with the operations leads to regular and close connections with the co-workers and shows that you are a manager who is not afraid of getting your hands dirty. This might, perhaps, often improve the conditions for managerial work. Managerial work should, after all, be related to, rather than decoupled from, the operations. There is little doubt that much managerial work is in reality closely connected to operational questions (we do not take managers' claims above or earlier in the book that they stay away from operations for granted), but the exaggerated tendency to claim the opposite says something about manager's desires to be seen and to see themselves in a particular way. The practice phobia suggests an identity theme. The efforts to achieve the pure point to a clear identity – the identity work is fairly distinct. It includes the following elements:

- As a manager, you belong to a different, higher category than your co-workers. You should be "up there".
- As a manager, you respect and behave well towards the lower category – as long as your co-workers know their role, you can allow them to be proactive.
- Rejecting vulgarities such as meddling or interfering in things underlines your good morals and a good upbringing.
- Superiority is emphasized through giving others the preconditions in a patriarchal spirit and "then looking ahead and maybe seeing what others do not see", you do not "waste your own or others' time by asking for irrelevant information" and are "strategically indispensable".

The identity work is facilitated to some extent by claims to orthodoxy and the clear drawing of boundaries (see Ashforth & Mael 1989). The latter is justified in moral terms. This alludes to a managerial ideology in which the world can be clearly divided into managers and others. Such categorical hierarchical divisions can, however, not be emphasized directly – this would eliminate the ideological effect, since the manager would appear pompous, patronizing and uncompromising. There is an attempt to conceal the elitist element. Such an element would clash with another central ideology: that everyone is important, that it is desirable to strive for equality and that differences should be concealed, or at least played down. In the organizations of our time, there is a conflict between the leadership ideal – the manager is important, and everything centres around this person's leadership – and the idea of the central importance of the co-workers. It is essential to move smoothly between these poles (Lundholm 2011). It is frequently stressed that everyone is equally important, yet sometimes managers are given a little more space, and their superior position is accentuated – before the equality is once again stressed. And so on. This alternating – ideologically (in the world of ideas) and interactively (in social situations) – facilitates adaption, but also complicates things for managers in their identity construction. In practice, it becomes a mixture, an oscillation, rather than something streamlined and consistent.

It is not easy to know which approach to take to others in the question of conflict between these standpoints: that everyone is (equally) important or that the manager is more important than everyone else. The statements above show that this is done by stressing the natural division of labour and separating oneself and others into belonging to different working worlds. Not adhering to your separated (superior) position is described in this respect as morally unacceptable: you interfere, meddle, take the decision-making rights away from people, micromanage and other unpleasant things. The practice phobia can then be seen as a question of fear of – further – obscuring your identity. The fear of doing the same as everyone else – getting stuck in the role of technician or some other professional role – and not clearly emphasizing your managerial position motivates this, perhaps somewhat exaggerated, drawing of boundaries with regard to operational questions. You steer – at least in your talk and actions – past the grey zone between the operational and the purely managerial over to a more streamlined and flawless managerial world – hierarchically (in terms of status) clearly superior and full of important matters (see Bacon's idea of the "smart people in suits and ties" – those from the pure, fine and important world which triggered his longing to become a manager). Caring about people and distancing yourself from the unhygienic practice offers a somewhat strange legitimacy and identity reinforcement – although it probably works for the managers themselves.

Both moral purism and practice phobia may appear as rather odd approaches but, as we have tried to show, they are very much in evidence and widely embraced by our managers. They suggest general identity claims of our time – we like to see ourselves as worthy and place ourselves in a superior status category. This appears to be particularly important for managers, and perhaps they have good opportunities to do so with credibility, at least for themselves. Yet, as has been repeatedly stressed, it is not without problems, and the practice phobia in particular can have an impact on the level of anxiety in the managerial life. We now address this.

DISTANCE TO AND KNOWLEDGE OF THE CORE BUSINESS – VERSIONS OF ANXIETY IN MANAGERIAL WORK

Many of our managers do not only have a slight practice phobia, but they also have a real fear of the operational business they lead, since they do not always fully understand it. Bert Bacon's village idiot problem can appear or at least threaten to become serious in certain situations and in interactions with co-workers. Technically competent managers may also experience the practice phobia (we saw this in Charlie Chase, who sees himself as being locked into activities), but it seems to be reinforced where such knowledge is lacking. Practice phobia and ignorance are seen to cause anxiety and worry among the managers that they are not always seen as sufficiently managerial or particularly knowledgeable about the core business. If the fear of not appearing sufficiently clearly as a manager (leader) is combined with the fear of not understanding the operational activities, two forms of anxiety – in terms of anxiety and nervousness – can be said to work together: the anxiety of not being sufficiently different from and superior to co-workers, and the anxiety of not understanding what, as a manager, you are expected to lead. This is about hierarchical and knowledge authority, respectively. The anxiety can come from within, that is to say low self-confidence or a slight feeling of neuroticism, or from the environment, which can signal imperfections or place the person in a particular cage-like compartment, which causes anxiety.

By starting from and combining these two forms of anxiety with the help of a four-field matrix, we can identify different managerial positions with regard to the practice phobia (see Figure 9.1).

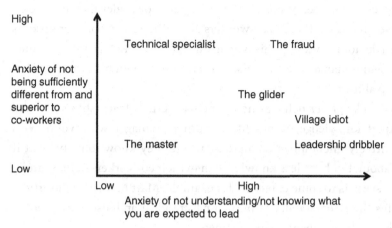

FIGURE 9.1 Anxiety positions

The technical specialist knows the business area, but worries about experiencing (receiving feedback about) weaknesses as manager and/or leader. This is a position where you are scared of not being sufficiently distinct or being seen as a competent manager/leader, but are drawn into and get stuck in the role of professional expert or professional. At the same time, you have little or no anxiety about what the core business involves, as a rule because you understand it (or are confident that you do not need to understand it). We can see this not only in many of our strategy-oriented managers (including managers C, N and P), all of whom say that they have difficulty getting away from their scientific and technical background and establishing a clear "manager and leader" identity, but also in Charlie Chase, whom others see as an expert.

The fraud experiences considerable weakness in both management and expert knowledge and feels of little use. High anxiety caused by fear of not looking like a manager is coupled with high anxiety regarding ignorance of the core business. Of our managers, Bert Bacon is perhaps the one who comes closest to this unfortunate position, largely as a result of ignorance of the business, which increases the anxiety of not being sufficiently managerial or leader-like. In Bacon's case, the worry that his co-workers are pulling the wool over his eyes and do not fully accept his managerial ability, which is not confirmed by senior managers either, also leads to doubt about his general leadership ability.

The glider believes he or she has certain leadership skills and expert knowledge, rather like a normal manager who works with relatively uncomplicated matters, where they know roughly what it is about, but have less knowledge than their co-workers in most areas. We see this to some extent in, for example, Matt Mooney, who articulates the understander of human nature ideal and also some knowledge of the company's core business.

The village idiot has even less of an insight into what people work with, but seeks comfort in the value of openness and the importance of asking silly questions. It is possible to compensate for ignorance and attempt to turn this to your advantage by mobilizing the co-workers' competence: the co-workers are involved, and given attention, confidence and other good things. If Bacon had not had such strong doubts about his leadership abilities, he would have been an outstanding example – now he fluctuates between the useful village idiot and the more problematic fraud.

The leadership dribbler is self-confident when it comes to general management/leadership theory and proves his or her identity by having confidence in co-workers and not interfering, but is not entirely sure that this is justified, and is afraid of being taken in. Dribblers are anxious about their lack of knowledge of the core business, but compensate for this with leadership ideas – for example, grand leadership and understander of human nature leadership – which make it possible for them to feel that they have a clear position as a leader. Ignorance of the substantial is not always felt to be a big problem, since the leader does not always have to be close to the business. We see this leadership dribbling in some of our managers, William White for one, who are concerned about their lack of knowledge of the business, and instead draw legitimacy and security from the role as leader.

The master, finally, sees himself as a good leader who knows the business well, as well as or even better than anyone else. Henry Harding does not express any worry about not appearing as a manager or being ignorant about the business. (He appears to be ignorant of some co-workers' negative assessment of him, but this does not affect his anxiety level, at least during the period of our study.) Harding's low level of anxiety can be seen as the consequence of his being very close to the business – "leadership orthodoxy" is of low value here – and having direct control in the core business as the result of his interest in, and knowledge of, the core business.

It should be noted that this characterization is not intended as an objective description of the skills of the managers, but that our aim is rather to capture experiences and anxiety levels (at a given point in time). As we have shown in this book, managers' self-understanding frequently does not match the impressions of others. Individuals often have an initial self-confidence and see themselves as brilliant managers, but problems and feedback from those around them may mean that they have to rethink. The level of anxiety can increase considerably. They might believe, for example, that ignorance of the business is not a problem; as a master, they may feel they do not have to concern themselves with what people work with or that they need to understand and contribute to the practice. But after a while, the ignorance can become embarrassing, and they go from being what the diagram shows as the position of master to leadership dribbler or to glider or village idiot or even fraud. The feeling of ignorance can be augmented and also affect their view of themselves in terms of leadership ability. Even if they believe themselves to be capable, there are some jobs where this is totally inadequate, and they may feel or fear that their environment will see them – now or later – as a fraud.

The situations of several of those we interviewed have changed radically during the time we have followed them. David Dean has gone from being what he saw as master (even if ignorance of the school world was a source of worry, it is not so technically specialized that it was a problem in terms of business knowledge) to fraud. Benjamin Book has experienced something similar, if less pronounced. Stuart Smart has also changed his situation. After feedback from his manager about a lack of self-insight, his anxiety level has shot up considerably along the vertical axis.

We can further illustrate our anxiety matrix with regard to the anxiety, doubt or worry managers may experience. The mechanics of this should not be overestimated, but understanding the business or being skilled in general leadership strongly reduces the level of anxiety. The situation is generally more difficult when they experience bigger problems with regard to both knowledge of the business and leadership – above all, if they receive feedback that suggests this.

We propose that the anxiety level can be roughly illustrated using the diagonal axis in the diagram (see Figure 9.2). As mentioned above, this is not an attempt to highlight managers' "objective" capability, but, rather, the focus is on their experiences and emotional state. It is possible to be relaxed but ineffective, or terrified but successful. (While the latter may not be so common, competent people can find themselves in a difficult outer situation which causes them to worry despite their merits.)

Relaxed is a position which expresses generally low levels of anxiety in both dimensions. Henry Harding is, as we have seen, the person in this material who best exemplifies this level of self-confidence and well-being.

Terrified is the direct opposite of the relaxed position. Here there are elements of anxiety and depression/despair. Bert Bacon is, as we have said, a clear example, but David Dean is also placed here, even if in his case it is the rejection of his leadership rather than ignorance of the school world which is the crucial problem.

Cold sweat is a kind of average position and is perhaps not uncommon among managers. The leadership dribbler, the village idiot, the glider and the technical specialist experience medium-high

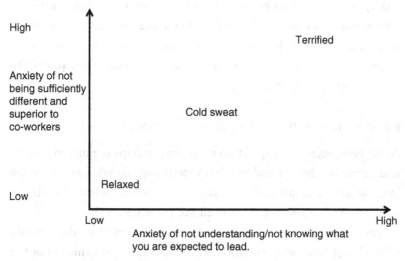

FIGURE 9.2 Anxiety strength

levels of anxiety – their emotional state is not always the best, but they get by.

There are different mixes of doubt about business knowledge and leadership ability for those in a cold sweat. If we disregard the extremes – technically competent but ineffective manager and good leader who does not understand what it is all about, respectively – we find people who know a fair bit about the business and think that their managerial work is going quite well, but who are nonetheless wrestling with questions to do with both meaning and relations. Identification with the managerial position is not entirely stable in terms of identity, since they are struggling with the degree of familiarity and intervention regarding the core business. We have, for example, Gerald Goodman and Steven Stone, who are both rather worried about whether they are, in fact, clear as leaders and who worry about where the boundaries for the meaning and status of the managerial work are drawn. They do not want to be too close to the practice, but at the same time they want to exert influence because they understand at least some parts of the business. Being trapped, like

Stone, in the dilemma between being a driving force, being decisive, taking over and being authoritarian, on the one hand, and being employee oriented, listening, restraining yourself, not using your competence (*the useless-or-idiot paradox*), on the other, paves the way for uncertainty and worry.

PRESENCE IN THE PRACTICE AND KNOWLEDGE

As we have seen, a key question for many, perhaps the majority of all managers, is whether and to what extent they should take a greater interest in the detail and substance of the actual work of their co-workers. Two terms we have used are presence in the practice and absence from the practice. Several managers believe that they should take a lot of interest in co-workers as individuals, but this is not the same as taking their starting point in what they do and accomplish, which appears to be dangerous territory. The practice phobia then justifies absence from the practice: that is to say, the manager maintains a distance to what the co-workers are doing and to operational questions.

This is, however, neither easy nor obvious. An interest in people and strategies – rather than work tasks and performance – does not always justify the manager being completely distanced from the core of the business (or primary practices; Reed 1985). The question must be where and in what to get involved. Where does the boundary lie between demanding information you do not need or interfering in details, and showing interest, wanting to know what is going on and making it clear that you think the core of the business and tangible achievements are central? While meddling is a bad thing, might it be permissible to offer a suggestion as to how the work can be done more efficiently? Different words can be used to refer to more or less the same thing, although this may be described and/or experienced differently. Managers often find themselves walking a tightrope not only between different ideals but also between different interpretations of one and the same way of approaching things.

The majority of the managers we have studied clearly incline towards an absence from the practice ideal – at least, that is how they portray their management. They are (or so they say) present in questions regarding the inner lives of individuals and in the question of strategic essentials, but rather absent when it comes to the work and operational matters. Is this successful? In this – as in most matters of leadership and managerial work – there are no obvious or universal answers. It is, of course, important to avoid doing something co-workers see as interference and meddling, as well as things they experience as disinterest, belittlement or lack of support for their work. It is difficult to have firm principles and offer advice here – as with most other things, it is essential to know the circumstances, local traditions and the capabilities, relationships and lines of reasoning of those involved. Some co-workers may interpret the manager who always acts in the same way as "snooping and controlling", while others see this as an expression of "interest and support".

More generally, we can see two main opposing principles in the question of what is a good point of departure for leadership efforts. Against the idea that *absence from the practice* is an ideal and that too much presence is the same as inferior (or weakened) management, we can equally claim that *presence in the practice* is central for good leadership, and that managers who are absent from the actual work process and keep a distance from operational questions are in a poor position to exercise efficient leadership. To put it bluntly: someone who suffers from practice phobia is unlikely to be a successful leader.

Our point here is *not* to make a firm claim. In our view, the assumption that absence from the practice is superior (morally, and possibly in terms of efficiency) can be challenged by a counter-assumption of the precedence of presence in the practice. Most managers – and co-workers – would do well to give this question careful consideration and decide what is relevant for them in the local context.

It goes without saying that management based on both absence from the practice and presence in the practice can be exercised in many ways and with different qualities, more or less in line with local conditions and the expectations and wishes of co-workers. Absence from the practice may mean monitoring and controlling remotely, with the manager making certain interventions when they are seen to be justified. By managing conditions, values and approaches, as well as by exerting direct influence on the psychology of individuals, the manager can have a lot of control over the way the work is done. Or the control can be minimized and handed over to the co-workers. Presence in the practice can mean the manager getting stuck in, setting a good example and setting the tone for the practical work. Or it might simply mean being present and showing interest in what people do and accomplish by following their work, rather than just looking at how they feel. A significant presence can also mean that the overview and long-term aspect of the managerial job is lost. The point is that the question of absence and presence is multidimensional.[2] Managers frequently fluctuate between absence and presence and between different ways of exercising absence- and presence-based managerial influence, with different emphasis on different elements. This is done with varying degrees of success.

GRAND LEADERSHIP, PRACTICE PHOBIA AND CONSTRUCTION OF LEADERSHIP

In this context, it is important to look at the way in which individuals construct leadership. Our overall standpoint is that leadership does not exist in any objective sense, but that it is about how people characterize, reason about and generally approach something that they call leadership. Grand leaders tend to tone down the employee approach in their portrayal of "the grand" and seek to associate leadership with senior management. They try to climb upwards in the symbolic food chain via a particular, grandiose sense of leadership.

---

[2] There are certain similarities between presence and absence in the practice and the traditional division in task- and relations-oriented leadership. Our concepts capture phenomena which are somewhat different and considerably more multi-dimensioned, which we hope is apparent in the above.

For many managers – who, in this respect, do not work as much with strategy as is traditionally believed – strategy becomes a means of raising themselves above the mundane, although what is constructed as "strategy" rarely has much to do with corporate strategies in a stricter sense.

Identifying with grand leadership may mean missing out on significant opportunities to influence. Carol Courage sees the fact that minor problems are sent up to her as an obstacle, rather than an opportunity to exercise leadership by trying to influence people's attitudes, mindsets and self-view so that they are stimulated to use their common sense and not report everything, including questions about coat racks, to her. She appears to take on these small problems, rather than systematically encourage her subordinates to act independently within given limits, using delegation and their own judgement. Leadership can be about making a well-planned division of labour work. Grand leadership is, in many cases, turned into a rather abstract, limited and splendid activity which is kept separate from the routine organizational processes.

This illustrates how strongly characterized many managers (and in some cases also their subordinates) are by a view that leadership means working with very big important questions: developing the organization, establishing overall harmony, working with "strategic matters", and so on. Leadership becomes something big and noble – splendid – where trivialities such as ensuring that the daily work goes smoothly do not really count (Alvesson 2013a). Mintzberg (2012, p. 327) points out, regarding leadership in managerial work:

> [Leadership] may be more enticing (than the nuts and bolts of the down-to-earth-manager), but that has led to an awful lot of hubris in organizations these days: heroic leadership disconnected from the requirements of plain old managing.

Many managers interpret leadership which enables people who work with administrative matters – janitorial questions – to function as simply a factor of disturbance rather than real leadership. But leading people who work in reception, cleaning services and suchlike is just as much (or little) a question of leadership as is focusing on questions such as company culture and long-term direction at meetings with more senior managers. When Nora Noble talks about "where things really happen", she is not referring to the core business but to a change effort. However, these do not often lead to much in the way of tangible activity (Alvesson & Sveningsson 2015). Perhaps leadership is something which, it is understood, is *not* done where things "really" happen, but is something extraordinary and symbolic, which looks good and does not involve much in the way of influence which will have consequences (cf. Lundholm 2011). Yet the feeling that this – which is often abstract and peripheral to the business – is "leadership for real" is rather common.

We find a contrast to these individuals' view of leadership as something outside the routine and the actual core business in Henry Harding, who specifically stresses active participation and a strong presence in the work. The meaning of "for real" varies. For some, "for real" means the daily business and the operational work, while for others it is what lies outside: strategy work, development projects, and so on. There is, of course, a risk that what is perceived as "for real" is mainly symbolic – it involves a lot of paperwork, talk, meetings, PowerPoint presentations and other "pseudo-real" matters in which "reality" is simulated. In other words, it can be "fake (or sham) leadership" (cf. Lundholm 2011). But this "pseudo-reality" can be interpreted as very positive, aesthetic, pedagogical, generating energy and providing identity. All this is achieved more easily if you manage to keep some distance away from the actual business – yet again, absence from the practice is the ideal. Grand leadership has the considerable advantage that you can distance yourself from the imperfections of the humdrum and the circumstances, at least as far as fantasy and approach are concerned. But for the majority, core activities and the complexities, imperfections and sluggishness these display are often in evidence. For most people, grand leadership is therefore something incomplete and not infrequently hollow. Not everyone is as disappointed and frustrated as Carol Courage, but the discrepancy between hopes, expectations and demands, on the one hand, and what organizational life as a rule offers, on the other, is often significant.

MANAGERIAL IDEALS – IS THE SOLUTION THE PROBLEM?

For the managers in this book, management – and specifically the opportunity to work with leadership – is the road to self-fulfilment. We see how a strongly idealized picture of managerial work and leadership – the manager as someone privileged, with a large degree of freedom to control and personify the managerial work – finds expression in the managers' ambitions to become managers and exercise leadership. This is a glorified picture of management which is often communicated in managerial and leadership education, the trade press, newspapers and popular media (see Mintzberg 2009). In a society dominated by superficial and seductive images, "professions" or occupations which match these images are given a special status – and today management appears to be the right way, perhaps more than any other profession, if our managers are to be believed. It is by attaining the position of a manager busy doing leadership that they will finally have the scope to realize themselves and blossom. The managerial job is portrayed here as superior to other – more controlled and therefore less worthy – jobs in terms of freedom, autonomy, responsibility and control. There is a strong identity aspect in this. Managers belong to a group which has a job which also has value in terms of personal prestige, rather than one less worthy – trivial – where you are controlled by forces over which you have no control. The term leader makes this very clear. As a leader you lead others. You play first fiddle.

Managerial work is, however, rather difficult and challenging, and being a manager is not always easy. Conflicting demands and unclear expectations mean that the managerial work is complex, uncertain, confusing and divided. Expectations which pull in different directions make it difficult at times to know which leg to stand on, and translating abstract behavioural ideals and good principles into how to act locally and in practice in actual and difficult situations is not always easy.

The consequences of the complexities and division of the managerial work are not only about being forced as a manager to devote yourself to different types of tasks (more controlled than controlling – *the control paradox*) but also about experiencing division in your thinking, preferences and emotion, which threatens and undermines the possibility of creating a coherent managerial identity which can support and direct the managerial work (see also Clarke et al. 2009; Watson 2009). The identity work is viewed by our managers as an ongoing process, lined with uncertainty, confusion and a certain fragility with respect to the identity constructions. In themselves, uncertainty and division are no great problem, but managers experience a strong influence towards a distinct ideal, and all our managers make strong identity claims (to be a coach, cultural change agent, humanist, and so on), which causes vulnerability and complications in an inconsistent world.

One of the recurring central contrasts and threats to the attempts to create a stable managerial identity is the abstract ideal of leadership, which proves to be difficult to translate and anchor locally in tangible relationships and organizational situations. Much of it sounds good on paper, but in practice it is often difficult to unilaterally live up to and shape the ideals and their joint connections to, and consequences for, practical action.

- Grand leadership clashes with demands for reporting, budgets and other operational matters. The strategic leadership becomes more of a symbolic ideal with little bearing on or relevance for what the manager actually does in the managerial work. The grand leader risks becoming peripheral for co-workers in most businesses: he or she is better at making PowerPoint presentations than in the actual business.
- Coaching ideals clash with demands for sensitivity to real wishes and problems which cannot be talked away. We have seen how an insistence on sticking to the idea of general coaching as leadership can clash with the co-

workers' practical and organization-specific demands and wishes. People often want the fundamental conditions for the business to be in order. Another aspect is that coaching is about things that people other than managers do as well, if not better than, say, experienced colleagues, consultants or others in the network.

- The understander of human nature ideal, which often has a special emphasis on humanitarian questions, clashes with demands for delivery and following up tasks which are sometimes felt to be neglected. The willingness to accept people's good motives and intentions clashes with the insight that individuals are not perfect and have less attractive sides. It is one thing to lavish praise and encouragement, another to give honest feedback and possibly insist that someone pulls their socks up.
- The ideal of the leader as a driving force and someone who sets the agenda and shows resolve – sometimes based on how you see your own personal traits – sometimes clashes with the ideal of playing a waiting game and instead letting others speak. Should you hold back your personal style when you believe that is the reason you get on and get things done?
- The authenticity ideal, in which natural traits find expression, clashes with the environment's imperfections (ungrateful co-workers, demands and wishes from the environment and the business, which by no means always allow the manager's ambitions for self-expression). Often what is required is adaption and diplomacy – and the concealing of all the manager's less attractive sides.

We see here that many fine ideals are not always easy to put into practice or to use as aims for how to behave and act when faced with daily operational and administrative demands and expectations to maintain adverse organizational machinery.

The conflicts and clashes between different ideals, and between ideals and reality, trigger and intensify efforts – identity work – to build a stable managerial identity which can act as a platform for self-esteem. This work often takes the form of an identity struggle which is characterized by compromising and adapting to the conditions, expectations and demands of organizational life. It is about complying with specific organizational situations rather than blindly following abstract ideals and principles. Sticking rigidly to the latter only reinforces the pressures and makes the management identity struggle more difficult. When it comes to the identity struggle, pragmatic rules of thumb for practical problem-solving – which lead to a certain situational flexibility and compliance in decisions and action – are often preferable to pure personal principles based on beautiful ideals (Wenglén 2005). But getting by pragmatically is nothing to write home about from an identity point of view, compared with clear positioning as a strategic leader, understander of human nature or authentic humanist.

The struggle is certainly less obvious in a number of cases where managers seemingly glide smoothly between different views of what they work with – they despise the leadership ideal, yet work with technical and administrative questions. Others see contradictions and frictions in the work – the specialist administrative and technical work is seen as frustrating deviations from, and obstacles to, what they believe they are naturally good at and what they want to do.

As was indicated in the list of points above, the solution – in its abstract and idealized forms of grand or humanistic leadership – is often the problem. The means, that is to say idealized leadership ideals, are often easy to identify with, but it is easy to fall into "the triumph of emptiness" (Alvesson 2013a). Neither attractive leadership ideals nor a belief in personal traits – the leader's psychology – are seen in our study to stabilize identity work, which instead normally demands considerable confirmation. What is more, social contexts are marginalized. Furthermore, the significance of a deeper understanding of the complexity and dynamics of organizational life is often lost.

TEN KEY THEMES IN MANAGERS' IDENTITY WORK

We can summarize our arguments and ideas put forward in this book by pointing to ten key themes. These concern different problems which managers are likely to face, in particular if they buy the ideals and recipes for leadership which are doing the rounds and which many, perhaps rather too uncritically, profess. The ten-point list is an essential input for self-reflection and caution, not only for managers but also for others in the management/leadership industry (authors, educators, HRM professionals, researchers and others).

1.   The confirmation pact

Popular management theories, in particular those of the more quasi-therapeutic variety, house a mutual confirmation logic – the manager confirms the co-worker, who confirms the manager – which gives rise to a striving for a confirmation pact for mutual identity reinforcement. It may not sound terribly important (and perhaps it not always is) but there is an obvious risk that this will help to reinforce the need for confirmation and offer an exaggerated picture of the manager as someone who represents this. The focus on "the manager's gaze" can undermine independence and critical reflection. It becomes particularly important for managers to be popular among appreciative co-workers, something which can be achieved at the expense of doing their job well. Managers and co-workers who crave confirmation can no doubt reach agreement, but it can lead to both psychological and effectivity costs. There are times when criticism and a strict task focus are useful.

2.   The leadership pact

Managers are frequently encouraged by organizational management to see themselves as leaders and strategists rather than managers, while at the same time being expected to work with conventional management rather than leadership. The leadership pact offers the opportunity for advancement upwards in the symbolic food chain through titles, business cards and symbolic promotion, although without corresponding substantial influence. The latter is, however, not always obvious in the pact, which is why an identity struggle often follows. The decoupling between leadership talk, on the one hand, and administrative and operational practice, on the other, gives rise to friction and sometimes conflict-filled identity work.

3.   The boomerang effect

Managers are encouraged and given the opportunity to profit from management ideas which are attractive in terms of identity – coach and cultural change agent. When these are fully assimilated, flexible behaviour becomes more difficult and an organizational world with partially different demands offers strong resistance. Strong ideals and identities rebound like a boomerang and make meaningful local and situational behaviour, and thereby appropriate management and a stable managerial identity, more difficult.

4.   The Hotel California effect

It is easy to check in and out of the world of abstract concepts via management and leadership education, but it is difficult to leave when you have developed a taste for the ideals. Many management concepts such as strategy and leadership are seductively inviting and alluring, since they are seen to involve power, influence, overview, prestige, image, strong identity and much more that is positive. The concepts are relatively easy to identify with but difficult to break free from when the incomplete reality does not live up to the perfect chart. Convincing and seductive concepts can thereby create identity deadlocks and identity traps which reduce flexibility and openness. This can lead to boomerang effects.

5.   The useless or idiot paradox (or Stone's dilemma)

Should you push others by taking command, as in the classic leadership ideal, and thereby abandon what you regard as the humanistic ideal, or should you give everyone the chance to speak in line with the ideal that everyone should participate and be acknowledged? The former can be seen as a deviation from what is right, the latter as foolish, since it should be one's own natural leadership ability that determines. No one wants to appear useless or as an idiot and find themselves in an identity dilemma where they do not know what leg to stand on. Many managers live partly in a conceptual world where it is possible to accept different ideals without too much friction. In practice, however, it is difficult to embody many of these smoothly and without a struggle.

6.   The irony of (in)dependence

Managers' assumed natural independence and strength rarely stand alone but must be constantly confirmed by the environment if they are to be maintained. Different problems in the feedback – confirmation which is ambiguous, negative or not forthcoming – give rise to identity shakiness and anxiety. Rather than being the natural independent leader hero who many stress is the platform for their management, they appear as someone who is dependent on confirmation. Rather than leading themselves, they may be controlled by the confirmation, or lack thereof, of their co-workers. This creates identity uncertainty and potentially unhealthy, mystified dependency relationships, where the co-workers secretly almost lead the manager, through more or less subtle signs of approval or disapproval.

7.   The moral illusion

Many are keen to appear as the morally perfect manager. However, the moral positioning of the managerial work – integrity and fairness – often goes wrong, not unsurprisingly, since the reality forces compromises and deviations from ideals which are too naïve and unrealistic. High moral principles are replaced by compromise, pragmatism and a willingness to adapt, which leads to identity traps, labyrinths and dead ends. But the fantasy of moral superiority and that this goes hand in hand with other good things (rather than that a high degree of integrity is a source of conflict) lives on.

8.   The paradox of authenticity

Many pursue the identity ideal of unicity and originality yet follow similar standardized recipes for managerial meaning. Like many other ideas, the authenticity ideal holds a special attraction – it is about genuineness and honesty. This sounds good but is difficult to achieve, since the range of tempting recipes or packages for management (leadership) encompasses most things and thereby makes it more difficult to be unique. What is more, the authenticity ideal is hard to realize in complex organizations – where role-play and politics are hard to avoid – and probably reinforces the identity struggle.

9.   *The psychology trap*

The psychologizing of management, encouraged by the media and leadership educators, means that managers interpret local and situational identity constructions – expressions for liking or disliking – as a result of their own innate personal style and morals rather than local interpretation and understanding. They confuse local identities – created in connection with specific interactions and relations– with essential personal qualities, which, in a change of context, leads to identity insecurity and an undermining of the managerial identity.

10.   *The managerial trap*

Given the problems and pressures we have pointed out, we might finally ask ourselves why management of all things is seen by many as the obvious road to self-realization. Personifying managerial work is often difficult, and self-realization does not exactly seem to be achieved in the way hoped. Based on the traits and interests of our managers – people, humanism, etc. – one might think of other professions where this could flourish on a greater scale and without all the problems which accompany the hardships of management. This does not, of course, prevent management from being an important, interesting and meaningful job for many. But the dream of a managerial job as the best platform for self-realization appears at times naïve.

A final word

As has been shown throughout the book, portrayals of managerial life justify a critical approach to many of the popular management theories, models and concepts which have taken root among people in the management business, often with unfortunate consequences. Against this it can, and should of course, be said that theories and models often encourage reflection and act as a source of inspiration and a deeper and broader understanding of organizations and ways of working. They can make it possible to problematize existing organizational environments – strategies, structures, routines, control and other ways of working – and contribute to diversity in the view of business as well as to development and renewal. In this respect, a development of the intellectual repertoire in organizations often has clear benefits and should be accepted and encouraged. However, this requires active reflection and consideration. Models and concepts have, as we have seen, a seductive, enticing side, which means that people want to identify with them quickly and often, without always giving much thought to their deeper significance and the relevance for their own work situation. In addition to the feeling of control, overview, power and identity, there is something aesthetically pleasing about formulations such as strategic leadership, which makes it difficult not to accept and adopt them, at least on a symbolic level. There is a superficiality and an idealization in this which sometimes makes the managerial work more difficult. You adopt an idea about something, which works well (initially) as an identity marker in certain contexts but which is difficult to work with and which therefore also undermines your identity. It is frustrating when you cannot work seriously with what you believe expresses part of who you are as a manager.

One alternative might be to attempt to develop a more reflective and distanced managerial style, in contrast to modern management models and concepts. This requires you to think carefully about what the various concepts and models represent – what they mean – in and for the individual managerial work and your own organizational environment. Tengblad (2012b) stresses, for example, the importance of experimenting and developing a kind of critical learning attitude which involves testing and cautiously trying out new ways of looking at managerial work and management based on local conditions and challenges. It is not a question of simply presenting yourself as, say, a strategic leader on your business card, on the golf course, in recruitment interviews and in formal speeches – or of telling your reflection in the mirror that you are a distinguished understander of human nature or humanist – but also of reflecting over the deeper meaning of the concepts and their relevance for how you see yourself and what you accomplish in your managerial work. It is a question of critically and independently interpreting concepts and giving them meaning, based on the interests and ambitions you have for your management, and on a realistic assessment of your own work situation and environment. As Mintzberg (2009) has pointed out, management is not in the first instance about grand, splendid leadership in some abstract and often unrealistic sense. It is better to try to bring about a "dialogue" with the concepts and try (critically) to be selective and assess what they can contribute in a meaningful sense – if, in fact, they can contribute anything at all in the local context. It might be sensible to stay away from much of what is popular and sounds good. This can be seen as an attempt to bring the concepts to life in tangible and local practice – to allow the reality, rather than the map, to control.

A well-considered link (that is to say, not mere wishful thinking) to one's own managerial position and the practical work situation encourages not only a certain critical distance and *independence* in relation to popular views of strategy and leadership, but normally also a certain realism in the application of concepts and theories which otherwise have a tendency – as we have seen in some of our cases – to lead to fantasies which appear to be decoupled from the organizational environment in which they are rather too active. We should perhaps add that there is, of course, nothing wrong with a little wishful thinking, as it can also provide inspiration and extra enthusiasm in the face of tough challenges and tasks. We all need our illusions to make us feel good. But too much of this – and there is an over-abundance in the leadership industry – causes, as we have seen, problems for many people. The important thing is to reduce too great a distance from the core business. Organizational development in modern organizations also involves participating in the everyday practical formulation – the decisions, processes and actions – of ways of working and organizational circumstances (structures, routines, culture, etc.). This fosters a non-psychological *intimacy* and presence; organizational development is sometimes referred to as handcraft, in which you risk getting your hands dirty (Mintzberg 2005). Many managers should perhaps focus less on psychology and more on work processes and results. Of course, it is right to treat people well, but in our narcissistic culture there is a tendency to be oversensitive when it comes to psychology and people's inner lives.

We would therefore like to issue a warning about the danger of applying theories and models without reflection or purely for the purpose of impression management. We could perhaps talk about a cautious and well-considered formulation with a focus on importance and relevance. This is undoubtedly something which can contribute to a certain restraint and possibly also encourage a certain intellectual autonomy with regard to the abundance of trendy words and terms which frame much of modern management thinking and which are also expressed by our managers, who are perhaps not as authentic and autonomous as they portray themselves. Instead of allowing themselves to be taken over and governed by various management flummery, a deeper reflection might stimulate them to be a little more distanced and take a more *ironic* approach to theories and models. We must recognize the imperfections in the world, and as managers, management educators and management researchers perhaps be rather less pretentious.

Appendix **Our method**

We base this book on a number of empirical projects in which, in addition to studying companies and other organizations, we have also focused on a selected group of individuals we see as being suitable for focused, in-depth studies. Some of the interviews and observations have been conducted by other researchers – Johan Alvehus, Tony Huzzard, Dan Kärreman, Daniel Nyberg, Jens Rennstam, Robyn Thomas and Robert Wenglén – who were, to varying degrees, active members of the research group Lund University Management and Organization Studies (Lumos) at Lund University at the time. We have had in-depth discussions of the interpretations within the research group, which is why we have a good understanding of the empirical despite not having conducted all the interviews ourselves. The quality of the interpretations has also been enhanced thanks to fruitful and creative group discussions. The selection is random; it includes people we have come into contact with in connection with broader organizational studies, for example managers of units we have studied in conjunction with studies of organizational change, knowledge work or similar. In our experience, there are great benefits in undertaking ambitious studies where rich material is of more importance than material which is broad and superficial. There are (too) many studies which have used questionnaires or one-off sixty-minute interviews. We are doubtful as to whether these can provide a qualified illustration of complex phenomena (Alvesson 2011a).

In this study, we have prioritized material which is deep and rich. But since we have been working with this for a relatively long period of time and have combined studies reported here with a range of other projects, we also have a large, broad foundation. Given the seriousness of our ambition, we have included a relatively large number of managers and working environments.

In order to gain depth, but also to give the reader the opportunity to become familiar with individuals and understand contexts, we have focused on thirteen managers whom we see as main actors. These have been studied closely, and we follow them throughout the book. We also have a number of secondary actors, who provide variation and supplement the main actors. Their appearances are more sporadic, but each appears more than once in the text. All those studied have, however, been carefully observed, and the text as a whole is a result of an analysis of the breadth of our entire material, which means we can claim that our main actors provide a realistically broad and representative picture. As we have said, however, we would like to emphasize the depth, context and understanding, as well as utilize the unique qualities found in the people we have studied. It is not least through what is unique that we can learn something interesting. Simply focusing on what applies to the majority or the average is not always rewarding.

We have a considerable breadth with regard to the types of organizations, and thereby a certain representativeness. Since we can see clear patterns, we believe that we have illuminated the circumstances with a certain generality, at least in Sweden, even though managers, managerial work and managerial identities naturally demonstrate great variation. However, we see a good knowledge product first and foremost not in terms of offering a kind of comprehensive description, but of drawing attention to ideas and insights which provide a deeper understanding. We can also learn a lot from non-typical cases. A unique case can provide insights of great value, even if the problem of creating misleading impressions or even overgeneralization must always be taken into account.

To achieve qualified empirical depth, it has been essential to get to know the managers and build relationships based on establishing a certain long-term view and trust. Identity is about how one sees oneself, and this requires confidence and reflection on the part of both researchers and those studied, something which is normally established through regular meetings and interviews. It is also important to be able to follow people over a period of time. Snapshot interviews on a single occasion do not provide an adequate opportunity to capture variation and change over time. We have interviewed all our main and secondary actors on a number of occasions and also had the opportunity to observe most of them in their places of work, often in interaction with co-workers. The secondary actors have been interviewed on fewer occasions, although often on more than one occasion. Most of the interviews with and observations of the managers were conducted between the years 2002 and 2009, mainly in the respective managers' organizations (occasionally also at the university or in other neutral places).

The majority of our actors have been formally interviewed between four and eight times, and to this we can add informal conversations where we have been given the opportunity to follow up on interesting themes. In all cases, we have also held formal interviews with several of the managers' co-workers (normally between three and twelve), both those with and without managerial titles. Formal interviews have been documented on tape or the equivalent and transcribed. Informal meetings and conversations have been regularly documented in writing. To this we can add extensive observations in each manager's workplace. These have been conducted mainly during different forms of interaction between managers and co-workers at different types of meetings. Sometimes these have been routine meetings and sometimes specific meetings to discuss, for example, strategy or organizational change. We have also, in some cases, participated in company events of varying degrees of formality, such as informal co-worker meetings, company information meetings, formal and less formal managerial dinners, parties and development days at conference centres. To this we can add numerous informal meetings and encounters during coffee breaks, at lunch and on other informal occasions. In all, interviews with co-workers and our observations have contributed to valuable knowledge about the managers' interactions in the organizational environment. Although our primary focus is on the managers' experiences and identity work, this does not take place in splendid isolation, but must be seen in relation to those around, relationships and behaviour. Management and leadership studies which focus solely on managers are often of dubious value.

As a result of the interviews and the informal conversations, we have been able to intensify the discussions with the managers at a later stage to include specific problems and challenges in the managerial life. From having initially focused strongly on roles, expectations and mandates which belong to the managerial role, we have increasingly moved the focus to the challenges of management and, in particular, how to reconcile the demands of management with self-view and managerial identity. Our questions have concerned how to reconcile the demands and expectations of management – what is difficult, stressful, and when do they feel inadequate and ignorant? – with how they understand their own capabilities and strengths. A great deal has, of course, centred on the managerial work and the organization (the content of the managerial work, meetings, interaction, co-workers, control, motivation, etc.), but we have also discussed the importance of background, experience of management education and other significant events in the lives of the main actors which have impacted the way in which they see themselves and their management (courses, management and leadership education, MBA, etc.).

Regular interviews, conversations with colleagues and observations of interaction between managers and co-workers have meant that we have constantly been able to return to and problematize identity claims. We have been able to follow up and track any significance of practices associated with specific identity claims such as leader, strategist, change actor and coach. Can we see a link between how the managers express themselves in interviews over time and how they actualize overall concepts such as leadership and how they behave in interaction with co-workers, or are there inconsistencies between these levels which give rise to ambiguities, inconsistencies, conflicts and direct contradictions? It is not unusual in management studies and management education to assume that there is a kind of harmony between these levels since what is said (or marked in questionnaires) is taken for granted. We have instead tried to be more open to the idea that speech, meaning and behaviour do not always match, but can instead be very different.

From what has been said above, it follows that we have not used a predetermined list of questions or followed a strict procedure to process the data. Obtaining qualified insights, producing portraits which communicate a strong feeling for experiences, context, dilemmas, thinking and feeling in relation to the identity themes, requires work with a deep, rich body of material. Holistic interpretations and reflection are more essential than codification and other mechanical procedures (Alvesson & Sköldberg 2009). An important principle of interpretation is to consider the nature of the interview statements. There is a naïve tendency to believe that these reflect "the reality", in other words that people describe things as they really are, or at least describe their understanding of "how things are". Yet interviews also reflect the fact that people are inclined to talk about things. They repeat assertions made in textbooks or the media (e.g. about their leadership). They are politically correct, work with impression management, and so on. These are important aspects of managerial work, which, after all, involves a lot of talking. This must be carefully assessed before giving the interview talk any substantial meaning, for example, seeing it as providing information about the identity theme (Alvesson 2011a). This should be done with the help of interpretation support, where interpretations of precise statements are alternated with a thorough consideration of the entirety of the information gathered – from interviews, observations and knowledge of discourses in society at a given point in time.

References

Alvesson, M. (2004), *Knowledge Work and Knowledge-Intensive Firms*. Oxford: Oxford University Press.

——— (2010), Self-doubters, strugglers, storytellers, surfers and others: Images of self-identities in organization studies. *Human Relations*, 63(2), pp. 193–217.

——— (2011a), *Interpreting Interviews*. London: Sage.

——— (2011b), Leader as saint. In M. Alvesson & A. Spicer (eds.), *Metaphors We Lead By*. London: Routledge.

——— (2013a), *The Triumph of Emptiness*. Oxford: Oxford University Press.

——— (2013b), *Understanding Organizational Culture*. London: Sage.

Alvesson, M. & Billing, Y.D. (2009), *Understanding Gender and Organization*. London: Sage.

Alvesson, M. & Kärreman, D. (2003), Att konstruera ledarskap: En studie av "Ledarskap" i praktiken. *Nordiske Organisasjonsstudier*, 5(2), pp. 62–60.

Alvesson, M. & Lundholm, S. (2014), *Personalchefers arbete och identitet: Strategi och strul*. Lund: Studentlitteratur.

Alvesson, M. & Sköldberg, K. (2009), *Reflexive Methodology*. London: Sage.

Alvesson, M. & Spicer, A. (eds.) (2011), *Metaphors We Lead By*. London: Routledge.

Alvesson, M. & Sveningsson, S. (2003a), The great disappearance act: Difficulties in doing "leadership". *Leadership Quarterly*, 14, pp. 359–381.

——— (2003b), The good visions, the bad micro-management and the ugly ambiguity: Contradictions of (non-)leadership in a knowledge-intensive company. *Organization Studies*, 24(6), pp. 961–988.

——— (2003c), Managers doing leadership: The extra-ordinarization of the mundane. *Human Relations*, 56(12), pp. 1435–1459.

——— (2011), Identity work in consultancy projects: Ambiguity and distribution of credit and blame. In C. Candlin & J. Crichton (eds.), *Discourses of Deficit*. London: Palgrave.

——— (2012), Un- and re-packing leadership: Context, relations, constructions and politics. In M. Uhl-Bien & S. Ospina (eds.), *Advancing Relational Leadership Theory* (pp. 203–225). Greenwich, CT: Information Age.

——— (2013), Authentic leadership critically reviewed. In D. Ladkin & C. Spiller (eds.), *Authentic Leadership: Clashes, Convergences and Coalescences* (pp. 39–54). Northampton, MA: Edward Elgar.

——— (2015), *Changing Organizational Culture: Cultural Change Work in Progress* (2nd edn.). London: Routledge.

Alvesson, M. & Thompson, P. (2005), Bureaucracy at work: Misunderstandings and mixed blessings. In P. du Gay (ed.), *The Values of Bureaucracy* (pp. 89–114). Oxford: Oxford University Press.

Alvesson, M. & Willmott, H. (2002), Identity regulation as organizational control: Producing the appropriate individual. *Journal of Management Studies*, *39*(5), pp. 619–645.

Andersson, T. & Tengblad, S. (2009), Medledarskap: Ledarskap som kollektiv initiativförmåga. In S. Jönsson & L. Strannegård (eds.), *Ledarskapsboken* (pp. 249–272). Malmö: Liber.

Ashforth, B.E. & Mael, F. (1989), Social identity theory and the organization. *Academy of Management Review*, *14*, pp. 20–39.

Avolio, B.J. & Gardner, W.L. (2005), Authentic leadership development: Getting to the root of positive forms of leadership. *Leadership Quarterly*, *16*, pp. 315–338.

Badaracco, J.L. (2002), *Leading Quietly: An Unorthodox Guide to Doing the Right Thing*. Boston, MA: Harvard Business School Press.

Balogun, J. & Johnson, G. (2004), Organizational restructuring and middle manager sense making. *Academy of Management Journal*, *47*(4), pp. 523–549.

Barbuto, J.E., Jr. & Wheeler, D.W. (2006), Scale development and construct clarification of servant leadership. *Group and Organization Management*, *31*(3), pp. 300–326.

Barnard, C.I. (1938), *The Functions of the Executive*. Cambridge, MA: Harvard Business Press.

Bass, B.M. & Riggio, R. (2006), *Transformational Leadership* (2nd edn.). New York: Psychology Press.

Bass, B.M. & Steidlmeier, P. (1999), Ethics, character, and authentic transformational leadership behavior. *Leadership Quarterly*, *10*, pp. 181–217.

Beer, M. & Nohria, N. (eds.) (2000), *Breaking the Code of Change*. Boston, MA: Harvard Business School Press.

Billing, Y. (2006), *Viljan till makt? Om kvinnor och identitet i chefsjobb*. Lund: Studentlitteratur.

Blake, R. & Mouton, J. (1964), *The Managerial Grid*. Houston: Gulf Publishing Company.

Blom, M. & Alvesson, M. (2014), Leadership on demand: Followers as initiators and inhibitors of managerial leadership. *Scandinavian Journal of Management*, 30(3), pp. 344–357.

Bolden, R., Hawkins, B., Gosling, J. & Taylor, S. (2011), *Exploring Leadership: Individual, Organizational and Societal Perspectives*. Oxford: Oxford University Press.

Borgert, L. (1992), *Organisation som mode: Kontrasterande bilder av svensk hälso- och sjukvård*. Thesis. Stockholm: Department of Business Administration, Stockholm University.

Bredin, K. & Söderlund, J. (2012), Project managers and career models: An exploratory comparative study. *International Journal of Project Management*, 1(2), pp. 1–14.

Brown, A. (2015), Identities and identity work in organizations. *International Journal of Management Reviews*, 17(1), pp. 20–40.

Burns, J.M. (1978), *Leadership*. New York: Harper & Row.

——— (2003), *Transforming Leadership*. New York: Grove.

Carlson, S. (1951), *Executive Behaviour: A Study of the Workload and the Working Methods of Managing Directors*. Stockholm: Smartbergs.

Carter, C., Clegg, S.R. & Kornberger, M. (2008), *A Very Short, Fairly Interesting and Reasonably Cheap Book about Studying Strategy*. London: Sage.

Caza, A. & Jackson, B. (2011), Authentic leadership. In A. Bryman, D. Collinson, K. Grint, B. Jackson & M. Uhl-Bien (eds.), *The Sage Handbook of Leadership* (pp. 352–364). London: Sage.

Clarke, C., Brown, A. & Hope Hailey, V. (2009), Working identities? Antagonistic discursive resources and managerial identity. *Human Relations*, 62(3), pp. 323–352.

Cogliser, C., Schriesheim, C., Scandura, T. & Gardner, W. (2009), Balance in leader and follower perceptions of leader-member exchange: Relationships with performance and work attitudes. *Leadership Quarterly*, 20, pp. 452–465.

Collins, J. (2001), *Good to Great: Why Some Companies Make the Leap – And Others Don't*. New York: HarperBusiness.

Collinson, D. (2005), Dialectics of leadership. *Human Relations*, 58(11), pp. 1419–1442.

Conger, J.A. & Kanungo, R.N. (1998), *Charismatic Leadership in Organizations*. Thousand Oaks, CA: Sage.

Crevani, L., Lindgren, M. & Packendorff, J. (2007), Shared leadership: A postheroic perspective on leadership as a collective construction. *International Journal of Leadership Studies*, 3(1), pp. 40–67.

—— (2010), Leadership, not leaders: On the study of leadership as practices and interactions. *Scandinavian Journal of Management, 26*, pp. 77–86.

Cunliffe, A. & Eriksen, M. (2011), Relational leadership. *Human Relations, 64*(11), pp. 1425–1449.

DiMaggio, P.J. & Powell, W.W. (1991), The iron cage revisited: Institutional isomorphism and collective rationality in organizational fields. In W.W. Powell & P.J. DiMaggio (eds.), *The New Institutionalism in Organizational Analysis* (pp. 1–38). Chicago, IL: Chicago University Press.

Dukerich, J.M., Kramer, R.M. & Parks, J.M. (1998), Identity in organizations: Building theory through conversations. In D.A. Whetten & P.C. Godfrey (eds.), *Identity in Organizations: Building Theory through Conversations* (pp. 245–256). Thousand Oaks, CA: Sage.

Dutton, J., Dukerich, J. & Harquail, C. (1994), Organizational images and member identification. *Administrative Science Quarterly, 39*(2), pp. 239–263.

Fairhurst, G.T. (2007), *Discursive Leadership: A Conversation with Leadership Psychology*. Thousand Oaks, CA: Sage.

Fayol, H. (1921/1949), *General and Industrial Management*. London: Pitman.

Fletcher, J.K. & Käufer, K. (2003), Shared leadership: Paradoxes and possibility. In C.L. Pearce & J.A. Conger (eds.), *Shared Leadership: Reframing the Hows and Whys of Leadership* (pp. 21–47). Thousand Oaks, CA: Sage.

Foley, M. (2010), *The Age of Absurdity*. London: Simon & Schuster.

George, B. (2003), *Authentic Leadership: Rediscovering the Secrets to Creating Lasting Value*. San Francisco, CA: Jossey-Bass.

George, E. (2000), Emotions and leadership: The role of emotional intelligence. *Human Relations, 53*(8), pp. 1027–1055.

Giddens, A. (1991), *Modernity and Self-Identity: Self and Society in the Late Modern Age*. Cambridge: Polity.

Grint, K. (2005a), *Leadership: Limits and Possibilities*. London: Palgrave Macmillan.

—— (2005b), Problems, problems, problems: The social construction of leadership. *Human Relations, 58*(11), pp. 1467–1494.

Gronn, P. (2002), Distributed leadership as a unit of analysis. *Leadership Quarterly, 13*, pp. 423–451.

Hambrick, D. & Mason, P. (1984), Upper echelons: The organization as a reflection of its top managers. *Academy of Management Review, 9*(2), pp. 193–206.

Hambrick, D. & Pettigrew, A. (2001), Upper echelons: Donald Hambrick on executives and strategy. *Academy of Management Executive, 15*(3), pp. 36–47.

Haslam, S.A. (2004), *Psychology of Organizations* (2nd edn.). London: Sage.

Heifetz, R. & Laurie, D. (1997), The work of leadership. *Harvard Business Review*, 75(1), pp. 124–134.

Helgesen, S. (1990), *Female Advantage: Women's Ways of Leadership*. New York: Doubleday/Currency.

Hersey, P. & Blanchard, K. (1982), *The Management of Organizational Behaviour: Utilizing Human Resources* (4th edn.). Englewood Cliffs, NJ: Prentice Hall.

Hill, L.A. (1992), *Becoming a Manager: Mastery of a New Identity*. Boston, MA: Harvard Business School Press.

Holmberg, I. & Tyrstrup, M. (2010), Well then – What now? An everyday approach to managerial leadership. *Leadership*, 6(4), pp. 353–372.

Huey, J. (1994), The new post-heroic leadership. *Fortune*, 21, pp. 42–50.

Isaacson, W. (2012), *Steve Jobs*. New York: Simon Schuster.

Jackall, R. (1988), *Moral Mazes: The World of Corporate Managers*. Oxford: Oxford University Press.

Jönsson, S. (1995), *Goda utsikter: Svenskt management i perspektiv*. Stockholm: Nerenius & Santérus.

Kairos Futures/Tidningen Chef (2006), Bäst på allt och aldrig nöjd.

Kärreman, D., Sveningsson, S. & Alvesson, M. (2002), The return of the machine bureaucracy? Management control in the work settings of professionals. *International Studies of Management and Organizations*, 32(2), pp. 70–92.

Katz, D. & Kahn, R.L. (1978), *The Social Psychology of Organizations* (2nd edn.). New York: Wiley.

Kenny, K., Whittle, A. & Willmott, H. (2011), *Understanding Identity and Organizations*. London: Sage.

Knights, D. & Vurdubakis, T. (1994), Foucault, power, resistance and all that. In J.M. Jermier, D. Knights & W.R. Nord (eds.), *Resistance and Power in Organizations* (pp. 167–198). London: Routledge.

Knights, D. & Willmott, H. (1989), Power and subjectivity at work: From degradation to subjugation in social relations. *Sociology*, 23(4), pp. 535–558.

Koot, W. & Sabelis, I. (2002), *Beyond Complexity: Paradoxes and Coping Strategies in Managerial Life*. Amsterdam: Rozenberg.

Kotter, J.P. (1996), *Leading Change*. Boston, MA: Harvard Business School Press.

Ladkin, D. (2010), *Rethinking Leadership: A New Look at Old Leadership Questions*. Cheltenham: Edward Elgar.

Ladkin, D. & Taylor, S.S. (2010), Enacting the "true self": Towards a theory of embodied authentic leadership. *The Leadership Quarterly*, 21(1), pp. 64–74.

Lasch, C. (1978), *The Culture of Narcissism*. New York: Norton.

Laurent, A. (1978), Managerial subordinacy: A neglected aspect of organizational hierarchies. *Academy of Management Review, 3*(2), pp. 220–230.

Lind, R. (2011), Organisationsledning: Rationell retorik och mångfacetterad praktik. In R. Lind & A. Ivarsson Westerberg (eds.), *Ledning av företag och förvaltningar: Former, förutsättningar, förändring* (pp. 31–60). Stockholm: SNS.

Lokaltidningen, Lund (2008), Det som de tycker är trist, tycker jag är roligt. 11 August, p. 6.

Løwendahl, B.R. (1997), *Strategic Management of Professional Service Firms.* Köpenhamn: Handelshøjskolens forlag.

Lundholm, S. (2011), *An Act of Balance: Hierarchy in Contemporary Work.* Thesis. Lund: Lund Business Press.

Luthans, F. & Avolio, B.J. (2003), Authentic leadership: A positive developmental approach. In K.S. Cameron, J.E. Dutton & R.E. Quinn (eds.), *Positive Organizational Scholarship: Foundations of a New Discipline* (pp. 241–261). San Francisco, CA: Berrett-Koehler.

Mastrangelo, A., Eddy, E.R. & Lorenzet, S.J. (2004), The importance of personal and professional leadership. *Leadership and Organization Development Journal, 25*(5), pp. 435–451.

McAdams, D. (1996), Personality, modernity, and the storied self: A contemporary framework for studying persons. *Psychological Inquiry, 7*(4), pp. 295–321.

McClelland, D. & Burnham, D. (1976), Power is the great motivator. *Harvard Business Review, 54*(2), pp. 100–110.

McSweeney, B. (2006), Are we living in a post-bureaucratic epoch? *Journal of Organizational Change Management, 19*(1), pp. 22–37.

Meindl, J.R., Ehrich, S.B. & Dukerich, J.M. (1985), The romance of leadership. *Administrative Science Quarterly, 30*, pp. 78–102.

Meyer, J., Boli, J. & Ramirez, F. (1987), Ontology and rationalization in the western cultural account. In G. Thomas, J. Meyer & F. Ramirez (eds.), *Institutional Structure Constituting the State, Society and the Individual* (pp. 12–37). Newbury Park, CA: Sage.

Mintzberg, H. (1973), *The Nature of Managerial Work.* New York: Harper & Row.

——— (1991), Managerial work: Forty years later. In S. Carlson (ed.), *Executive Behaviour.* Reprinted with contributions by Henry Mintzberg and Rosemary Stewart. Uppsala: Acta Universitatis Upsaliensis.

——— (1998), Covert leadership: Notes on managing professionals. *Harvard Business Review*, November–December, pp. 140–147.

—— (2005), The magic number seven – Plus or minus a couple of managers. *Academy of Management Learning and Education, 4*(2), pp. 244–247.

—— (2009), *Managing*. San Francisco, CA: Berrett-Koehler.

—— (2012), That research on managing be developed. In S. Tengblad (ed.), *The Work of Managers* (pp. 327–328). Oxford: Oxford University Press.

Mintzberg, H. & McHugh, A. (1985), Strategy formation in an adhocracy. *Administrative Science Quarterly, 30*, pp. 160–197.

Montgomery, C.A. (2008), Putting leadership back into strategy. *Harvard Business Review, 1*, pp. 33–39.

Niehoff, B., Enz, C. & Grover, R.A. (1990), The impact of top-management actions on employee attitudes and perceptions. *Group and Organization Studies, 15*, pp. 337–352.

Norrman Brandt, E. (2012), *Ny chef: Praktisk och mental beredskap för ledare.* Stockholm: Sanoma utbildning.

Nyberg, D. & Sveningsson, S. (2014), Paradoxes of authentic leadership: Leadership identity struggles. *Leadership*.

Ogbonna, E. & Wilkinson, B. (2003), The false promise of organizational culture change. *Journal of Management Studies, 40*, pp. 1151–1178.

Pearce, C.L. & Manz, C.C. (2005), The new silver bullets of leadership: The importance of self- and shared leadership in knowledge work. *Organizational Dynamics, 34*(2), s. 130–140.

Peterson, D.B. & Hicks, M.D. (1996), *Leader as Coach: Strategies for Coaching and Developing Others*. Minneapolis: Personnel Decisions International.

Pettigrew, A. & Whipp, R. (1991), *Managing Change for Competitive Success.* Oxford: Wiley & Blackwell.

Pfeffer, J. (1977), The ambiguity of leadership. *Academy of Management Review, 2*(1), pp. 104–112.

Reed, M. (1985), *Redirections in Organizational Analysis*. London: Tavistock.

Rennstam, J. (2007), *Engineering Work: On Peer Reviewing as a Method of Horizontal Control*. Lund Studies in Economics and Management, 93. Lund: Lund Business Press.

Schaefer, S. (2014), *Managerial Ignorance – A Study of How Managers Organise for Creativity*. Lund: Lund University Press.

Sennett, R. (1977), *The Fall of Public Man*. New York: Random House.

—— (1998), *The Corrosion of Character: The Personal Consequences of Work in the New Capitalism*. New York: Norton.

Shamir, B. (2007), From passive recipients to active co-producers: Followers' role in the leadership process. In B. Shamir, R. Pillai, M. Bligh & M. Uhl-Bien (eds.),

Follower-Centered Perspectives on Leadership: A Tribute to the Memory of James R. Meindl (pp. ix–xxxix). Greenwich, CT: Information Age Publishing.

Shamir, B. & Eilam, G. (2005), What's your story? A life-stories approach to authentic leadership development. *Leadership Quarterly*, 16, pp. 395–417.

Shotter, J. & Gergen, K. (eds.) (1989), *Texts of Identity*. London: Sage.

Sims, D. (2003), Between the millstones: A narrative account of the vulnerability of middle managers' storying. *Human Relations*, 56(10), pp. 1195–1211.

Sinclair, A. (2011), Being leaders: Identities and identity work in leadership. In A. Bryman, D. Collinson, K. Grint, B. Jackson & M. Uhl-Bien (eds.), *The Sage Handbook of Leadership* (pp. 508–517). London: Sage.

Sluss, D. & Ashforth, B. (2007), Relational identity and identification: Defining ourselves through work relationships. *Academy of Management Review*, 32(1), pp. 9–32.

Smircich, L. & Morgan, G. (1982), Leadership: The management of meaning. *Journal of Applied Behavioural Science*, 18, pp. 257–273.

Sparrowe, R.T. (2005), Authentic leadership and the narrative self. *Leadership Quarterly*, 16, pp. 419–439.

Spector, B. (2014), Flawed from the "get-go": Lee Iacocca and the origins of transformational leadership. *Leadership*, 10, pp. 362–379.

Stogdill, R.M. (1974), *Handbook of Leadership: A Survey of Theory and Research*. New York: Free Press.

Sveningsson, S., Alvehus, J. & Alvesson, M. (2012), Managerial leadership: Identities, processes, and interactions. In S. Tengblad (ed.), *The Work of Managers* (pp. 69–86). Oxford: Oxford University Press.

Sveningsson, S. & Alvesson, M. (2003), Managing managerial identities: Organizational fragmentation, discourse and identity struggle. *Human Relations*, 56(10), pp. 1–31.

——— (2010), *Ledarskap*. Malmö: Liber.

Sveningsson, S. & Blom, M. (2011), Leaders as buddies. In M. Alvesson & A. Spicer (eds.), *Metaphors We Lead By: Understanding Leadership in the Real World* (pp. 96–117). London: Routledge.

Sveningsson, S., Kärreman, D. & Alvesson, M. (2009), Ledarskap i kunskap sintensiva verksamheter: Hjälteideal och vardagsmagi. In I.S. Jönsson & L. Strannegård (eds.), *Ledarskapsboken* (pp. 30–57). Malmö: Liber.

Sveningsson, S. & Larsson, M. (2006), Fantasies of leadership: Identity work. *Leadership*, 2(2), pp. 203–224.

Tengblad, S. (2003), Classic, but not seminal: Revisiting the pioneering study of managerial work. *Scandinavian Journal of Management*, 19(1), pp. 85–101.

—— (2006), *Aktörer och institutionell teori*. GRI report, 10. Gothenburg: GRI.

—— (ed.) (2012a), *The Work of Managers: Towards a Practice Theory of Management*. Oxford: Oxford University Press.

—— (2012b), Conclusions and the way forward: Towards a practice theory of management. In S. Tengblad (ed.), *The Work of Managers* (pp. 337–356). Oxford: Oxford University Press.

Tengblad, S. & Vie, E.O. (2012), Management in practice: Overview of classic studies of managerial work. In S. Tengblad (ed.), *The Work of Managers* (pp. 18–46). Oxford: Oxford University Press.

Tyrstrup, M. (1993), *Företagsledares arbete: En longitudinell studie av arbetet i en företagsledning*. Stockholm: EFI.

—— (2002), *Tidens furstar: Om tid, företagsledning och ledarskap*. Lund: Studentlitteratur.

Uhl-Bien, M. (2006), Relational leadership theory: Exploring the social processes of leadership and organizing. *Leadership Quarterly*, *17*(6), pp. 654–676.

Wallander, J. (2003), *Decentralisation – Why and How to Make It Work, the Handelsbanken Way*. Stockholm: SNS.

Watson, T.J. (2001), *In Search of Management: Culture, Chaos and Control in Managerial Work* (2nd edn.). London: Thomson Learning.

—— (2004), HRM and critical social science analysis. *Journal of Management Studies*, *41*(3), pp. 447–467.

—— (2008), Managing identity: Identity work, personal predicaments and structural circumstances. *Organisation*, *15*(1), pp. 121–143.

—— (2009), Narrative, life-story and the management of identity: A case study in autobiographical identity work. *Human Relations*, *62*(3), pp. 425–452.

Wenglén, R. (2005), *Från dum till klok? En studie av mellanchefers lärande*. Lund Studies in Economics and Management, 81. Lund: Lund Business Press.

Western, S. (2008), *Leadership: A Critical Text*. Thousand Oaks, CA: Sage.

Wilkins, A. & Ouchi, W. (1983), Efficient cultures: Exploring the relationship between culture and organizational performance. *Administrative Science Quarterly*, *28*, pp. 468–481.

Wolvén, L.-E. (2012), *Machiavelli, de tio budorden och det moderna ledarskapet*. Lund: Studentlitteratur.

Wright, P.L. (1996), *Managerial Leadership*. London: Routledge.

Yammarino, F.J., Dionne, S.D., Schriesheim, C.A. & Dansereau, F. (2008), Authentic leadership and positive organizational behaviour: A meso, multi-level perspective. *Leadership Quarterly*, *19*, pp. 693–707.

Ybema, S. (2004), Managerial postalgia: Projecting a golden future. *Journal of Managerial Psychology*, *19*(8), pp. 825–841.

Ybema, S., Keenoy, T., Oswick, T., Beverungen, A., Ellis, N. & Sabelis, I. (2009), Articulating identities. *Human Relations*, *62*(3), pp. 299–322.

Yukl, G.A. (1989), Managerial leadership: A review of theory and research. *Journal of Management*, *15*, pp. 215–289.

Zaleznik, A. (1977), Managers and leaders: Are they different? *Harvard Business Review*, May–June, pp. 67–68.

—— (1997), Real work. *Harvard Business Review*, 75(6), 53–63.

Index

Printed in the United States
By Bookmasters